VALOUR IN THE TRENCHES!

By the same author

The Colonel's Table
Reveille & Retribution
Spit & Polish
Friend & Foe
On Laffan's Plain
'K' Boat Catastrophe
Chitrál Charlie

VALOUR IN THE TRENCHES!

'Bombo' Pollard
VC MC* DCM HAC
in The Great War

NS Nash

In memory of
9332G A/Sergeant Ernest Simmons HAC
1898-1963
For turning a boy into a man

Pen & Sword
MILITARY

First published in Great Britain in 2011 by
Pen & Sword Military
an imprint of
Pen & Sword Books Ltd
47 Church Street
Barnsley
South Yorkshire
S70 2AS

ISBN 978 1 84884 447 6

A CIP catalogue record for this book is
available from the British Library

Typeset in Ehrhardt by Chic Media Ltd

Printed and bound in England
by MPG

Pen & Sword Books Ltd incorporates the imprints of
Pen & Sword Aviation, Pen & Sword Maritime,
Pen & Sword Military, Pen & Sword Family History,
Wharncliffe Local History, Wharncliffe True Crime,
Wharncliffe Transport, Pen & Sword Discovery, Pen & Sword Select,
Pen & Sword Military Classics, Leo Cooper, Remember When,
The Praetorian Press, Seaforth Publishing and Frontline Publishing

For a complete list of Pen & Sword titles please contact
PEN & SWORD BOOKS LIMITED
47 Church Street, Barnsley, South Yorkshire S70 2AS, England
E-mail: enquiries@pen-and-sword.co.uk
Website: www.pen-and-sword.co.uk

Contents

List of Illustrations

Acknowledgements

A book such as this can never be the unaided work of a single person and I have been particularly fortunate in the quality of the support that I have been given.

Key to the writing of this book was the active support of Alfred Pollard's family and I am indebted to Mr Richard Chown, his nephew, and Miss Christine Chown, his great-niece, both of whom gave me enthusiastic and practical assistance. Not least as representatives of the Chown family, they gave permission for me to quote from Alfred Pollard's war memoir, *Fire-Eater*. Further to that they gave me access to family photographs – and their memories of Alfred Pollard.

I could not have completed this biography without the buttress of the Honourable Artillery Company where Brigadier Digby O'Lone, the Chief Executive of the HAC, smoothed my path.

Miss Justine Taylor, the Archivist of the HAC, gave unstintingly of her time and expertise. She involved herself in the minutiae of my research and met my every request with a smile and a refreshing 'can do' attitude. Mrs Cristina Kennedy copied photographs from the archive – a tedious job, and my thanks go to her for her time. A number of the photographs in this book are taken from HAC sources, principally from the regimental journal of the 1920s and 1930s.

James Colquhoun, a Pollard aficionado, most generously shared his research with me, and I acknowledge, in addition, his advice and the use of his maps. He read a draft of the book and made helpful observations.

The sketches of Adrian Hill have appeared in countless HAC publications and are reproduced here with grateful acknowledgement to the unknown copyright holder. Hill was at the scene of some of the action described and knew the participants – I believe he would be content for his work to be associated with Alfred Pollard and 'Bill' Haine.

My researchers Peter Gallagher and Jeff Birch who know their way around the National Archives at Kew were, as always, towers of strength. This is the third book that I have completed with their skilled assistance.

I am only too aware that, without the encouragement and gentle direction of Brigadier Henry Wilson, my commissioning editor at Pen & Sword Ltd, I would not have even made it to the 'start-line', although I believe in modern parlance that is now called the 'point of departure'. My text editor at Pen & Sword Ltd was Linne Matthews; her scholarship made the text that much more intelligible and the editing process enjoyable at least for me.

Contemporaneous accounts of the engagements in which Alfred Pollard fought have been mined in order to capture the atmosphere of the day. Central to this is the work of Major G Goold Walker DSO, MC, who wrote *The Honourable Artillery Company 1914-1919*, which has been an invaluable source. All references to Goold Walker are in connection with this book unless otherwise specified.

Catherine Boylan wrote a masterly paper for the *Journal of the Society for Army Historical Research* in the spring 2004 edition. This paper, entitled *Fearless Fighter, Tender Romantic: The Paradox of Alfred Oliver Pollard*, alerted me to several lines of research of his post-war life that I would otherwise have missed. I have quoted from Catherine Boylan's paper and I acknowledge, very gratefully, her contribution and encouragement to me in writing this biography of Alfred Pollard.

Finally, Lieutenant Colonel Tom Gowans, soldier/'schoolie' that he is, generously applied his particular brand of common sense to the project. His enthusiasm was invaluable and his support and friendship a constant joy.

Tank Nash
Malmesbury,
2011

Preface

The First World War involved the active participation of many millions of young men of many nations and several million of these young men died. The British Army had expanded very rapidly from 257,000 men in 1914 to over three million by 1918. The expansion was so rapid that the training given to the influx of enthusiastic volunteers was cursory and, in the early days of the war, the brunt of the fighting fell upon the relatively small regular army. It was the civilians, volunteers and conscripts of the Territorial Forces that reinforced and eventually provided the overwhelming majority of Britain's manpower. This book tells the story of just one of those territorial, volunteer soldiers. The 21-year-old civilian who is the subject of this book became one of the most decorated soldiers of the war and is still a legend today.

He was a remarkable man and in his early life he had an unusual and compassionless attitude, but that was offset by his extraordinary devotion to a young lady who did not return his affections. His bravery and unalloyed patriotism are beyond question and both were of such unflagging consistency that Alfred Oliver Pollard has been the subject of several studies by academics, seeking to uncover the secret of his valour.

I have quoted from his autobiography at some length, and this is because it is better that he be judged on the basis of his words, not mine. Any judgements that are passed are mine, unless attributed elsewhere.

This book seeks to provide a record of Alfred Pollard's exploits, putting his courage into the wider context of his life and the times in which he lived.

Chapter 1

The End and the Beginning

'The setting up of soldiers.'

1914–1960

It was 0830hrs on Sunday, December 1960, and Bournemouth was gearing itself up for Christmas but, in the meantime, the town was being assailed by a violent storm. Heavy rain was falling, being driven by a strong wind with gale force gusts.

At 18 Queen's Park Gardens, Alfred Pollard, one of Bournemouth's most distinguished residents, could hear the wind howling outside. Although never a gregarious person, he too was looking forward to the festivities, despite the continuing worry he had over the health of Violet, his dear wife of thirty-five years.

Violet fussed around him in their modest home on that Sunday morning, but she was clearly very unwell and in the care of the doctors. On the table beside his chair was a copy of *Wrong Verdict*, the most recent of the sixty-one books he had written and had published over the previous thirty years. His sixty-second book – *Forged Evidence* – he had completed only three months earlier and he looked forward to seeing a copy of that joining the row of his other published work that filled a small bookcase in the lounge, early in the New Year.

Alfred Pollard had not always been an author; he was once a soldier and a very good one. That was all years ago but now, as old age beckoned, there was time to speculate upon the many men he had killed with bullet, bomb and bayonet, time to recall laughing comrades whose lives were snuffed out in an instant or who died, slowly, in shrieking agony. He had survived the horrors of the First World War and had been decorated four times for acts of extraordinary bravery. He still carried in his body splinters from German grenades and shells.

He recalled vividly the horror of contact with that first corpse – the rotting remains of a French soldier that he had inadvertently come to grips with in his early days in the trenches and of the unutterably awful stench that erupted when his pickaxe pierced the body of another soldier, long since buried but unmarked.

How could he forget the crack of the bullet that missed its target and the spray of blood, bone and brain when it did not? He remembered vividly the scream of one of the Huns as he shot him in the stomach – but then he had had no choice. Engraved on his mind were the cheerful faces of the living and also the grey, waxy faces of the dead, the prayers of the Padre, the shrill call of the whistles, the crump of artillery shells and the lethal shower of white-hot steel fragments that followed. He recalled the impact and pain of shell and grenade splinters, lying in hospital beds, pretty nursing sisters – one in particular. What had happened to her? What of his brother Frank, his idol – long dead but not forgotten. Ernest Boyle, 'Ossy', Sherry Bryan, 'Billiken', Marrs, Percy Lewis, Hughesdon, Freter, George Thorpe and Hoblyn – dear old Harry.

He could smell the putrefaction of a thousand corpses, the stink of the latrines and the discomfort of being lousy. He remembered the rats, the cold food, the driving rain, the unremitting heat, the dust and the bone-aching cold. He recalled the pleasure of clean water to drink and hot water in which to bathe. But, above all else, his abiding and most treasured memory was the comradeship and bravery of the men who had served beside him in his trench and their shared pride in the Regiment. A young queen was on the throne now. He had served her grandfather, met him several times, good chap; he too was proud of their regiment.

He recalled the thrill of seeing and holding his first book, *Pirdale Island*. It was as good as a medal … but that was thirty years ago. Ruefully, Alfred concluded that even after sixty-two books authorship was a difficult and badly rewarded way to make a living. However, he was fortunate. Plots came to him relatively easily and he did not find that writing was arduous. He had never suffered from 'writer's block' and his output had been described by others as 'prolific'. On that basis, he could go on for ages yet, turning out two books a year and looking forward to his royalties, such as they were.

He was fit, well perhaps a bit overweight, but at sixty-seven, he certainly had no intention of making an appointment with his maker just yet. When that time did come he would have no regrets and he would face the prospect of death with equanimity – he had been at the very door many times before. Indeed, he had knocked, several times, but had been denied admittance. He had done his duty, found favour with his comrades and when his time was up, then so be it.

He had killed German soldiers, many of them, but he had not kept score. Back then in the trenches he had felt and felt now, '*neither pity nor fear*'. That was his view then and he had no cause to change it.

The storm raged outside and as the Dorset coast was being battered, Alfred recalled winter nights like this in the trenches. He remembered the impossibility of keeping warm and dry, icy water draining down one's neck, cold wet fingers grasping a greasy weapon. Then there was the thick, clinging mud underfoot and the smell, always the smell of putrefaction, ordure and unwashed bodies.

Even on awful days like this, Bournemouth certainly beat the hell out of trench life.

Then he heard a clatter from the garden. He muttered under his breath and rising from his chair made for the window. He could see that the wind had blown down a panel of the garden fence. Decisive as he had ever been, he muttered under his breath and made his way to the door …

* * *

The consensus seems to be that an appropriate place to start a biography is at the beginning and, on that traditional and sound basis it must be recorded that Alfred Oliver Pollard (AOP) had been born into a safe and secure middle-class family on 4 May 1893. At the time the family home was a house called 'Rycroft' in Melbourne Road, Wallington, Surrey. Soon after his birth the family moved to 'Tilbury', 2 Belmont Road, in February 1894, and it was here that James Pollard, his father, had died in 1933, having seen one of his sons achieve international fame.

Alfred was the second son, and fifth child, of Yorkshireman, 34-year-old James Alfred Pollard, who hailed from Heckmondwike and was married to Ada Jane Pollard (née Payne). She had been born two years after her husband, in Ryde, on the Isle of Wight.

James Frank, who was the first-born of James and Ada, was now a lively three- nearly four-year-old. He had been born on 23 June 1889 and welcomed the birth of a baby brother, to whom he would soon be very close. They had three sisters. These were Lily Ada, born in 1885, Eva Kate, 1887, and Amy Grace, who arrived in 1891.

James Alfred Pollard was well able to care for his young family as he had a secure job with the Alliance Assurance Company in their offices in the St. James's Street branch. He was professionally qualified and a Fellow of the Chartered Insurance Institute (FII).

The family home was and is a substantial building; it was certainly sufficiently so to house a family of seven and a live-in maid. 'Tilbury' today is a sad sight. The house has been split into eight flats, and the garden in which the Pollard children once played has long gone and is now an unattractive car park, approached past the 'wheelie bins' of the flat dwellers.

Alfred Oliver Pollard and his siblings grew up in Wallington, then an attractive village on the outskirts of London, but now a rather dreary suburb. Victorian England was a country with no doubts as to its place in the world. The Royal Navy ruled the waves and the Army, supported by locally enlisted troops, ensured that, in all those parts of the map coloured pink, the Queen's peace held sway. The ever-reclusive Queen Victoria still had nine years of her illustrious reign to run. However, the British century was running to a close and rebellion was afoot in South Africa.

When war broke out against the Boers any number of myths were destroyed. It was discovered that the Army that had been so devastatingly effective against African and Arab tribesmen was a deal less capable of dealing with the fast moving, guerrilla type of opposition provided by the determined and skilled Boers.

The two small boys almost certainly stood in the streets and cheered as British troops marched off to war to die at Colenso, Nooitgedacht, Sanna's Post and Spion Kop.

Descendants of James A Pollard

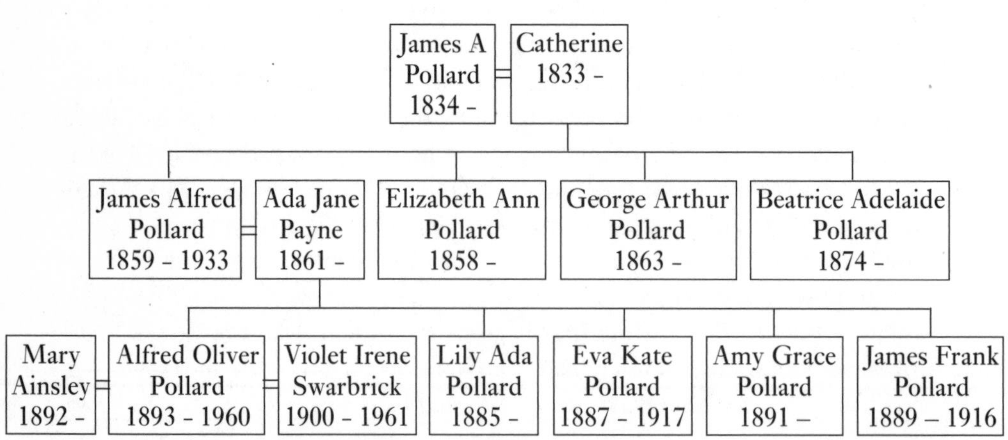

The Boer War was still raging when, in January 1901, Queen Victoria died and the world changed forever. The two small boys grew into young men. Alfred's education is not well recorded other than that he attended Merchant Taylors' School from 1906 to 1908. During this period the school was located in a complex of medieval buildings behind Smithfield Market and was readily accessible for a boy living in Wallington. The school later relocated to its present campus at Northwood. Alfred advanced from thirteen to fifteen, but that was clearly not the sum of his education, although assiduous research has found no other educational record.

In 1909 James Frank Pollard (always called 'Frank'), by now aged eighteen, joined the HAC. We can safely presume that he had been 'invited' to join because the Honourable Artillery Company did not offer an open door to any Tom, Dick or James.

As a new member he had first to 'take the King's shilling' and enlist as a soldier and then, suitably proposed and seconded, he appeared before the Court of Assistants and was admitted to membership of the Civil Company. He had, in effect, joined a club, and an exclusive one at that. He signed his name in the Great Vellum Roll, a document that already held the signatures of the Great and the Good over the previous 350 years.

The function, the aim, of the HAC then, and still today, was '*the setting up of soldiers*' and Frank probably regaled his younger brother with tales of what went on, on drill nights and at 'camp'. He undoubtedly explained that on parade the HAC was 'strict particular' but off parade very relaxed and informal. Members had social relationships that transcended rank although, as in any society, members tended to relate to their peer group. Informality did not extend as far as either the Regimental Sergeant-Major (RSM) or the Commanding Officer (CO) – and nor should they.

Frank explained to his younger brother that the HAC was organized like a battalion of the Foot Guards and that some of the key staff were regular soldiers – not least the RSM. Where the Foot Guards wore gold (well, brass, in effect) the HAC wore silver. Similarly, lance corporals of the HAC wore two stripes (not the normal one stripe) and that was by the explicit command of the old Queen. These and other snippets all added to the message that was loud and clear – it was a privilege to be a member of the HAC.

The hard lessons learned on the dusty plains of South Africa between 1899 and 1902 had generated significant change in the Army and in the manner that it operated. Not the least was that the need for enhanced skill-at-arms was recognized and acted upon.

The year 1906 had seen the start of major reforms to the structure of the Army and these were driven by the Secretary of State for War, Richard Haldane. His were the first significant alterations to the organization of the Army since the Childers Reforms of the early 1880s, and they were somewhat belatedly put in place to recognize deficiencies identified during the Boer War, which had ended in 1902.

Haldane formed the Expeditionary Force, which was designed for overseas service in the event of major war, and at the same time, made arrangements that the Force would be provided with the logistic and supporting elements that modern war demanded.

Cognizant that sending the bulk of the regular army overseas would make the UK base vulnerable, he created the Territorial Force by grouping the disparate Volunteers, Militia, and Yeomanry units together in the Territorial and Reserve Forces Act of 1907 – and this was just before Frank Pollard joined the HAC. Haldane had the foresight to institute the Officer Training Corps in universities and what were then called 'public schools' (but are now described as the more politically correct 'independent schools'). World War I would underscore Haldane's wisdom in this regard.

It was suggested, by a tidy-minded jobsworth of the day, that the Honourable Artillery Company would be re-designated '26th Battalion, The London Regiment', Similarly, the Inns of Court Regiment was to be awarded the appellation the 27th Battalion. Both of these ancient organizations treated the unattractive and impertinent suggestion with the contempt it deserved – they ignored it and, like a bad smell, it went away.

However, the political reforms had an immediate effect on the HAC and, as a result of the transfer of the Company to this new Territorial Force, there was a considerable influx of recruits, 533 new members being admitted in 1908, whereas the yearly average had hitherto been about seventy. In 1909 Frank Pollard became one of 1,066 active, that is to say, serving members.

Frank Pollard was at 'camp' at Bulford, Wiltshire, when King Edward VII died in May 1910. Camp was abandoned and the Company journeyed back to London for the funeral of its Captain-General.

In 1911 Frank Pollard was almost certainly involved in the celebrations for the Coronation of King George V because the HAC was always at the centre of public events in London and there would have been guards to find, routes to line and much social activity to enjoy at Armoury House, the home of the HAC in City Road. Alfred Pollard learned about the HAC and its doings at his brother's feet and it left a very strong impression.

The Territorial Force settled down during the next three years, but by then, dark clouds were forming over Europe and in June 1914 the awful progress to war was initiated in Sarajevo. The British public was not averse to war – indeed, a significant proportion looked forward to it as a means of asserting national pride and putting all those foreigners in their place.

They got their way when HMG declared war on Germany on 4 August 1914. AOP remarked that:

> At that date, August bank holiday, I was twenty-one years and three months, a clerk in the St. James's Street Branch of the Alliance Assurance Company and utterly irresponsible. My chief interests in life were rugger in the winter, tennis in the summer and dancing all the year round.
>
> Girls? Of course!

> They added a spice to life in the same way that one uses salt to season food. With the exception of one, with whom I had believed myself in love with from the age of eighteen, none had any influence over me. I invested the one with every feminine virtue and shut my eyes to the fact that her real self might fall short of the wonderful creature of my imagination. She was two years my senior and thought me rather a silly ass.

Alfred Oliver Pollard (AOP) was no different to 99% of young men with his interest in games, girls, and gadding about. However, he was markedly different in that he was patently besotted with this one lady. She remained unnamed throughout the 271 pages of his autobiography[1] – even though it was originally published in 1932, some fourteen years after the event.

Frank Pollard was twenty-five and young Alfred was twenty-one. The latter, 6 foot 2 inches of rugby-playing bone and muscle. He was a good looking chap and no doubt the ladies noticed that too, although there is not a shred of evidence that AOP had a relationship of any degree with someone of the opposite sex.

In late summer of 1914 there was an ill-judged and oft repeated statement that 'the war would be over by Christmas'. One of the results of this optimistic forecast was that Britain was gripped, initially, by a war fever and many young men rushed to join the Colours because they did not want to 'miss the fun'. Haldane's Expeditionary Force of regular soldiers embarked for France to face its first test. War having now been declared, Pollard commented that:

> Our branch at St. James's Street had a staff of twenty-seven, ten of whom were Territorials. Mobilization left us short-handed. The official attitude was one of annoyance. No Territorials would be sent overseas – the war would be over by Christmas – and no one else could be spared from the office to take part in a protracted holiday, playing at soldiers and guarding railways … Every time I could I slipped away from my desk and went into the street and bought a paper, which I devoured eagerly in the basement. With an optimistic belief in the British flag, I expected to read that we were victorious all along the line. Instead, the news was guarded. The Germans were advancing through Belgium … I could see the red-coated sentries parading up and down outside St. James's Palace … the march and tramp of feet sent the blood coursing through my veins. The voices of my ancestors were calling, calling. A poster on the walls of Marlborough House stated that recruits were needed.[2]

AOP was a curious emotional mixture and at times, he was readily moved.

He said that when standing outside Wellington Barracks he watched a party of khaki-clad Guardsmen leave for the front:

> The crowds were cheering. I joined in, but my voice was choked and there were tears in my eyes. Tears of envy at their good fortune. How could I be left behind? Was it Patriotism that stirred me? That is the name for it, I suppose.

The following day he confronted 'the Secretary' in charge of the St. James's Street branch of the Alliance Assurance Company and asked for leave to join the Army. The request was turned down and Alfred took the rejection calmly and on the chin, understanding fully that from the Company's point of view, his leaving was highly undesirable. 'You'll always remember I asked you, Sir,' riposted Alfred.

He speculated later that, as the Secretary did not enquire what was meant by the remark, perhaps he had thought that the initial request had been merely to salve the young man's conscience for not yet being in uniform. At the close of play that afternoon Alfred left the office with no intention of ever returning. It was a bold step because, as he readily realized, if indeed the war was over by Christmas, then he was out of a job and he was not even a soldier, either. On examining his motivation he admitted[3] that he had had enough of clerking for an Assurance Company and emigration to Canada was an option he had been considering. He said, with refreshing honesty, 'The opportunity for freedom from the slavery of desk routine was probably as big a contributory factor as patriotism in the shaping of my destiny.'

Fired by his brother Frank's stories of the HAC, AOP would settle for nothing less and the following morning, the Saturday of the August bank holiday, he found that Armoury House had been completely besieged by men wanting to volunteer. Overwhelmed by the flood, the iron gates that bar entry to the Artillery Garden were closed. A notice decorated the gates with the stark advice that *'No more volunteers are needed'*.

Alfred Pollard was only one of the many in City Road that day. It is probable that somewhere in the melee there were a very young Mr. Reginald Haine and a Mr. Thomas Pryce, and of these two we shall hear more later. Another one was a Mr. ERM Fryer[4], who recorded that:

> The Inns of Court wouldn't look at anyone who hadn't previously been a soldier of some sort: I hadn't. So I went further up the street to the HAC and found a crowd waiting outside the gate on a similar mission: but I was fortunately with a friend, Elwes, who was a nephew of the Colonel of the Regiment, Lord Denbigh, so after he had convinced the sentries of this fact (and nothing would make them believe it at first) we

> were admitted to the orderly room, and filled up various forms, and then were told to return next day, as the Regiment was full up and awaiting War Office sanction to form two new companies.
>
> In the light of future events it is hard to realize how difficult it was to get into the Army in those days, even as a private soldier. Next day, the 8th, we were duly elected members of the HAC and paid our subscription of two guineas, for this was no ordinary regiment, but more like a soldiering club, where candidates had to be proposed and seconded by members.

Pollard had no similar, high-priced connections and as the crowd drifted away, Alfred Oliver Pollard stayed. He was made of stern stuff and he hung around in the bleak environs of City Road for three hours until, at about 1130hrs, the notice was removed and the gates swung open. AOP was first through the gap and he ran the 150 yards to burst through the doors of Armoury House. An hour later, medically examined and pronounced fit, he was attested 'joined the Army' and assumed the appellation Private AO Pollard HAC[5]. He then paid his subscription and signed the Vellum Roll. He was not just a soldier but, in addition, he had also joined a unique society.

Reginald Haine had a different story to tell and he explained that:

> A friend phoned me (on the Monday morning) and said, 'What are you doing about the war?' Well I had thought nothing about it at all.
>
> He said, 'I have joined my brother's regiment, which is the Honourable Artillery Company. If you like come along, I can get you in.'
>
> At lunchtime I left the office in Southampton Row, went along to Armoury House in the City Road, and there was my friend waiting for me. There was a queue of about a thousand people trying to enlist at the time, all in the HAC – it went right down City Road. But my friend came along the queue and pulled me out of it and said, 'Come along!' so I went right up to the front, where I was met by a sergeant–major at a desk. My friend introduced me …
>
> He, (the Sergeant-Major) said, 'Are you willing to join?'
>
> I said, 'Yes Sir.'
>
> He said, 'Well, how old are you?'
>
> I said, 'I am eighteen and one month.'
>
> He said, 'Do you mean nineteen and one month?'
>
> So I thought a moment and said, 'Yes Sir.'
>
> He said 'Right-ho, well sign here please. You realise you can go overseas?'
>
> So that was my introduction to the Army.[6]

Alfred Pollard and Reginald Haine may have been delighted with their lot but Frank Pollard was suffering agonies of frustration – he wanted to get at the enemy, and as far as he could see, it was going to take far too long if he stayed and waited with his comrades in the HAC.

In 1914 the Colonel of the HAC was the Earl of Denbigh and Desmond, and in late August, he visited the Company, which had been drawn up in 'open square'. He addressed the uniformed element of the Company and AOP described the address as a 'harangue'. Denbigh certainly did not intend to give that unfortunate impression but nevertheless, at the end of his speech he called for volunteers willing to go to the front to step forward. Alfred Pollard observed that:

> I fully expected the response to be unanimous. I could not understand that everyone was not filled with the same fever as myself. If they did not want to fight, why the deuce were they in khaki? Forty-two per cent expressed their willingness to serve. The following day the sheep were separated from the goats. First Battalion HAC came into being.[7]

Evelyn Fryer[8] was present and he saw it slightly differently, like this:

> The law was that no Territorial regiment could be sent abroad unless it volunteered, or, in other words, if a certain proportion of the men did so. So we were asked to volunteer, and at first the response was disappointing, and it did not reach the required number. Next day, Lord Denbigh addressed the Battalion, most eloquently, and put the case so well that 89%, if I remember correctly, volunteered. As a result of this, we were ordered to hurry on our training with a view to proceeding to France at an early date.

The re-organization that followed found AOP in Number Eight section of 10 Platoon in 'C' Company. Sergeant Pritchard, a friend of Frank Pollard, commanded Number Eight section, which also included Malcolm Lewis, an old friend. Very quickly, Alfred chummed up with Harry Hoblyn, a big man 'with a twinkle in his eye and a heart of gold.'[9] The third of the group was Ernest Chaland, who was the product of a French father and English mother. These three, soon to be known as 'The Trinity', became inseparable and Pollard remarked that 'even the non-commissioned officers treated us with respect.' That might indicate that they threw their weight around, probably physically, because that is the order of things in a barrack room.

Generations of soldiers will attest to the fact that one's early days in uniform are not designed by the Army to provide entertainment or amusement. AOP peeled potatoes, swept floors, washed out latrines and in his spare time worked on his boots and cap strap. There was, of course, drill – there is always drill. The large area of tarmac that fronts Armoury House rang to the sound of steel-shod heels being 'raised 12 inches and driven down 15'.

The route marches around London's streets and parks were declared, by Alfred, to be 'fun', and he and his fellow recruits sang as they marched - but apparently not everyone sang the same song. This discordant but happy group were even happier when they were marched to HM Tower of London to be issued with their rifles. The weapons were obsolete, albeit functional and lethal.

AOP's mind set at this time would never have been known if he had not chosen to reveal it many years later in his book *Fire-Eater*. His precise form of words is chilling and something of a contrast to the man moved to tears at the sight of others going off to war:

> The rifles were of an old pattern[10] which had been discarded in the Army for years. But they were rifles. Handling mine for the first time gave me a thrill which is with me to this day. I was armed. It was a weapon designed to kill. I wanted to kill - not because I hated the enemy but because the primitive instinct was strong in me to fight.
>
> A bayonet was supplied with the rifle. How many times I examined that bayonet in secret, feeling its edge and gloating over it. The desire to get to the front had become an obsession.

By 23 August the news was that the 'Contemptible Little Army'[11] was retreating in the face of a massive and well co-ordinated German thrust. Frank Pollard had not waited to get into the fight and, on 15 August 1914, he 'deserted' and promptly enlisted in the 1st Battalion, Grenadier Guards under the name of 'Frank Thompson'.[12] It was as 17341 Guardsman Thompson that Frank Pollard fought his war.

The Battalion formed for the morning muster parade, the roll was called and, predictably, Private James Frank Pollard was found to be missing. Alfred was summoned from the ranks by the Adjutant, Captain MG Douglas[13] who questioned him on the whereabouts of his elder brother. AOP reports that Captain Douglas was very tall and 'superlatively thin'. He was known as 'the Pull-through' because he was likened, by some wag in the ranks, to the cord, brass-weighted at its end, used for cleaning the barrel of a rifle.

Alfred was unable to say where his brother was and he suspected that he was not believed. This interrogation, described by AOP as a 'pantomime', was repeated on the next six mornings. Speaking of his brother, Alfred said:

He was my only brother, four years older than me, one of the finest athletes I have ever come across. I had spent a lifetime worshipping his exploits. No torture has ever been invented would have dragged his secret from me.

To use the time-honoured phrase, 'The company and battalion lines were searched but no trace could be found of him and he was placed on the report.' Frank Pollard was duly marked as a 'deserter'. It is presumed that this was because the HAC had been warned for overseas service. The legal difference between 'absence' and 'desertion' is vast and the penalties commensurately more severe for the latter offence. Changing one's name is a rock-solid proof of desertion. Alfred remarked: 'I had achieved fame. I was the brother of the only deserter in the history of the oldest regiment in the British Army.[14] What a distinction!'

The 1st Battalion HAC was moved to 'camp' at Aveley, Essex, on 12 September, but before departing for deepest Essex, the Battalion was first inspected by HM King George V, the Captain-General. After the King had reviewed the 1,000 officers and men, the Battalion marched through the City of London and exercised its right to do so 'with bayonets fixed, colours flying and drums beating'. 'We learnt later the value of old privileges and customs, together with that wonderful thing, "esprit de corps".'[15] The Lord Mayor[16] took the salute as the column marched past the Mansion House, however, the stationmaster did not inspect any tickets when the Battalion en-trained at St. Pancras Station.

On 17 September 1914, at Aveley in a tented camp, 'officers' swords were sharpened and rifles and bayonets were issued.'[17] Eight Section occupied a single tent and found that when soldiers live cheek by jowl they quickly learn each other's foibles and develop the especial form of comradeship that sustains them when life becomes uncomfortable. Pollard mistakenly speaks of exciting days spent on the ranges at Pirbright as being 'an easy march away'. The war diary speaks of 'Rainham Ranges', later called Purfleet Ranges. Located on the Thames marshes, which are quite close to Aveley, the range complex was in use until the mid 1960s and is now a nature reserve. Speaking of this musketry camp, during which he fired only fifteen rounds, AOP said:

> To me it was the most exhilarating experience of my life. Every time I looked along the sights I saw a German. Already I hated the whole German nation, for no other reason that they were our enemies. My aim was deadly and I was complimented by our platoon sergeant, Sergeant Harrap, on it.

Sergeant Harrap and Pollard were deluding themselves. Fifteen rounds are barely sufficient for a novice to zero his weapon at short range and certainly not enough to identify anything other than a potentially competent weapon handler – certainly not a marksman. However, Harrap's remark fuelled Alfred's overweening self-confidence and not for the better, either.

The Battalion was 1,000 strong but its establishment was for only 800 'other ranks'. Reductions had to be made and Pollard and his two friends made it their business to ensure that they were not among those to be left behind. It appears that, in Eight Section, they made the decision, having been 'consulted' on the selection process. Afterwards, AOP said smugly of The Trinity, 'Already we were making ourselves felt.' The unattractive attitude of The Trinity was further exemplified by Pollard's account of one of their last days in England before embarking for France. He recorded that:

> Another incident serves to show our growing power. The camp was surrounded by a high wall. The village which lay outside was 'out of bounds'. The Trinity were thirsty and The Trinity decided to have a drink to celebrate our departure to the front. Walls were built to be scaled. The village boasted only one pub. Several sergeants, privileged people, were enjoying themselves when we arrived. No one took any notice of us. We left at closing time.[18]

This short quotation paints a further picture of an overly self-assured young man and his friends. The use of the word 'power' is mildly disturbing. AOP was only twenty-one years of age and, like every 21-year-old soldier since time began, he was immature and unworldly. It remained to be seen if like a fine wine he would mature to greatness or, like a lesser vintage, turn sour.

Evelyn Fryer cheerfully admitted to being an inadequate soldier and he was not one of the 800 originally selected. Nevertheless, he lobbied any officer who would give him a hearing and, eventually, he had some success. As he later wrote:

> That evening I was called in and told that the Company had been made up to strength without my valuable services, but that if I liked to take on the job of officer's servant and groom to the Machine-Gun Officer, I could go to France. Well, this was what the Yanks would call a bit of a 'proposition'. I didn't know one end of a horse from the other, and except for fagging when a lower boy at Eton, had no experience in the servant line. Anyhow, I decided to take the job, and reported, full of fear and trembling, to my new lord and master, Lieut. Holliday, of the M.G. section. Later in the evening I was introduced to my horse, a long-legged chestnut with, mercifully, a reputation for quietude.

Reg Haine and Tom Pryce were among the 800. They were on nodding terms with AOP and were on parade the day that the regimental historian, Major G Goold Walker, recorded in his very dry manner that 'The 1st Battalion, recruited up to war strength, was inspected by His Majesty King George V in the Artillery ground on 12 September 1914 and sailed for France on the 18th.'

Those are the facts but, they should be expanded upon to reflect the atmosphere of the time. For the men on parade it was a very special event indeed. For the King, the Captain-General, only the very best would do. Mere excellence was not enough. Rehearsals had been held: kit buffed and polished, imprecations issued and national pride dusted down. The King pronounced himself satisfied with his 'Company'. Beer was taken in oceanic amounts after the 'dismiss'.

At dawn on 18 September 1914 the Battalion paraded, marched to the station and boarded a train for Southampton. Pollard entertained no doubts or concerns as to what lay ahead and he commented on embarkation day in the following, very up-beat, terms:

> There were 800 of us, every man a public school boy. Our average height was 5 feet 10 inches. Without a doubt we were the finest battalion that ever crossed the water. Every man was a potential officer. Later, when the country needed officers of the right type, the War Office realized the error of using such material as that which composed the First Battalion of the Honourable Artillery Company as ordinary soldiers. Hundreds were killed as privates who could have commanded companies from the first day they joined.[19]

These remarks were made well after the event. Pollard's view on the waste of potential officers is not original thought. It is rather the oft expressed view of many others, but only after hundreds of potential officers had been killed in the guise of private men.

By the standards of the twenty-first century there is a flavour of superiority in many of Pollard's remarks, and by the curious standards of the twenty-first century, he could be termed a snob. However, 100 years ago social distinctions were much more clearly defined and the blunt fact is that the products of 'public schools' did assume a position of superiority because a man's accent and education were the critical yardsticks by which one was judged – in the main, their superiority was cheerfully acknowledged by those who were less well educated.

In Southampton docks the twenty-nine officers and 800 men of 1st Battalion, the Honourable Artillery Company,[20] 1 HAC, as it was now designated, looked with disfavour on a cattle boat recently returned from Australia. She was the SS *Westmeath*.[21] She was not designed to take human cargo and most certainly not the gentlemen from the Artillery Garden: thankfully, it was to be a short voyage.

Pollard took the chance to pen a quick note to his mother and then voiced his regrets at:

> Not having seen the lady of my dreams. I believed that she was away in the country visiting friends and had no idea of the sentiment with which I surrounded her. I was a knight going on a crusade. She was my ever-gentle lady. I carried her favour in the form of a lace handkerchief of hers which I had stolen.

These sentiments are in sharp contrast with some of his other less sensitive pronouncements and taken as a package some might conclude that, in September 1914, Alfred Pollard still had some 'growing up' to do.

Notes

1 AO Pollard, *Fire-Eater*. This was then re-published by The Naval & Military Press. See pages 223 and 238.
2 AO Pollard, *Fire-Eater*, p21.
3 AO Pollard, *Fire-Eater*, p23.
4 ERM Fryer, *Memoirs of a Grenadier*, 1921. Fryer joined the HAC on the same day as Pollard. He went to France with 1 HAC but was quickly commissioned into the Grenadier Guards in April 1915. He served in 2nd Battalion, rose to the rank of captain and was awarded the MC.
5 The ranks of the HAC were swollen by lapsed members returning to the Colours and by new volunteers. In all, 14,000 men were admitted and every one passed through the Court of Assistants in the time-honoured way. This was sufficient to produce two Infantry battalions, a Reserve battalion, four Horse Artillery batteries, a Siege battery, two Reserve batteries and the Depot. Source: G Goold Walker, *The Honourable Artillery Company 1537-1947*, p242.
6 Max Arthur, *Forgotten Voices of the Great War, p8-9.*
7 AO Pollard, *Fire-Eater*, p26.
8 Evelyn RM Fryer, *Memoirs of a Grenadier.*
9 AO Pollard, *Fire-Eater*, p26.
10 Probably Lee Metford rifles of pre-Boer War vintage.
11 An Army order issued by Emperor William II on 19 August 1914 pronounced that, 'It is my Royal and Imperial command that you concentrate your energies, for the immediate present, upon one single purpose, and that is that you address all your skill and all the valour of my soldiers to exterminate first the treacherous English and walk over General French's contemptible little army.' *Source Records of the Great War*, Vol. II, ed. Charles F Horne, National Alumni, 1923.
12 Some sources give his pseudonym as Tompson.
13 Captain Douglas – later Lieutenant Colonel MG Douglas DSO, MC.
14 Frank Pollard remains the only 'deserter' in the 475-year history of the HAC. However, it was not quite as simple as that, as a later chapter reveals.
15 ERM Fryer, *Memoirs of a Grenadier.*

16 Colonel Sir Charles Johnston (1848-1933).
17 War diary, 1st Battalion HAC, September 1914.
18 AO Pollard, *Fire-Eater*, p28.
19 AO Pollard, *Fire-Eater*, p28.
20 G Goold Walker, *The Honourable Artillery Company in the Great War 1914-1919*, p18.
21 The ship was built in 1903 and originally named SS *Everton Grange*. She flew the flag of the Union Steamship Company of New Zealand and was employed transporting cattle. In 1911 she was renamed *Westmeath*. In 1917 she was torpedoed in the Channel but limped back to port. In 1925 she was sold and renamed *Nordico*. She was broken up in 1928. Her bell hangs in Armoury House.

Chapter 2

France

'He had presumed, mistakenly, that the Honourable Artillery Company had something to do with "artillery".'

September-November 1914

The arrival of 1 HAC in France was something of an anti-climax. The port used for the docking of *Westmeath* and the disembarkation of the Battalion was St. Nazaire on the Atlantic coast of France. This port had been selected because the Channel ports were thought to be at risk: in the fluid state of the fighting at the time they could easily have been lost.

The Battalion did not march straight to the front line, much as AOP would have preferred, but instead it was quartered in a tented camp just outside the town. Here they met old hands – those who had been in France perhaps a month longer.

The lamp was swung – vigorously – by soldiers from the Army Service Corps (ASC) and Royal Army Medical Corps (RAMC), but they did not impress Pollard. He had a low opinion of the RAMC, unlike most soldiers who recognized that their lives could be in the hands of the RAMC any day soon. Pollard said, and repeated it more than once, that RAMC stood for 'rob all my comrades'. This was an all-embracing conclusion for which, in September 1914, he had not a shred of evidence. His firmly held view of the entire RAMC was based on one single incident later in his service that involved only one member of a vast and very worthy corps.

'C' Company was moved on to Nantes and was employed labouring in the Ordnance Depot. The smart well-educated men of the HAC, who were busting to get at the enemy, were invited not only to mark time but to act as labourers to load trains with war stores for the front. It was a disappointing form of employment but 1 HAC got on with the job with as much goodwill as it could muster in the circumstances.

Of The Trinity, two spoke fluent French. Pollard did not, and on this basis,

Harry Hoblyn and Ernest Chaland told Alfred that they were going into town to meet a local dignitary. In due course the trio marched up to the imposing entrance of a significant mansion that occupied a dominating position on one of the main thoroughfares of Nantes.

Alfred was just a little impressed.

The three private soldiers were ushered into a large and tastefully well-furnished room. They seated themselves and after a short pause, a door opened and into the room paraded about a dozen young women. Pollard recorded that:

> All were stark naked – with the exception of their shoes and stockings. They paraded solemnly round the room to show off their points whilst Madame, their keeper, invited us to make our choice. The one who appealed to me was a little brunette called Mugette. I said so to Ernest, who called her over.
>
> She came over and sat on my knee.
>
> Then she kissed me.
>
> It was very nice.
>
> Closer inspection revealed a scar above her left breast. I asked her what it was: Chaland interpreted. She shrugged her dainty shoulders and said that a horrid drunken soldier had bitten her there in an abandonment of passion the week before.
>
> Two minutes later I was out of the house enjoying God's fresh air. I only visited one other brothel the whole time I was in France.[1]

Pollard's hasty exit from the brothel, presumably in shock at the naked young woman's reasonable and doubtless truthful explanation, poses the question: in what sort of establishment did he think he had been? AOP was not a worldly man and the chances are that he was a virgin at the time. Mugette was, almost certainly, the first naked woman he had ever seen or touched. Most men would be impressed by his extraordinary restraint in the circumstances; others might judge him to be 'wet' and a few would understand that in that setting he just had no idea how to proceed.

On several scores, flight was a good option to exercise.

In Britain, the nation was rocked by a series of dreadful naval disasters and not the least of these was when on 22 September 1914, U-9 sank the three obsolete cruisers *Hogue*, *Cressy* and *Aboukir* 'before breakfast' with massive loss of life. Earlier, the sinking of HM ships *Amphion*, *Pathfinder* and *Pegasus* had cast a doubt on the invincibility of the Royal Navy. The German submarine campaign, which was to drive Britain to its knees, had commenced. However, these events might just as well have been on a different planet as far as AOP was concerned.

1 HAC was occupied in Nantes for about six weeks. It was a period of complete safety and without incident of a military nature. However, there were ample administrative duties and one of these was mounting a guard over German prisoners receiving treatment at the military hospital. The Trinity contrived to be selected for this chore under the command of an NCO. It was the first time Pollard had a chance to look the enemy in the eye and he said that 'Even to be near them, gave me a feeling that I was nearer the firing line.'

During this guard Pollard came to the assistance of a nursing sister who was in difficulty dealing with a recalcitrant and drunken British soldier. He was much taken with the Sister, who by dint of her calling and qualification would have been an officer. She was to reappear in his life two years later.

The guard gave Alfred and Harry the opportunity to set up dinner with two of the nurses and the evening was a great success. All manner of delights seemed to be on the near horizon and as result both young men saw that Nantes was not without its attractions. Quite what Alfred planned, with his track record, is not specified.

They manipulated, manoeuvred and schemed to get back on hospital guard but without success because the Company Sergeant-Major was on their case and he was having none of it. Instead he detailed them off for the incredibly designated 'Armed Porridge Guard'. On the quay, near an old and decrepit tramp steamer, the *Lousy Ann* (a corruption of *Louisaine*), the guard was required to secure the porridge that was cooked in bulk each night in a vast cauldron for service at breakfast. The affront to Pollard's dignity was huge. He was a soldier, not any soldier, but an HAC soldier, and he was guarding … bloody porridge. 'Ye Gods!' he commented feelingly.

It must be presumed that someone or some organization was likely to steal the porridge – why that should be remains a mystery to this day.

The nurses being unavailable, or at least unreachable, Pollard transferred his attentions to an attractive girl who worked in a local estaminet. Despite his limited French, Alfred assiduously pursued this flower of French womanhood. It all seemed to be going rather well when he decided to:

> Tell her of the wonderful girl I had left behind in England. To prove my devotion to the absent one I showed her the lace handkerchief which I treasured. She snatched it from me and refused to give it back. I can only think that I used the wrong words … As far as I know Suzanne still has my handkerchief. I never saw either her or it again.[2]

The weather turned colder and as it did so, in very early November 1914, the 1st Bn HAC was ordered toward the front, to St. Omer. The journey took three days, in a train that advanced only at walking pace. AOP and his friends were fortunate that they were crammed eight to a compartment. Nevertheless, this was to be preferred to the cattle trucks to which some of the more unfortunate members of the Battalion were consigned. Pollard's group, by dint of careful stowage of their kit, was able to establish two bridge fours. The train was unlit and the winter nights were getting longer, but the games continued through the night after AOP and his comrades had stolen an oil lamp from the gentlemen's toilet on Rouen Station. Much later, in 1932, Alfred Pollard still had that oil lamp and he said that it was a 'treasured souvenir'.

The arrival in St. Omer was every bit as anti-climactic as the arrival in St. Nazaire and it dawned on Alfred Pollard that soldiering was not 'all fix bayonets and charge' – there was a great deal of hanging about involved before one got to that point.

The Battalion was quartered in French barracks that dated back to 1815 and he speculated that the place had not been cleaned since Napoleon's troops had marched out. The Battalion was required to find a guard for GHQ and all those selected were 6-footers. To the amusement of his friends, Harry Hoblyn was rejected because he was only 5 feet 11 inches. Pollard saw all the generals of the day pass before his 'presented arms' and noted sourly that the Great Men paid no heed to the guard. That is the way of things in the Army but thereafter, AOP always empathized with the guardsmen at Buckingham Palace.

Meanwhile, and elsewhere in the Battalion, Fryer was not enjoying his role as an officer's servant and he said:

> During all this time I was showing no skill whatever either as a groom or a servant: my horse showed a distressing lack of discipline and my master's boots were never clean nor his shaving water hot. Consequently one day at Le Mans the boots being even dirtier than usual and the shaving water even more tepid, my master, to whose patience up to now I pay a generous tribute, rose in his wrath and rebuked me: whereupon I applied, somewhat insubordinately, I fear, to return to my old section in Number 2 Company. This was duly arranged, and everyone was very nice about it.

It would seem that abject failure, in any capacity, for a member of the HAC was not the cause for any form of censure and certainly not retribution. A little after this incident Fryer's company was sent to Boulogne and he commented on his stay there in these terms:

> At Boulogne we did various duties, including several funeral parties for men who had died of wounds in hospital. It was here that we really got our first sight of the horrors of war, as the hospitals were all full, and car loads of fresh wounded were constantly arriving. I shall never forget the

> shiver which went down my back when doing a funeral party at the Casino hospital: on our way we passed a large marquee with its door open, and inside what looked like a whole lot of men sleeping, wrapped up in blankets. I remember thinking what a nasty, draughty place to put sick men to sleep, when it dawned on me that they were all dead men waiting to be buried. One got hardened to this sort of thing, but it was unpleasant at the time.

The state of unpreparedness of 1 HAC at this stage is illustrated by this extract from the Battalion's war diary:

> General Chichester & his Brigade Major … were notified we had never fired our rifles.[3] He seemed rather astonished but interested and promised every assistance.
>
> 3 Nov. 1914. … The CO met General Lambton (Military Secretary to the C-in-C) and said he hoped HAC would be given a fair chance and not thrown into action too soon and suggested they should first go in reserve in order to become accustomed to shell and rifle fire as by this means better results would be obtained. He also said we had 600 recruits and the men had never had a chance of sighting their rifles.
>
> 4 November 1914. (The CO's conversations with authorities evidently took effect) Rifle range in town-ditch allotted to us all day. No. 1 Coy, Signallers and Pioneers all had five shots each at silhouette targets. Found rifles mostly sighted 50 yards low. Light bad but shooting excellent. Informed by Brigade Major that remaining companies could fire on following days but this excellent scheme was not fulfilled as orders came in the evening for the whole Battalion to proceed to Bailleul.

As it was bidden, on 5 November, the Battalion en-bussed[4] in a fleet of red London buses and was transported to Bailleul in some state. The enemy had been ejected from the village only a week before and there was ample evidence of the fighting. Fryer recorded that:

> On November 10th we went up in support to some small night operation: there was a terrific cannonade, and I remember being almost inarticulate with fear, and quite unable to prevent my knees from knocking together. I don't think it was till the 12th that we got our first shells close. It was NOT nice.

It was decided that 1 HAC would join the Lahore Division, a component of the Indian Army, commanded by Major General James Willcocks and located around the village of La Bassée. The unit formed-up and marched to join its new master. When it arrived the new master was vastly disappointed with what he saw. He had presumed, mistakenly, that the Honourable Artillery Company had something to do with 'artillery'. He was neither the first nor the last to make that mistake.[5]

Someone had to decide what to do with the HAC and, in the meantime, Lieutenant General Sir Horace Smith-Dorrien inspected the Battalion. He pronounced it to be 'a fine body of men'. The fine body of men were then put to work digging trenches. Fryer observed on the Corps Commander's inspection as follows:

> He gave us a wonderful address, full of optimism, though I think he must have been intentionally over-optimistic so that we should not have the 'wind up' during our first turn of duty in the trenches. He said he didn't think the war would last long, and that 85% of the German shells were duds. They must have improved their output soon after, as we found they burst only too well.

With reference to the trench digging, AOP said that:

> We set about it quite cheerily without taking the slightest precautions to make ourselves as inconspicuous as possible. The first day we were unmolested. The second, Fritz decided to give us a lesson. There was a noise like an express train at an incredible speed. A metallic clap, a cloud of smoke billowed out 100 yards in front of us about 50 feet from the ground. A shell! High explosive shrapnel! A woolly bear, as this type was aptly named.
>
> I leaned on my spade and watched, fascinated. I was really under fire. My pulse raced with excitement. A second shell followed the first, then a third. There was a commotion a little way along the line. Men were running. Someone rushed by calling for the doctor. A direct hit, we had suffered our first casualty.[6]

Pollard was incorrect. The very first casualty in 1 HAC had been Lance Corporal Claude Smart, who had been killed in an accident at Le Mans on 26 October 1914. In fact, this minor artillery stonk, on 14 November 1914, was an inconsequential incident in the context of a world war. However, it was the occasion when the first member of 1st Bn HAC was killed in action.

He was Private FJ Milne.

Francis Milne had joined the HAC three weeks after Pollard and ten weeks later, he was dead. The artillery strike caused eleven casualties and, of these, only Milne died. If AOP felt concern for his fallen comrades he did not express it and did not give any of them a name.

At this stage in the war, Alfred Pollard did not appear to realize that artillery fire, by its very nature, takes its victims by the most random and cruellest of selections. AOP could so very easily have been the first fatal HAC casualty in World War I, and had he drawn that short straw, then the lives of many, some of them German and certainly that of this biographer, would have been very different. It might even have been Milne who went on to win the Victoria Cross.

This incident was merely an introduction to shell fire. Later, Alfred Pollard and his comrades in 1 HAC were to receive their full share of incoming artillery, under which the Battalion was to suffer significant losses. To be under shell fire is one of the most awesome and terrifying experiences. By 1915, the effective use of artillery had been a feature of the battlefield for over 200 years. The mere passage of time does not alter the horror.

Vernon Scannell, a member of 51st Highland Division in Normandy in 1944, writing about events that lay thirty years or so in the future, said:[7]

> The fury of artillery is a cold, mechanical fury, but its intent is personal. When you are under its fire you are the sole target. All of that shrieking, whining venom is directed at you and at no one else. You hunch in your hole in the ground, reduce yourself into as small a thing as you can become, and you harden your muscles in a pitiful attempt at defying the jagged, burning teeth of the shrapnel. Involuntarily you curl up into the foetal position except that your hands go down to protect your genitalia. This instinct to defend the place of generation against the forces of annihilation was universal. Many resorted to a litany of repetitive swearing, a sort of profane mantra to dull their fear.
>
> Scannell continued:
>
> The same soldier went on to describe the psychological collapse of the most warlike member of their company. It took place in the cellar of a farmhouse. This battle-shock casualty was curled up on the floor, howling and sobbing. 'The smart, keen young soldier was now transformed into something that was at once pitiful and disgusting. The neatly-shaped, alert features had melted and blurred, the mouth was sagging and the whole face, dirty and stubbled, seemed swollen and was smeared with tears and snot. He made bleating noises, crying for his mother. As well as a feeling of slightly sadistic contempt, the observer became aware of a kind of envy of the boy's shameless surrender to his terror.'

Notes

1 AO Pollard, *Fire-Eater*, p31.
2 AO Pollard, *Fire-Eater*, p33.
3 This was misleading because the Battalion had spent time on Purfleet Ranges before embarking for France. They had not fired many rounds but they had fired their weapons.
4 En-trained, de-trained, en-bussed are words much loved by the Army. It quite likes 'de-buss', too.
5 'Artillery' in the title is of medieval origin when 'artillery' was the word applied to any form of firearm or missile weapon.
6 AO Pollard, *Fire-Eater*, p36.
7 Vernon Scannell, *Argument of Kings*, London, 1987, p165.

Chapter 3

Action!

'A cook was required in the Company officers' mess. I volunteered and became the cook. I have never been able to decide why I took this job on. I knew absolutely nothing about cooking.'

November 1914–May 1915

It was on 21 November 1914 that 1 HAC went into the line for the first time. Company by company they went in for a twenty-four-hour rotation and introduction to trench life. It did not take long for the comfortably raised young men to decide that this was no way for a well brought up lad to spend his time.

The trenches were wet, very cold, and with an absolute dearth of creature comforts. It was something of a relief to be withdrawn on 3 December for an inspection by the Captain-General although it was less than three months since the King had inspected the Regiment at Armoury House. Some of Pollard's comrades were blasé about this constant contact with the Monarch. Significantly, it was the first time that a reigning monarch had been with his army in the field since Dettingen, in 1743.

King George V, 'the Sailor King', had an affinity to his servicemen and throughout the duration of the war, he often demonstrated a sincere concern for their well-being, coupled with an acute awareness of the military and political factors that placed them in harm's way. He certainly displayed more compassion than many of his generals and accordingly, he enjoyed the unqualified affection of his 'Company'.

A number of senior regular officers were present[1] at the parade on 3 December and were shaken and bemused when 'Regimental Fire' was given to the King by companies as he passed down their lines.[2] They probably wondered how they should respond. They had no need to do so as it was absolutely nothing to do with them – it was an HAC, a family matter.

On 9 December the Battalion left Bailleul to join the 7 Brigade of the 3rd

Division under the command of Major General Haldane and went into the line for the first time as a complete entity. It took over trenches in front of Spanbroek Molen. Goold Walker said with great authority that:

> The trenches were shallow, mud-filled ditches, dominated by the German line: the parapets were often only breast-high: the approaches were open and bullet-swept. It rained incessantly, with frost and snow at intervals.

Units that found themselves alongside the HAC were nonplussed to discover that their comrades had actually been proposed and seconded to join their regiment and what is more, they then *paid a subscription* [author's italics] to live in the mud and among the dead and detritus of war.

Mr. SB Wood[3] recalled that when the HAC were relieving a Royal Fusilier battalion one dirty night in 1914, a voice politely enquired: 'Oo are yer?'

The resulting explanation was greeted with the remark, 'Lor mates, come and 'ave a look at these blokes wot's paid to come 'ere.'

In similar fashion, Mr. Wood recalled that when being relieved by another cockney battalion, one of the incoming soldiers asked what the trenches were like. Before a reply could be given another cockney voice chimed in, 'Don't worry, Bill; wot's good enough fer the 'onerables is good enough fer us.'

AOP found the march into the trenches an exciting journey as he stumbled through the dark night. There was to be no talking and no smoking but as the 800 men made their way through the mud the clinking of the equipment provided a muted military overture for what lay ahead.

For many, it was to be death.

Once in the trenches every third man was put on guard and Alfred, rifle loaded and cocked, was prepared. 'I was determined to sell my life dearly,' he said. There were the usual alarms and on one occasion an unfortunate stray cow, moving around in no man's land, paid with its life for making a noise as it attracted fire from both sides. It was at this time that the Commanding Officer won the respect of Pollard, who commented:

> I think we owe more than we appreciated to Colonel Treffry for the tactful way he handled the Battalion at this time.[4] He knew the type of men he was commanding – every one was from a public school, delicately brought up, unused to roughing it. He insisted on our being broken in by degrees. There is not the slightest doubt that, had he allowed us to be pitchforked straight into the thick of things, we should not have given such a good account of ourselves.[5]

The men adapted to trench life but not to the infestation of lice. The opportunity to bath and change clothes daily did not exist and the lice were a constant and unremitting torment. The routine was for companies to spend about three days in the line, a further three days in support and then a period in billets. These were commandeered buildings well to the rear where the men could sleep, wash and relax.

The Battalion was 'working the 'F' trenches in front of Kemmel', and to get there AOP recorded that:

> Winter was upon us and it was bitterly cold. From Kemmel village we left the road and proceeded across country. Part of the route (to 'F' trench) traversed a turnip field. I had been detailed to help carry ammunition for the Vickers guns in two heavy boxes in addition to my rifle. Every time I stepped on a turnip I slipped. Stray bullets from the German line hummed through the air. Once while crossing a ditch, I fell. My out-flung hand came in contact with a slimy something that gave to the touch. It was the face of a Frenchman who had been lying dead for some months. It was my first experience of Death. I wondered whether it would ever be my fate to lie like that uncared for and uncaring.
>
> The trench, when we reached it, was half full of mud and water.[6] We set to work to try to drain it. Our efforts were hampered by the fact that the French, who had first occupied it, had buried their dead in the bottom and sides. Every stroke of the pick encountered a body. The smell! Ugh!
>
> The cold was terrible. Standing in water as we were it was impossible to keep warm. I kept beating my feet against the parapet to keep them from going to sleep. We lived for the rum ration which was all too meagre. I was in a traverse trench with The Trinity and 'Scully' Hull. We swore that when we got out we would have a roast goose and a jolly good tuck-in.

The 'good tuck in', when it came, was when 'C' Company was withdrawn to billets. It was rabbit instead of goose, but the plum pudding, cake and chocolate from home all washed down with *vin rouge* and coffee was more than good enough.

When Pollard returned to the line he was better equipped and was well provided with mittens, scarves and spare socks. In their absence 1 Wilts, who had relieved the HAC, had made a great improvement to the trenches. The German trenches opposite were about 200 yards distant and they were manned by a Bavarian battalion that contained a disconcertingly high number of excellent shots. Sniping occupied both sides and the HAC lost a number of men to head shots, but the majority of casualties were caused by the incessant shelling.

AOP said that he fired about fifty rounds a day, usually from around a sand bag, eschewing the steel plates with loop-holes. He described these as 'a snare and a delusion, as several men were killed by a bullet coming right through the plate'. He was learning his trade and made sure that he did not fire more than a few shots before he moved further down the trench. Ideally he would have moved to a prepared position after every shot. He did not record whether or not his fire was 'effective' – that is to say, did he hit any of his chosen targets? A trained sniper would not fire unless certain of a hit, but that was subtlety probably lost on AOP.

Although he may have been enthusiastic, unskilled snipers did not make old bones on the Western Front and he was most fortunate not to attract counter-fire.

In the early days of the war, an isolated death by gunshot was often attributed to 'a stray round', and on this topic Martin Pegler[7] commented:

> However, as the war became more static, the British soldiers began to notice that that even in quiet parts of the line, the number of men dropping from bullet wounds to the head was beyond the simple explanation of being hit by a "stray". On average, a line battalion could expect between twelve and eighteen casualties a day, most from rifle fire. From the earliest days of 1914 the German snipers dominated the front lines, and their prowess was soon legendry. In a vain attempt to combat the growing menace, the British used whatever they could lay their hands onto provide makeshift sniping positions, but the men had no training and were often frighteningly naïve.

This naivety is well illustrated by William Skipp[8], who recounted that:

> We had a sniper's post, which was just a sheet of metal … a hole big enough to put the end of a rifle through. We had two boys, they were orphans and they had been brought up together. They were standing in the trenches and one said, "What's this George, have a look through here," and no sooner had he approached it than down he went with a bullet through his forehead. Now his friend was so flabbergasted he too had a look and less than two minutes later he was down in the trench with his friend.

That sad anecdote was endorsed by Reginald Haine when he was recalling his time as a private man during the awful winter of 1914–15. He said, sagely, that 'The finest training in warfare is warfare itself. In a fortnight you learn more than in two years of any training can teach you. And so, before the end of the year, we were a very seasoned battalion and – I might say it without bragging – we were as good as any regular battalion in the line.'[9]

Christmas was spent in the line. At midnight on Christmas Eve, 'We sang all the carols we could remember: the whole Company in one huge chorus. After we had exhausted our repertoire there was a lull. Then the Bavarians started (to sing) in their trenches.'

There were some, elsewhere in the line, who were unable to sing.
A sketch by Adrian Hill.[10] (HAC Archives)

The cold was intense and relief was welcomed. The 4-mile march out of the line to Locre surprisingly exhausted the very fit AOP and on arrival at his billet, he collapsed. He woke with a raging fever, and when the medical officer was called, he diagnosed jaundice and Alfred Pollard was evacuated to hospital.

Pollard was not the only one in need of medical help as casualties slowly mounted. One officer and seventy men were killed before Kemmel, Elzenwalle, Dickebusch and St. Eloi. All of these obscure little villages with little-known names are long since forgotten. In their vicinity, however, a further 250 all ranks were hospitalized for frostbite, exhaustion and exposure. These casualties – over 300 in number – were incurred without the Battalion making a single aggressive move. The weather and shell fire did the damage.

AOP was sent back to a base hospital to recover but he suffered agonies of self-reproach at leaving his comrades and imagined that he would have been classified as a 'miker' or shirker. He begged the doctor not to repatriate him and the doctor readily agreed because, he opined, Pollard had no more got jaundice than he had. Pollard was discharged from hospital on 4 January – 'thrown out', in his words. That freezing night was spent travelling in a cattle truck, en route to Rouen, and he observed that it was a wonder he didn't get a fresh chill.

At Rouen Alfred found himself in a holding camp and he met up with the first draft of replacements for his battalion. He was delighted to be among friends and enjoyed being able to play the 'old soldier' on the basis of his few weeks' service at the front.

The draft was required to rise at 0600hrs each morning but AOP was disinclined to join them. 'I felt to do the same would be undignified,' he explained. The camp was tented and covered a very wide area. Alfred found a tent set aside for men who had not yet arrived. He scrounged three blankets and established himself in a large tent, which he had all to himself. He was quite snug, remained in his blankets until a gentlemanly 0930hrs, when he took a leisurely breakfast at the YMCA. He did no fatigues, parades or drills because he was clearly not on anyone's nominal roll. He was unaccounted for, spare, and as a result, left entirely to his own devices.

It could not last.

It didn't.

On the eighth morning, the flap of the tent was cast aside and the Camp Sergeant-Major made a brisk and martial entry into Alfred Pollard's life. He was a regular soldier and his mission in life was to sort out people like Pollard. He asked, in an ominously quiet voice, for an explanation for Pollard's horizontal position so late in the day and for his absence from other forms of productive activity. Pollard relates how he explained that 'coming from the line', as he had, he had no idea about camp routine.[11] The CSM, who had not yet been in 'the line', was outraged by Pollard's calculated insolence. Pollard was ordered to report to the orderly room at 1200hrs.

The young man had not the least intention of so doing – he made his way over to the HAC draft and found that it was to parade at 1100hrs to march to the station. Pollard attended his first parade and lost himself among the other 300: he boarded the train and was soon reunited with 'C' Company. He speculated, in 1932, that the CSM was probably still looking for him.

Goold Walker recorded, clinically, that throughout the remainder of this winter of almost unimaginable hardship and misery for the troops, the HAC took its turn in the line. Sometimes during the period of so-called 'rest' out of the line, the men would be engaged all night on fatigue parties carrying material up to the trenches. Casualties mounted steadily until, on 13 January 1915, a draft of four officers and 300 men arrived from the 2nd Battalion to fill the gaps. The 301st was Alfred Oliver Pollard.

One of these draftees was Private HS Clapham. Clapham was a willing but less enthusiastic soldier than Pollard and he wrote about his experience of nine months in France.[12] He recorded the prosaic routine of trench life by saying that on 24 January 1915:

> I was on guard for an hour three times during the night and, in accordance with instructions, fired a round at nothing every ten minutes or so. Apparently it is quite safe to keep your head over the parapet at night if you duck when a star shell flares to the ground. It is impossible to see anything sufficiently clearly to aim straight … the other men in the section are the nicest chaps I have met in this game and we have really quite a good time.

Back with his Company AOP caught up with his mail and was ecstatic to receive a letter from the girl who had been constantly in his thoughts. She did not write regularly or often but, as he admitted:

> Every time she wrote it gave me hope. Poor fool that I was, I read between the lines things that were never there. A phrase intended to cheer me up became an endearment. She had joined The London Hospital staff as a probationer nurse. Heroine worship made her a second Florence Nightingale.

There were changes in the Battalion's officers and a number of promotions made. Private Harry Hoblyn became a lance corporal. Three of the sergeants were commissioned[13] and one, 'Duggie' Davis, asked Pollard to be his servant. AOP gave the matter some thought and he concluded:

> A change was taking place in me at this time. I crossed to France a mere boy, my outlook restricted. War was changing me into a man. I had not yet emerged from my chrysalis, but experience was making me more self-reliant. I began to realize the strength of my own personality. (Being a servant) would not make difference to my going into the line. If it had I would have refused. On the other hand it gave me something to do when we were out as an alternative to fatigues. It also promised a trifle more physical comfort.
>
> I accepted.
>
> I went further. A cook was required in the Company officers' mess. I volunteered and became the cook. I have never been able to decide why I took this job on. I knew absolutely nothing about cooking … Somebody had to do it and I suppose I decided I would rather be poisoned by my own hand than by someone else's.[14]

Pollard was most emphatically not a good servant and Davis had, figuratively, shot himself in the foot. The Company officers' mess was a small room at the rear of the local grocer's shop several hundred yards behind the lines. The grocer's wife or widow was an elderly lady of some sixty summers who lived alone with her daughter, a spinster of a certain age. At twenty-one, Pollard would have viewed the daughter, who was probably about thirty-five, as being ancient. Both the ladies were good cooks and they seemed to take sufficient of a shine to the strapping Pollard that they took on his catering duties. Pollard was swift to confess his manifold deficiencies in the servant department. He admitted:

> I have never in my life been much good at getting up early in the morning. To have to get myself out of bed, prepare early morning tea for the mess, rouse Duggie, brush his clothes and clean his boots and then cook breakfast was beyond me. Something had to go.
>
> That something was Duggie.
>
> I'm afraid that he usually cleaned his own boots and brushed his own clothes. His bath I used to leave ready overnight.[15] From Duggie's point of view I was the worst servant that ever happened. But, thanks to Madame I was a very efficient cook.
>
> After all, everything was on my side. It was impossible to vary the menu very much. Meat, when we got a bit outside a tin, invariably consisted of frozen beef. The only alternative was pork, which could be obtained from the local butcher. Otherwise my job consisted of wielding a tin-opener. And of course the servants had to come first. We took the pick; the officers had what was left. I well remembered one day I was standing in front of the stove cooking some succulent pork chops which I had wrested from the butcher after a fierce argument. Laurie MacArthur, the Mess President, came into the kitchen rubbing his hands attracted by the appetising odour.
>
> 'Splendid fellow, Pollard,' he cried enthusiastically. 'It looks as though we are going to have a damned good lunch today.'
>
> I turned slowly from the fire, my fork poised in my hand.
>
> 'Yours is stew, Sir,' I gently disillusioned him.
>
> He retired crestfallen. Stew from the Company cooker figured very prominently on the menu. Of course the officers were very raw or they would never have stood the treatment we gave them. Later on when I held a commission myself, I was in a position to out-general my servant in all the tricks he tried on me.

There was, however, a different facet to life, as Clapham explained when he quoted from an entry in his diary made on 4 February 1915:

> The trench was originally a German one and then held by the French … Apparently the Huns used the bodies of the dead to form the nucleus of the parapet and the resulting stench is horrible. In some places can be seen a foot or a hand sticking out of the trench wall and one's hands stink from the mud which clings to them. I saw a large captive balloon. We were all watching it and discussing if it were British or Hun when there was a sudden crack and X – who had risen to his feet … fell back onto another man who caught him in his arms. For a second one hardly realized what had happened, but the salmon on my biscuit was speckled red and white. And as we laid X down, we saw a furrow across the back of his head, from which his brains protruded. I don't think he could have felt anything at all, but he made inarticulate noises for three parts of an hour before he died. Poor K who caught him as he fell, is very young and could do nothing but lean against the parapet and say 'Oh God'. It was the first time I had seen death in wartime, and it was upsetting even to me.[16]

Whist in the Locre area on 25 February 1915, Sergeant Harrap, who had encouraged AOP at Purfleet Ranges, was very seriously wounded (but survived). During this period there were scant resources behind the HAC to back it up and the CO enquired of the Brigade Commander if he did not think it unwise to entrust such an important section of the line to his raw Territorials. The Brigadier shrugged and replied, 'At any rate, they won't run away. They would fight to the last man.' When 21-year-old Alfred heard of this conversation he concurred fully with his brigade commander. 'He was right,' he said sagely.

The attrition suffered by the Battalion was mirrored elsewhere in the division and, notwithstanding the need to reinforce 1 HAC, twenty-three private soldiers were selected by Colonel Treffry and sent to the Worcesters, Wiltshires, South Lancashires and Royal Irish Rifles. They were given no additional training and reported as second lieutenants. Pollard was sorry to lose one of his chums, 'Black' Scott,[17] who went to the Wiltshire Regiment. He was killed very soon after and several of that batch of twenty-three were dead even before they were gazetted.

The British Army was at its obstinate and stupid worst and it was personified in the shape of the Brigade Commander. This officer informed Colonel Treffry that GHQ had decided that these twenty-three men – or those still living and still being paid as privates – would not be gazetted until they had been through an officer cadets' school, which had recently been created at Bailleul. What is more, he, the Brigadier, could or would do nothing about the matter. We do not know if the Brigadier stamped his foot at this juncture physically, but he certainly did metaphorically.

The Brigade Commander clearly did not know who he was doing business with and Colonel Treffry was having nothing of this nonsense. He protested very strongly indeed. He said that he had encouraged these men to volunteer and it was on the basis of his assurance that they would be commissioned at once that they had come forward. The men who had been killed whilst acting as second lieutenants and wearing the badges of the rank would have died as private men under this unfair, unjust ruling. It was monstrous, and Treffry did not mince words in saying so.

It is little wonder that the men of 1 HAC thought that the sun rose and set on their CO because he went over the Brigadier's head to the Divisional Commander. He drew another complete blank here and honour would have been satisfied if, at this stage, he had given up. This was not Treffry's style and he promptly asked to see the Corps Commander, Lieutenant General Sir Charles Ferguson. Treffry put his case very strongly and, for his trouble, was threatened with the sack.

However, he still did not give up.

Treffry now elevated the issue to the level of the Army Commander. Lieutenant colonels do not habitually operate in these rarefied climes but Treffry was undaunted and when, by happy chance, General Sir Horace Smith-Dorrien visited the Battalion very soon after, Treffry laid out the case and argued it passionately.

Smith-Dorrien was convinced by the argument and he said he would take the matter up with the Adjutant General. He was as good as his word and promptly did so. Within two weeks, at the end of March, the *London Gazette* published the twenty-three names, appointing them all to a commission.

A number of other soldiers were promoted to fill gaps in the NCO ranks and Pollard was less than impressed by the promotion process – not the first British soldier to be so. He had reservations about the quality of some of the officer replacements and in addition felt that 'a man who had served two months in France was worth five men from home'. This endorses the view expressed by Haine (see page 28). He asserted that some of those who failed to make the grade were sent home, promoted and blocked the path of others. He says, somewhat defensively, he had no aspiration for a commission in January 1915. He claimed that he 'was happy in the carefree life of a private. My ambition to reach the line was satisfied: a new one was born within me. I wanted to take part in an attack.'

On 8 March 1915, command of 'C' Company passed from 'Fanny' Ward to Captain EPC Boyle,[18] who was the opposite from the hard-driving Ward. Boyle had come straight from England and he instantly won the respect and admiration of the officers' mess cook, who described him as:

> A kindly personality who understood men and how to get the best out of them. He was the finest soldier we ever had in the regiment. He never knew fear in any shape or form and always carried himself bolt upright in situations where most men crawled on their hands and knees. I gave him my allegiance from the first day I met him. His example and, I am proud to say, friendship, made me the Fire-Eater I afterwards became.[19]

That is an amazing tribute from a man with a chest full of medals for gallantry. It is clear that Boyle really was an exceptional soldier and leader. The mess held a dinner to mark the change of command and Colonel Treffry attended. Pollard promised to produce a six-course meal and in his book, lists the menu with which this reader will not be burdened, but suffice to say that AOP made a good fist of it and was called into the dining room to receive the Commanding Officer's congratulations.

Captain Boyle was not a young man. He was born in 1860, had joined the HAC as far back as 1886, served in the South African War and now, twenty-nine years later, at the advanced age of fifty-five, he had an immediate impact on his new command.

Ernest Boyle ordered all manner of culinary delights to be sent out from England and he announced that the officers' servants were to have a share of these mouth-watering and expensive adjuncts to the issued ration. It was a master stroke and AOP said that 'It was all very well to help ourselves when the extras were forbidden but it was a different matter when they were freely and generously offered.'

Boyle fired in young Alfred an ambition to do better, so much so that he sent home to his mother for cookery books, but the first recipe he opened started 'take a dozen oysters …' He opened an adjacent window and hurled the book across the street. A dozen oysters in Locre in February 1915? Not really.

When the Company was in the line Lieutenant Davis was usually with Captain Boyle at Company HQ and thus Pollard was close to hand when he heard Boyle announce that he was going to examine the barbed wire in front of the 'C' Company position. He asked for a volunteer to accompany him.

Pollard volunteered and thereafter 'Went everywhere with him.' Boyle was a father figure to Pollard and he set the younger man an example that Pollard sought to emulate from their first shared sally.

This first expedition was the first time that AOP had had cause to wander about in no man's land and he was 'thrilled to the core'. There was nothing between him and the German machine-guns. He felt very vulnerable; as well he might, every time a Very flare or star shell lit the sky. The effort of standing absolutely still until the illumination had faded, caused the adrenaline to flow. However, this was man's work and Pollard lived in hope that they would encounter a German patrol. It seems that Boyle spent time every night making these nocturnal patrols without apparent reason and Pollard suggested that 'It soothed his great fighting spirit to feel that he was exposed to certain death should we be discovered.' For Pollard, these excursions made life worth living. 'The danger acted like a drug, quickening my pulse. At last I was doing something worthwhile. I was as happy as a sand boy.'

AOP wrote constantly to his mother – always addressed as 'Mater'. His letters were of no great significance other than they chronicled the mundane and un-interesting routine of trench life. He wrote of near misses, of comrades wounded or killed. He had a very close relationship with his mother and his autobiography was dedicated to her but his father rarely figures in his correspondence. He relished letters from home but daily, he yearned to hear from his 'Lady' – more often than not he was disappointed.

On 16 March 1915, 2nd Lieutenant Horace Link joined the Battalion. He was to spend a great deal of his time with AOP over the next eighteen months or so and they got to know each other well.

It was in March 1915, after four months in the line, that Pollard first saw serious action, albeit as a spectator. As an eye witness his account is valuable and what he saw had a considerable effect upon him. He recorded that:

> An attack was delivered from the trenches on my right. We were not actually in it but we had a first-rate view of the whole affair, which was the next best thing. A British attack! How it stirred me! The British position was the slope of one hill: the German on the other. A shallow valley lay between. Our front-line trench was almost at the foot of the slope: the German being about 200 yards distant and half-way up to the crest of the rise. The strong-point to be attacked was called Spanbroek Moulin, nick-named by us the 'Moulin Rouge'. Behind in the distance rose the spire of Wytschaete Church.
>
> Davis's platoon (of which AOP was one) was in the support trench 100 yards or so behind our front line and almost on a level with the German front line. I was … in such a position … to have a perfect view of the whole show.
>
> The attack was timed for three o'clock in the afternoon but, owing to mist, it was postponed until later. It was preceded by a pitiable barrage of artillery fire, which consisted of a few salvos from our two batteries. Then a detachment of the Wilts (Probably, 1st Bn, The Wiltshire Regiment) swarmed over the parapet of the trenches on our immediate right.

The attack was launched.

Poor devils! They did not get very far. The Huns, warned by our unusual artillery activity, were prepared. As the first of our troops made an appearance the hitherto hidden shutters protecting four machine-guns which formed the armament of the Moulin Rouge were slid back.

The guns opened fire. Nothing could live in such a storm of lead.

The attacking troops went down like ninepins. One officer got about fifty yards. He was a big fellow and carried a rifle and bayonet which he waved over his head. Gallant fellow!

I ought to have been frightened. I ought to have realized the futility of infantry trying to cross open ground in the face of concentrated machine-gun fire. I ought to have prayed that it might never be my lot to be sent to certain death on such a mission.

Instead my blood raced through my arteries and veins, and I was filled with such a rage as I have never experienced in my life before. The Hun became my enemy then. He was mowing down my countrymen who were helpless to retaliate. Had not the merest thread of discipline restrained me I should have leapt the parapet and rushed down the slope of the hill, the blood lust in my heart? As it was I rested my rifle on a sand bag and fired as rapidly as I could work the bolt and trigger.[20]

The German machine-guns attracted by the fire coming from 1 HAC swept the parapet of the support trench, of which they had clear line of sight, and rounds thudded into the sand bags or whined on, overhead. In the meantime, no man's land was littered thickly with the gallant men from Salisbury, Warminster, Devizes, Malmesbury and countless small Wiltshire villages. It was quite evident that the attack on Moulin Rouge had failed miserably. Like many others who had witnessed the debacle that had unfolded before their eyes, AOP sought to analyse the reasons for failure.

It was not difficult.

Pollard placed the blame firmly on the inept artillery bombardment, which was insufficiently heavy and which left intact the four murderously lethal machine-guns firing in defilade and laying down an impenetrable beaten zone. He concluded that if one of the pairs of guns had been knocked out there would have been a gap through which the attackers could have reached the German line. He said soberly, obviously and accurately, 'It is impossible for the bravest man in the world to advance in the teeth of a machine-gun.' Pollard had found the charge of the Wiltshires an emotional experience and added:

To me the failure was a distinct shock. I had always believed the British infantry to be invincible: to see them (sic) rendered impotent was a

> revelation which dismayed me. Their courage was unquestioned. My national pride swelled in me and a lump came to my throat as I remembered how those men had gone forward to their deaths. The officer who had shown so noble an example set me a standard which I kept in mind all through the campaign. I should be proud to die in similar circumstances … but the affair of the Moulin Rouge made a deep and lasting impression on my mind. One lesson which I took to heart is indirectly responsible for my being alive today. I realized that bravery by itself is useless against modern weapons of war. Strategy and guile must also be employed to attain success. The most notable example of my putting this theory into practice was on the occasion of my winning the Victoria Cross … appreciated the truth of the axiom that 'discretion is the better part of valour'.

It transpired that, previously, Colonel Treffry had received orders to detail two captains to observe the artillery barrage and that he, his second-in-command and adjutant were to similarly observe from further back. The task was carried out and Treffry duly reported on the ineffectiveness of the gunnery. The report displeased the Brigade Commander. His brigade major rejected the report and insisted that the two captains were to undertake a personal and detailed examination of the enemy wire that night. Treffry realized that this was tantamount to ordering the two officers to their deaths and he insisted on being given the order in writing. Once more his strength of character and iron determination carried the day. The order, which seemed to have originated with the Brigade Major, was rescinded.

Alfred Pollard took a critical look at his officers. For Captain Boyle he had nothing but unqualified admiration. Others he found to be wanting. One officer he described as 'Bewildered, and although he had no fear for himself he developed a dread the he might be unable to lead his men across no man's land. From that hour his efficiency as a combatant officer was finished.' Quite how Pollard knew the inner workings of this officer's brain he did not explain.

Another officer he considered to be 'over-excited' and he said that 'I formed the opinion that I should not care to have to trust his judgment in a crisis.' Nevertheless, Pollard was quick to add that this officer did not lack personal courage but, unfortunately this courage was nullified by his highly-strung personality and his likely lack of control. Speaking of this particular officer he recounted an incident that took place just as the Wiltshires' operation stuttered to a close.

It would seem that Pollard busied himself getting some water to boil. He was on his hands and knees when someone delivered an enormous kick to his bottom ('posterior', as Pollard primly records). Pollard sprawled forward and all but demolished the cooker. A voice howled: 'Get up on the parapet man! Don't skulk down there! What are you doing?'

Pollard turned round to find the officer towering over him. His face was flushed and his eyes were starting out of his head. His lips twitched and his voice was almost falsetto. Pollard stared up into his eyes and replied: 'Making you a cup of tea, Sir.'

The officer made no reply but later in the day, made an indirect apology. In Pollard's opinion, rightly so, for he commented, confidently, that 'Even in those early days I had achieved a reputation which was incompatible with cowardice.'[21]

AOP was a hard judge but he recognized bravery when he saw it and recorded an incident that he described as 'a demonstration of mind over matter'. A signaller, called Evans, was on duty in his trench and was patently terrified. He was shaking uncontrollably with fear. He could only hold his instrument to his ear with difficulty. Poor Evans was close to the end of his tether. Suddenly the line went dead and it was evident that the line had been cut. 'Without a moment's hesitation, he climbed out of the trench in search of the break. His duty was to keep the line intact and, personal fear or no personal fear, his duty was carried out to the letter.'

Evans would have been vastly flattered in later life, if indeed he survived,[22] to know that he had attracted the admiration of one who was to become a regimental and national hero.

In Flanders, winter conducted a fighting withdrawal in the face of a spring offensive. Spring made forays into winter's territory and gained ground. The frost was weakened and no longer made its dawn appearance coating men and weapons in a white sheet. The sun made intermittent sallies over the trenches and the water table dropped slightly in support. Spring finally carried the day. Winter capitulated and the weather turned for the better. It had been a long and very hard winter.

1 HAC was withdrawn for four short days and then repositioned, further north, to St. Eloi and the delights of 'P' trench. There had been heavy fighting hereabouts only days before. The Germans had breached the British line and the consequent re-organization had called for new but incomplete trenches without any form of shelter – this heralded more digging for AOP and his friends. The Trinity was not as cohesive as hitherto because Harry had by now been promoted to sergeant and as such had to distance himself slightly from his friends – a situation that Pollard understood.

The Battalion moved into 'P' trenches from 4 April until 31 May, and alternated with the remains of 1 Wilts. During that period two officers were wounded and 125 other ranks were killed and wounded. This level of attrition applied to every line battalion.

This part of the line introduced to the HAC two fearsome German weapons designed to kill every last one of them. The first was the trench mortar, which fired a projectile filled with 1,200lbs of high explosive. This lethal shell was of low velocity and apprehensive British soldiers could see the incoming shell turning over slowly in flight. The bursting shell assailed the eardrums. Pollard was able to watch this weapon in action when he saw 5th Bn Royal Northumberland Fusiliers, holding a trench off to a flank, bombarded at some length. Most of the Fusiliers were evacuated to the HAC part of the line whilst the rain of mortar shells descended and they were spared. The unfortunates who had been left to man the trench suffered awful casualties.

An interesting statistic[23] discovered by the RAMC when it conducted a study after the war, showed that it was myth to suppose that it was German machine-guns that caused the most damage. It was true that 39% of wounds were caused by small arms fire (rifle and machine-gun) but by a very wide margin the majority – 58%, in fact – of British casualties were the result of artillery fire in all its different guises, of which the trench mortar was only one. Two per cent of all wounds were caused by grenades and a miniscule 0.32% was bayonet wounds. It would be reasonable to presume that the statistics for German casualties were similar. Although it took boots on the ground to win a war it can not be disputed that the artillery was 'the Queen of the Battlefield'.

The second fearsome weapon was gas. The opposition had used gas for the first time, against the Canadians holding the line just north of the Ypres salient, on 22 April 1915. Pollard had just been issued with a gas mask and he counted himself lucky not to have been on the receiving end of that first delivery. He had great faith in his gas mask and it was only after the event that he revised his view.

The Battalion was now in billets in Dickebusche. Pollard, who was still much affected by the slaughter of the Wiltshires and of the '5th Fusiliers', felt that acting as an officer's servant and mess cook he was not contributing much to the bigger picture. He asked to be relieved of both jobs and, thankfully, returned to Number Eight section. The day he took up his old place Captain Boyle promoted him to lance corporal and said that it was only his employment in the mess that had prevented his promotion earlier.

Nothing ever stays the same and very shortly afterwards, on 19 April 1915, The Trinity were sitting in a room at the back of a grocer's shop (different grocer!) drinking champagne, as you do when you have the chance, despite being involved in a war to end all wars. Glasses were fully charged when long range German guns started to shell the town. They were firing air bursts and the shrapnel had a devastating effect, especially upon the civilian population.

Sergeant Harry Hoblyn decided that he had to see what he could do and strode off into the maelstrom. Alfred and Ernest stayed to finish the bottle.

The Battalion had been ordered to occupy a prepared position behind the town but as the German guns were 'too long' they ran into fire that they would have avoided had they not moved. The two drinking chums looked out of a convenient window, 'Fanny' Ward caught sight of them and ordered then to rejoin their Company but first they went in search of Harry and found him lying badly wounded in both legs. His injuries were severe, he was evacuated and after a year in hospital he was discharged from the Army.[24]

The original 'Trinity' was no more but the compensation was that Pollard's greatest friend, Percy Lewis, arrived as part of a new draft. Lewis had been roundly rejected for service because he had chronic valvular disease. To his great credit he would not take 'no' for an answer and hawked himself around every recruiting office in London. Eventually, Lewis got into the Army and the HAC by the pragmatic expedient of getting someone else to attend a medical in his name – simple, really. The spirit of men like Lewis, and he was probably not an isolated case, is noteworthy.

The next time that 1 HAC went into the line, Percy Lewis found out what he had signed up for. The Battalion were in support of a minor attack dismissed by Pollard as 'Not nearly as exciting as Moulin Rouge', but nevertheless, it was his baptism of fire. Withdrawn to a support line 'C' Company was detailed to carry railway lines about 2 miles. Six men to a rail made for very arduous work with the taller men bearing a disproportionate part of the load – not least Pollard who was, of course, 6 feet 2 inches. Lewis had a weak heart; he should not have been there but gamely he played his part and it nearly killed him. The next night, 'C' Company was detailed off for trench digging, always unpopular, hard physical work. As the Company bent to its task it was strongly motivated to get below ground level by a machine-gun that pointed in their direction. This gun was firing speculative bursts, some of which were uncomfortably close. That exercise nearly did for Lewis, too.

On 4 May AOP marked his twenty-second birthday, and in schoolboy style, it was marked with a very large cake from home. Pollard did experience the pangs of homesickness, less for his mother but more for his 'Lady'. He cheerfully admitted:

> I wanted to see Her whom I now thought of … as my girl. I suppose I possess a strong strain of romantic sentiment. I had heard from her about once a month – just friendly newsy letters such as she might have written to any male acquaintance. In that womanless world of the forward area I had weaved into them thoughts they had never been intended to express. I persuaded myself that each wish for my health

> concealed a special meaning: each box of chocolates or packet of cigarettes I regarded as a special token. I hugged her image to my heart. I was fighting for England, but now England was personified by her. She was my ever gentle lady, for whom, if necessary, I would lay down my life. I wanted leave. Yes I wanted to go home and tell her of my love so that when I returned – and in my egotism, I had no doubt of her response – I should have the knowledge of our bond always with me to urge me to greater effort.[25]

These are the words of a very seriously besotted young man, recalled very vividly, sixteen years later with extraordinary and compelling honesty. The reader of this book, when young, may also have felt to some degree the mental turmoil that young Alfred was going through.

Unrequited love is the grist to the mill for novelists and song writers and it can be painful. For most of us these adolescent yearnings soon pass and reality takes over. Pollard was to be tortured for some time yet and his Lady – still unnamed, occupied his every waking thought.

Notes

1 'Regimental fire' is a compliment paid by members of the HAC on appropriate occasions. It consists of each individual shouting 'Zay' nine times whilst moving his right hand backward and forward across his body.

It is un-nerving to one attending a dinner for the first time, and having drunk the loyal toast, to hear the command, 'Regimental Fire … Present!

The origin of the custom is long since lost and even Goold Walker, the HAC historian, could not throw any light on the subject. However, the *Evening Standard* published a letter on 24 September 1960 in which the correspondent said that 'The custom dates from the early days of hand grenades when soldiers were taught to say this syllable (zay) nine times to count out the correct period between drawing the pin and throwing the weapon.' Fifty years on, this glib explanation has yet to be accepted as a reasonable explanation at Armoury House.

2 G Goold Walker, *The Honourable Artillery Company in the Great War 1914-1919*, p23.

3 The *Evening News*, 24 January 1930.

4 Later, Colonel E Treffry CMG, OBE.

5 AO Pollard, *Fire-Eater*, p39.

6 The British line ran through Flanders, it was low-lying, agricultural land but even in dry weather, the water table was very near the surface. Any digging quickly hit water. The winter of 1914-15 was particularly severe and the constant rain, snow and sleet all combined to add to the mud and misery.

7 M Pegler, *Out of Nowhere – A History of Military Sniping*, p80.

8 Corporal W Skipp, quoted in Arthur Max, *Forgotten Voices of the Great War*, Ebury Press, 2002.

9 Max Arthur, *Lest We Forget*, p121.

10 Adrian Keith Graham Hill (1895-1977) was born in Charlton and educated at Dulwich College and St. John's Wood School of Art. He also studied at The Royal College of Art.

He was admitted to the HAC on 18 Nov 1914 and joined 2nd Bn HAC. He was posted to 1st Bn on 26 November 1916 as a lance corporal.

Two months later he was promoted to corporal. This status was relinquished only three weeks later and he reverted to the ranks. He was employed as a sniper, and that being a highly hazardous task, he was clearly an above average soldier. He combined his martial activities with his artistic bent and whilst on active service he sketched the scenes about him and created some memorable images.

He became an official war artist and on 27 December 1917, he was appointed 'Temporary Honorary 2nd Lieutenant'. This is a rank as rare as hens' teeth – perhaps unique.

After the war he combined teaching with his painting and almost by chance, whilst recovering from an illness, he was exposed to 'occupational therapy'. He discovered the therapeutic benefits of art and thereafter contributed hugely to the British Red Cross in this field, coining the phrase 'art therapy', which he saw as a valid medical option for many patients.

He wrote a number of books, one of which – *Art versus Illness* (published in 1945) – expounded his ideas.

Hill knew Pollard and Haine and was with 1 HAC for the actions around Gavrelle in April 1917.

11 AO Pollard, *Fire-Eater*, p47.

12 HS Clapham, *Mud and Khaki*, p27. This book is a short but acclaimed account of trench life. Clapham was commissioned into the RAOC in 1916 and died in 1961.

13 It is unusual for an NCO in the British Army to be commissioned and to remain with his original unit, for obvious reasons. However, as this narrative reveals, that happened very frequently in the HAC, which did not accept officers of other cap badges and drew only from its own resources for officers.

14 AO Pollard, *Fire-Eater*, p49.

15 To offer his officer a cold bath every morning and get away with it, is less an indictment of Pollard but it speaks volumes about Duggie Davis. He was a chartered accountant before he enlisted, survived the war but died of pneumonia on 27 January 1919, aged twenty-nine, whilst serving with 2 HAC.

16 HA Clapham, *Mud and Khaki*, p49.

17 Walter Elvin 'Black' Scott, joined the HAC on 6 May 1914. He was commissioned into the Wiltshire Regiment in February 1915 and killed in action on 6 May 1915 whilst serving with 1st Bn Wiltshires. His photograph appears later in this book.

18 Later A/Lieutenant Colonel EPC Boyle DSO, who was killed at Beaumont Hamel in 1916. The Archivist of the HAC pointed out that there are two different versions for the order of Boyle's first names – either ECP or EPC. He signed the vellum book as 'Ernest Patrick Charles' and his regimental number register entry has this too. But all other HAC records, including his memorial service order of service, have ECP. The comprehensive list of all HAC members uses 'EPC', which is how he signed on joining. This book uses EPC throughout.

19 AO Pollard, *Fire-Eater*, p51.

20 AO Pollard, *Fire-Eater*, p57.

21 AO Pollard, *Fire-Eater*, p61.

22 A Private SJ Evans was killed at Beaucourt some months later. It may, of course, not have been the same man.

23 Major TJ Mitchell and Miss GM Smith, *Official History of the War, Casualties and Medical Statistics*, Imperial War Museum (re-printed), London, 1997.

24 Harry Hoblyn's wounds never did heal and seventeen years later, they still had to be dressed each day. He died in 1957.

25 AO Pollard, *Fire-Eater*, p69.

Chapter 4

The Salient

'The Huns are all around us, on five sides out of six, and bullets and trench-mortar shells can come from any of those five sides.'

June 1915

The Second battle of Ypres had come to a bloody conclusion on 25 May 1915. Gas had been employed by the Germans for the first time and this had been a factor in their seizing sufficient territory to reduce the size of the infamous Ypres Salient and to make the British hold all the more tenuous. The Germans had won control of Bellewaarde Ridge and possession of this modest piece of high ground was much to the disadvantage of the British units that faced it.

The war diary carries the following entries for 5-6 June 1915 (edited slightly by the author):

> The Battalion has orders to go to the Ramparts, Ypres. Today was spent morning refitting and were then inspected by CO. In the afternoon The Battalion marched off via Lamertinge, arrived at about 7pm. and relieved 3rd Dragoon Guards of the Cavalry Division in the Hooge Sector, the reserve dug-outs being in Ypres. Soon after arriving and while men were getting into billets the Ramparts were shelled, a usual occurrence in the afternoon – several shells fell near the billets and one onto a house in which the stretcher bearers were – Pte. Pilgrim P was killed. Pte. Hame AW was wounded and died of his wounds on 8 June. LCpl. Charles LP was wounded. These three men were all stretcher bearers and the first casualties among this section. The dugouts were not too good except those actually in the walls of the Ramparts Ypres.
>
> All companies and HQ were in the Ramparts. The town is in a terrible state of destruction though fairly clean as far as bodies go owing to work done by engineers and cleaning parties. A great deal has been burnt down by them (the Germans) and in places burning is still going on. Early in morning a pigeon alighting on a roof bought down a large

> tile on the head of and wounded Pte. Fairhead. At night the whole of the available men (over 400) went up to Hooge carrying barbed wire knife rests in a very heavy & long fatigue. Most of the men had bruised shoulders next day and the procession in single file must have reached for a mile & a half. Capt. Douglas was in charge and with only two guides great difficulty was experienced in keeping men closed up. About Hooge the place was very lively and three men were hit during the journey, they were Ptes. Scott-Robertson G, Hunt HF, Krauss WD.

'Fatigues' were cordially loathed. The story goes that a large body of men were observed involved in the most strenuous labour, at night, in pouring rain, with thick mud underfoot. A general officer who chanced upon them enquired of an aide, 'Who are these men, a Labour battalion I suppose?'

The ADC replied, 'No General, it's that battalion you withdrew from the line. They are resting.'

Pollard, now ensconced in the ramparts, had a brief chance to visit what was left of a once lovely city. He saw the biggest shell hole of his experience. It was 65 feet across and 30 feet deep. He reported that 'Seventeen horses were buried in the bottom of this vast hole but without making any discernible difference to its appearance.'

In his memoirs he goes to some length to describe the process by which he bought for his 'Lady' an elegant lace handkerchief but only after having been teased outrageously by the young French sales women who insisted on showing him the frilly knickers of the day, all to his acute embarrassment. This does rather point to Pollard being a rather prim, straight-laced chap and far removed from the wenching 'jack-the-lad' that, perhaps, he sometimes aspired to be.

Soon after the arrival of the HAC, German shelling started in earnest and what was left of the fair city of Ypres was quickly laid waste. This destruction was not the least of the tragedies of the Great War. After the war the massive reparation demanded from the defeated German nation for the re-construction of Ypres played into the political hands of the National Socialists and was a small factor that led, eventually, to the rise of Hitler.

1 HAC was allocated billets in cellars[1] under the ramparts of the city. The Ypres area was described by AOP as 'interesting' although most soldiers considered the Ypres Salient to be a suburb of hell and sharing the same post code.

Pollard made it his business, literally, to unearth as much wine as he could, having heard that the civilian population had buried its wine stocks before fleeing or falling victim to the shelling.

At that time, 'C' Company was closely confined to the safety of its billets. However, on the remarkably thin excuse of mounting a concert party, AOP was released to find a grand piano. The ruins were ransacked and eventually a piano was found. It was carted back to the cellars, where willing hands helped with it.

It was very heavy - it would be. It was crammed with wine.

The concert party never got off the ground as 'C' Company moved up into the line that same night. Pollard said that 'I am very much afraid that some members of 'C' Company were looking at the war through rosier-coloured spectacles than the Ypres Salient warranted.'

On 8 June Pollard wrote to his mother, who lovingly kept all of his letters, and advised her that:

> We are in a very interesting part of the line, and I am looking forward to some fun in the sniping line. We are going to these trenches for the first time tonight. I hear that in one place there is a chateau in the hands of the Huns whilst we hold the stables thereof. Rather a deadlock. What! I think we certainly shall have some fun there. The only trouble is that as we have been in reserve, we have eaten most of our extras, and consequently we shall have to live on rations entirely in the trench.

Alfred Pollard was ill-advised to describe sniping as 'fun' and twenty-seven years later, a high-grade sniping expert had this to say:

> The most dangerous individual soldier … is the sniper. I mean the real sniper, the lone wolf. He is deadly. He is feared more than the tank, more than the aeroplane he wages his own deadly little war … If you decide to become a sniper then the die is cast … your life will be in your own hands. There is no one to help you. Inefficiency, carelessness, over confidence – just one little slip and you are a goner. So learn all you can before you venture out to shoot men.[2]

Alfred Pollard was pitting himself against some of the most effective snipers in the world and he was most fortunate to survive these further and extended amateur sniping expeditions. No other British soldier ever described service in the Salient as 'fun' and none, of sound mind, looked forward to service in the forward trenches where life expectancy was markedly shorter. There was many a bigger and a bloodier battle than that fought by 1 HAC on 16 June 1915, but on this occasion and in this place the shelling was as bad as it gets. The Battalion occupied a position at the very apex of the triangle forming the Ypres Salient: consequently the Battalion was shelled from the front and from both flanks. The shelling was the cause of most of its casualties.

By this stage of the war, woods were fast being reduced to matchwood.
A sketch by Adrian Hill (HAC Archives)

HS Clapham said, amplifying and confirming Pollard's earlier supposition:

> So far as I can tell, we were near the point of a small triangle, with the Huns on two sides of us. On the third night we moved into the point itself. The wood tapers out, and from the end we passed up the side of a water-logged communication trench into what appeared to be the neck of a bottle. Two trenches run out a short distance apart, but they do not actually join at the end. One stops near the stables at the Chateau of Hooge, and from that point there is a bit of communication trench to the stables themselves. We hold the stables, the Huns own the Chateau: and they are only 15 yards from the end of the trench. It was very easy grenade range. The stables are falling to pieces, but what is left of the Chateau is a big square fort of stone with sand-bagged windows. The Huns are all around us, on five sides out of six, and bullets and trench-mortar shells can come from any of those five sides. We ourselves can fire at them, both in front and at the back, but luckily they dare not shell us, as they would probably get hurt themselves.[3]

In the 'Hooge pocket' the Battalion was in a truly unenviable situation. The 'march in' had been dangerous: the three-day tour was even more so. The 'Chateau' that Pollard had alluded to stood at the pinnacle of the Salient but was by now no more than a pile of stones. Pollard explained that he had expected to see the shell of the original chateau – wishful thinking because the building had been obliterated.

At this close proximity it was to mutual advantage to be alert, defensive but not aggressive. A careless shot could provoke a blood bath. Both sides watched and waited.

'C' Company was placed off to the left and here the front lines were further apart – a distance of about 150-200 yards. The message was passed that there was to be an attack and 1 HAC, of 7 Brigade, was to form part of the second wave. AOP was beside himself at the prospect and, in his own words:

> At last! I was as excited as a girl going to her first dance. But even then I was not satisfied. We were not going to make the charge but were to go over in support behind the first line. I was terribly disappointed. All the fun would be over before we reached the enemy position. At least so I thought in my ignorance. I was a little worried about Ernest. He had a presentiment that he was going to be killed and nothing I could say would alter his conviction; he went even so far as to write home and say goodbye to his father, so firm was his conviction. The possibility did not in the least affect his great natural courage. His only fear was that he should be wiped out in the initial advance before he had a chance to take two or three of the enemy with him. I myself had no such morbid thoughts. I simply looked upon the coming adventure much the same way that I looked forward to an exciting game of rugger before the war. I wanted to distinguish myself and I was determined to seize any chance that came my way. I also wanted to christen my bayonet, although I did not see much chance of that in the second line. Roll on the hours until we move off. Let us get at them![4]

Private HS Clapham saw it all rather differently:

> Yesterday we were told we were 'for it' on the 16th and ever since then great preparations have been taking place. We have arranged to leave all our spare food and effects with a pal in the transport. Our section commander has been attached to the Salvage Corps, so he does not go up with us. He has appointed a substitute, and made a list of men who are to take charge of the section in turn, if things go wrong: I come some way down so I am not likely to have much responsibility. Everyone is suffering from 'wind up' and I suppose a certain amount of 'wind' is natural. I certainly feel it myself, although I try not to show it.
>
> Anyway we shall see what we shall see … it is blazing hot but, we do not move until evening, so that will not hurt.[5]

Those few lines do not do justice to the mayhem of Hooge that summer day. Most of the soldiers were frightened, resolved, resigned, fatalistic or any combination of those. Only Pollard was enthused, expectant and excited. It begs the question, was his attitude abnormal? It was certainly not the norm and so 'abnormal' is a fair description.

The build-up for the attack was conducted in the sizzling heat of summer. Ammunition, food, medical supplies, water, and trench stores were all brought forward on horse-drawn limbers. There was an air of expectancy, which was enhanced (or exacerbated) by the heavy traffic. Fatigue parties, dispatch riders and fully equipped infantry were all about the King's business.

The HAC had to make a long approach march across open fields and some distance to a new position prior to the attack. The men were quiet and contemplative. It was a very hot day and they sweated under their 60lb packs. The Adjutant at the head of the Battalion alongside his colonel was suddenly swept from his horse by shell fire. It was a single round – a stray, but it was just as effective. The Adjutant was not killed but the incident had a sobering effect on men who had been pretty sober to start with.

The Battalion halted for a meal in late afternoon and this was provided from the 'cookers'. Replete, cigarettes smoked and with packs on, the men watched the cookers drive off to safety whilst they once more trudged toward the enemy in the slowly gathering dusk. They moved into single file and advanced up a railway line. For a man of his height Pollard found the spacing of the sleepers very uncomfortable because they did not fit his gait. They were either too far apart or too close, no matter how he adjusted his stride. The Battalion reached the shallow trenches that were to be their start line and spent an uneasy and uncomfortable night thinking about the morrow. Once more, Pollard reiterates, 'I felt no trace of fear or even nervousness: only an anxiety to get started. The hours seemed interminable. Would the dawn never come?'

The Company Commander was obliged to nominate two men as a 'link' with 1 Lincolns who the HAC were to support. Captain Boyle picked a man called Springfield[6] ('Springy', to his friends) – and Lance Corporal Pollard. Both soldiers were delighted to be chosen and Pollard in particular enthused, 'I was to take part in a real charge. With luck I might bayonet a Hun.'

Here, briefly, we leave Pollard thirsting for action – just one man alone with his ambition. Reportage of a battle is inevitably somewhat blinkered as the reporter can only observe that which enters his ken. He sees only a small portion of a much bigger canvas and is stretched to put the events into context. Someone once said that 'the horizon, when seen from a trench, is very limited.' Jünger[7] endorsed that view and remarked that 'Shell-hole and trench have a limited horizon … the range of vision extends no further than a bomb throw.'

Hynes[8] was even more specific and he said, 'No man will see much of the battle he's in: and what he does see he will not remember as other men who were there will.'

On that basis, the experience of Pollard when he saw his first action on 16 June 1915 needs to be put into a broader context. There are two accounts that the regimental historian judged to be worthy of inclusion in his definitive work.[9] The first of these is Colonel Treffry's formal observations as recorded in the Battalion war diary:

> Punctually at 2.30 am on June 16th, our bombardment of the German line started, and increased in violence until 4.15, when the assault was launched. The first line was carried straight away. Those of the enemy who were alive were much too dazed to offer any resistance. The second line was also carried at once, and the assault pushed on to the German third line and carried that also all three lines within the space of half an hour. As soon as I heard that the first line was carried, that the assault had gone on, and that 'D' Company HAC had mustered in the fire trenches, I ordered Douglas with that Company to go forward. No sooner had I said the word 'Go', than they were over the parapet like steeplechasers. It really was splendid to see the eagerness with which they went over the top. 'B' and 'C' Companies went over next almost simultaneously. I had just sent a note to the Brigadier informing him that all Companies HAC had moved to their tasks, when I was hit in the head by a piece of shrapnel. This was a little after 5 am. Bowman, the Orderly-Room Sergeant, assisted me to the dressing station adjoining our front fire trench. After I had had my head dressed I returned to Battalion Headquarters and, after some little while, learned that the Companies were in position, and that they had got on with their job splendidly. I also learned that Major Ward, the Second-in-Command, had been hit early in the day, also Captain Boyle and several other officers, but that so far the casualties among the men were not out of proportion. I was rather anxious about the communication trench, but I had an early report that it had been completed and that Captain Lankester had moved forward with the remnant of his Company to assist in driving off the counter-attack.
>
> It is very difficult in an account of this kind to single out any particular officer or man when all did so remarkably well, but probably the most thankless job of the lot was that of 'A' Company, who could at first take no part in the fighting, but had to dig, under a concentrated bombardment and furious cross machine-gun fire, until their task was completed or they were knocked out. Captain Lankester and CSM

Murray behaved with the utmost gallantry, and set a magnificent example. Lankester walked up and down most of the time, encouraging his men and smoking a big cigar, and it was astonishing that he had not been hit then (later in the day he was hit).

CSM Murray carried no less than seven wounded men who were lying in the open across 150 yards of this fire-swept zone to comparative safety. He was afterwards awarded the DCM for these acts of gallantry. Captain Douglas, to whom I had to hand over the command about 1 pm, also behaved with admirable judgment and cool-headedness. In fact, all the officers and men behaved splendidly, and it was the proudest moment of my life when a staff officer came into the shelter which I was sharing as Headquarters with other COs and as far as I remember, spoke as follows:

'The confusion up in front is appalling. Units seem to be inextricably mixed up, but there is one unit which is properly organized, is altogether, knows what it has to do and has done it dam' well, and that is the HAC.'

With regard to the confusion in the front line, mentioned by the staff officer just referred to, I ascertained in conversation with officers afterwards that this confusion was caused by a certain want of co-operation between our own artillery and infantry. Very shortly after that, another staff officer came in, and said:

'Well, if I have never seen 'stickers' in my life before, I have seen them today, and they are the HAC; the Boche will never shift them.'

I said to Sergeant Bowman, who had been endeavouring for several hours to get me to go back, '*Nunc Dimittis*. "I can go now",' as in these few sentences I felt that I had been amply rewarded for any effort or work that I had put in for the old regiment.

Our machine-gun section, under Captain Holliday, took its four guns into action and did most admirably. Captain Holliday never showed to better advantage than in the firing line. Captain Osmond did admirably as Acting Adjutant, and to his efforts and contempt of danger in moving about from one Company to another, seeing that proper touch was kept, is due in a great measure the fact that the Battalion remained an organized unit throughout the day. He had a marvellous escape. He was occupying a bay with fifteen Fusiliers when a salvo of 5.9s landed in the bay, burying everyone. He alone got out alive. The Battalion was relieved on the night of June 16-17th by the 1st Gordon Highlanders.

During this action no one behaved with more steadfast courage or showed a greater devotion to duty than our Medical Officer, Captain

> Carnwath. He had his aid post in our original front line and from the time of the first assault when the wounded commenced to come in, in fact even before that time, he was at his post and remained there all through the 16th, all through the night of 16-17th, and all through the 17th, on the latter day searching about for any who might have been overlooked and wanted aid. His unit had been relieved and gone down but he still carried on until no further wounded could be found. This had been the spirit in which Carnwath had worked ever since the Battalion came out and I am sure all ranks of the HAC will agree that no more sympathetic, human or devoted medical officer was ever attached to a unit.
>
> Of Captain Mayhew, the Quartermaster, 'Uncle George', as we all delight to call him, I may say that no CO was better served or unit more thoroughly looked after than by him. I personally owe him an immense debt of gratitude. Never once did anything go wrong in his department, and his cheerfulness and tact when times were most trying were of inestimable value to us all.
>
> Of the officers and men, happy is the CO who can get such a type to command. Their loyalty to their CO and their devotion to duty were beyond any words of mine, and as regards their discipline I need only say that from August 28th, 1914, to June 16th, 1915, the Battalion had a clean sheet. Their cheerfulness was infectious, and with that splendid regimental spirit, which insists that whatever happens, whatever has to be put up with, whatever has to be gone through, the regiment must not be let down, is it any wonder that they went from success to success, or that a distinguished General should say to me, 'Colonel. Your men act on me as a tonic!' Of the fighting officers during this early part of the war one might write indefinitely: their loyalty and devotion to me I shall never forget, and if I mention two or three names it is not that I am picking them out above the others, it is merely because they are no longer with us. With officers of the type of Ernest Boyle, Ted Ellis, Schiff, Newton and Tatham, all of whom were absolutely fearless and cheerful under any circumstances, it is no surprise that the 1st HAC has helped to add another glorious page to the history of the old Regiment.

This was the big picture as seen by the Commander but a person who was not in the thick of the action – and nor should he have been. The approbation of the Battalion's superior headquarters was important to Treffry and, at his level, his concern was the performance of the Battalion as an entity.

HS Clapham was, in the modern vernacular 'at the other end of the food chain' and as such right in the thick of the action. His view of the same engagement contrasts in style and content to that of his Colonel. His account of what followed has since become a classic of its type. His diary entry dated 19 June reported that:

> At 4.15 pm a whistle blew. The men in the front line went over the top and we scrambled out and took their places in the front trench. In front of us was a small field, with grass knee-high, split diagonally by an old footpath. On the other side of the field was a belt of trees, known as 'Y' Wood, in which lay the first Hun trench. In a few minutes flags went up there, to show that it had been captured and that the troops were going on. Another whistle and we ourselves scrambled over the parapet and sprinted across the field. Personally I was so over-weighted that I could only amble, and I remember being intensely amused at the sight of a little chap in front of me, who seemed in even worse case than myself. Without thinking much about it, I took the diagonal path, as the line of least resistance, and most of my section did the same.
>
> When I dropped into the Hun trench, I found it a great place, only 3 feet wide and at least eight deep, and beautifully made of white sand bags, back and front. At that spot there was no sign of any damage by our shells, but a number of dead Huns lay in the bottom. There was a sniper's post just where I fell in, a comfortable little square hole, fitted with seats and shelves, bottles of beer, tinned meats and a fine helmet hanging on a hook.

First, Clapham took time out to 'liberate' the fine helmet and he set it to one side. The task facing the assaulting troops was re-aligning the German wire, which had to be moved from what was now the rear of the trench to the new front. He described the wire as 'rotten stuff' because it was laid in loose coils and the 'knife rests' upon which it was placed were only knee height. The wire was transferred without undue difficulty and satisfied with a job well done, Clapham and his comrades congratulated themselves. They were premature and they were not to enjoy the security offered by the realigned wire because it appeared that their initial advance had been oblique and they were too far to the right. Clapham's platoon moved to the left through a narrow wood, really little more that a hedgerow, but as yet undamaged by shell fire. They joined another company of 1 HAC, heads down, busily engaged in digging a new communication trench, rearwards to the earlier British front line. Clapham commented that:

> Here there was really no trench at all. One or more of our own big shells had burst in the middle, filling it up for a distance of 10 yards and practically destroying both parapet and parados. Some of us started

> building up the parapet with sand bags, and I saw 'the twins' merrily at work hauling out dead Huns at least twice their own size. There was a hedge along the back of the trench, so I scrambled through a hole in it, piled my pack, rifle and other things, including the helmet, on the further side, and started again on the wire. Hereabouts it was much better stuff, and it took us some time to get it across and pegged down. We had just got the last knife-rest across, when I saw a man who was placing sand bags on the parapet from the further side, swivel round, throw his legs into the trench, and collapse in a heap in the bottom. Several others were already lying there, and for the first time, I realized that a regular hail of machine-gun bullets was sweeping over the trench. I made a dive for my pack, but I found that my pet helmet had disappeared. Quite a string of wounded and masterless men had passed down the back of the hedge, while I was working, and one of them must have thought it a good souvenir to take into hospital.
>
> We all started work at a feverish pace, digging out the trench and building up some sort of shelter in front. One chap, a very nice kid, was bowled over almost at once with a bullet in the groin, and lay in the trench kicking and shrieking while we worked.

It seemed that the attack had taken a number of other trenches, two of which were now firmly in British hands. Clapham's platoon was ordered to reinforce its defences and consolidate the position. This position, the gentlemen of the HAC were told, was to be 'held at all costs'. This unappetising instruction did not bode well for the immediate future.

Visibility from the trench was limited by the height of the grass waving gently in the breeze to the front. This grassy vista extended to a low mound 'several hundred yards' away and this marked the line of the next objective. The British were at a disadvantage because the Germans held the high ground, such as it was, in Bellewaarde Wood and Hooge Chateau. The only cover was afforded by a spur of 'Y' Wood.

Clapham toiled away with his shovel filling sand bags. He had filled a bag and positioned it on the parapet when he looked down and saw:

> A slight movement in the earth between my feet, I stopped and scraped away the soil with my fingers and found what seemed like palpitating flesh. It proved to be a man's cheek, and a few minutes' work uncovered his head. I poured a little water down his throat and two or three of us dug out the rest of him. He was undamaged except for his feet and ankles, which were a mass of pulp. He recovered consciousness as we worked. The first thing he said was in English, 'What Corps are you?' He

was a big man and told us that he was forty-five and had only been a soldier for a fortnight. We dragged him out and laid him under the hedge. There was nothing else we could do for him. He had another drink later, but he must have died in the course of the day. I am afraid we forgot all about him, but nothing could have lived there until evening.

The Captain was the next to go. He insisted on standing on the parados, directing operations, and got a bullet in the lungs. He could walk, and two men were detailed to take him down to the dressing station. One came back to be killed later in the day, but the other stopped a bullet en route, and followed the Captain.

When we had got our big Hun out, he left a hole in the ground, and we found a dead arm and hand projecting from the bottom. We dug about but did not seem to be able to find the body, and when I seized the sleeve and pulled, the arm came out of the ground by itself. We had to dig deeper for our own sake, but there was nothing else left, except messy earth, which seemed to have been driven into the side of the trench. The man helping me turned sick, for it wasn't pretty work, but I claimed a substitute and between us we carted out a barrowful in wetter sheets and dumped it under the hedge. After that I had had enough myself.

In the late afternoon, at about 1730hrs, German artillery played over the newly occupied British position and the accurate shelling turned Clapham's communications trench and the two traverses from which the communications trench ran into a death trap.

Unfortunately, wounded men were passing through the area and the German fire fell upon the stream of casualties. The carnage was frightful and all the trenches were soon choked with dead and dying men. The trenches became impassable and passage was only possible on top of the parapet. That was a very hazardous option.

The shelling was unremitting and 1 HAC casualties added to the butcher's bill. Clapham was flattened by a sand bag that had been thrown by the blast of a shell. It landed on his head and he was lucky to survive. He said that 'it nearly broke my neck.' The impact of the sand bag, weighing perhaps 20lbs was, not surprisingly, sufficient to make Clapham feel unwell. His situation was worsened because not only was it unbearably hot but the bombardment had filled the air with choking dust. Clapham recalled that although:

One was parched up, one dared not use much of one's water. One never knew how long it must last. I came off better than most in that respect, for I had taken the precaution of carrying two water bottles, knowing that one would never last me. The worst of it was the inaction. Every minute several shells fell within a few yards and covered us with dust, and the smell of the explosives poisoned one's mouth. All one could do was to crouch against the parapet and pant for breath, expecting every moment to be one's last. And this went on for hours. One began to long for the shell which would put an end to everything, but in time one's nerves became almost numbed, and one lay like a log until roused.

I think it must have been mid-day when something happened. An alarm was given and we manned the parapet, to see some scores of men retreating at a run from the trench in front. They ran right over us, men of half a dozen battalions, and many dropped on the way. As they passed, something was said of gas, but it appeared that nearly all the officers in the two front trenches had been killed or wounded, someone had raised an alarm of gas and the men had panicked and run. A lot of the runaways insisted on gathering by the hedge just behind us, in spite of our warnings not to do so, and I saw at least twenty hit with shrapnel, within a few yards of us.

The Brigade Major arrived, cursing, and called upon some of our men to advance and reoccupy the trench in front. He led them himself and they made a very fine dash across. I do not think more than twenty fell, and they reoccupied that trench, and, I believe, the third also, before the Huns realized that they were empty.

The bombardment continued unabated and Clapham and his comrades discovered that most of their weapons were clogged with dust and inoperable. They set to, to clean their rifles and this mundane activity did serve, in small part, to distract them from the incessant shelling. It was noted that at this stage there was no counter-bombardment fire and Clapham surmised, with remarkable equanimity, that the British were probably conserving their ammunition. Looking up from rifle cleaning Clapham saw:

The runaways began to return. They had been turned back, in some cases at the point of the revolver, but when their first panic had been overcome, they came back quite willingly, although they must have lost heavily in the process. They crowded into our trench, until there was hardly room to move a limb.

It was scorchingly hot and no one could eat, although I tried to do so. All day long – the longest day I ever spent – we were constantly covered with debris from the shell bursts. Great pieces fell all about us, and, packed like herrings, we crowded in the bottom of the trench. Hardly anything could be done for the wounded. If their wounds were slight, they generally risked a dash to the rear. Every now and then we stood to in expectation of a counter-attack, but none developed.

About 6 pm the worst moment of the day came. The Huns started to bombard us with a shell which was quite new to us. It sounded like a gigantic fire cracker, with two distinct explosions. These shells came over just above the parapet, in a flood, much more quickly than we could count them. After a quarter of an hour of this sort of thing, there was a sudden crash in the trench and 10 feet of the parapet, just beyond me, was blown away and everyone around blinded by the dust. With my first glance I saw what looked like half a dozen bodies, mingled with sand bags, and then I smelt gas and realized that these were gas shells. I had my respirator on in a hurry and most of our men were as quick.

The others were slower and suffered for it. One man was sick all over the sand bags and another was coughing his heart up. We pulled four men out of the debris unharmed. One was unconscious and died of gas later. Another was hopelessly smashed up and must have got it full in the chest. We all thought that this was the end and almost hoped for it, but luckily the gas shells stopped, and after a quarter of an hour we could take off our respirators. I started in at once to build up the parapet again, for we had been laid open to the world in front, but the gas lingered about the hole for hours, and I had to give up delving in the bottom for a time. As it was it made me feel very sick.

A counter-attack actually commenced as soon as the bombardment ceased and we had to stand to again. My rifle had been broken in two pieces, but there were plenty of spare ones lying about now. I tried four, however, before I could get one to act at all. All were jammed and that one was very stiff. As we leaned over the parapet, I saw the body of a Hun lying 20 yards out in front. It commenced to writhe and finally sat up. I suppose the gas had caught him. The man standing next me, a corporal in a county battalion, raised his rifle and before I could stop him, sent a bullet into the body. It was a rotten thing to see, but I suppose it was really a merciful end for the poor chap, better than his own gas at any rate.

The men in the front trenches had got it as badly as we had, and if the counter-attack was pressed, it did not seem humanly possible, in the condition we were in, to offer a successful defence. One man kept worrying us all by asking what we were to do if the Huns did us in, whether surrender or run! Fortunately our own guns started and apparently caught the Huns massing. The counter-attack accordingly crumpled up.

In the midst of it all, someone realized that the big gap in the parapet could not be manned, and four of us, including myself, were ordered to lie down behind what was left of the parados and cover the gap with our rifles. It was uncomfortable work, as the gas fumes were still very niffy and the place was a jumble of dead bodies. We could not stand up to clear them away, and, in order to get a place at all, I had to lie across the body of a gigantic Hun.

As soon as things quietened down a bit, we had a chance to look round. Since the morning most of the branches of the trees in the wood had gone and many of the trunks had become mere splintered poles. Something else had changed also, and for a time I could not make out what it was. Then it suddenly flashed across my mind that the thick hedge at the back of the trench had entirely disappeared. It was right in the path of the storm of gas shells and they had carried it away. We managed to get some sort of parapet erected in the end. It was more or less bullet-proof at any rate. At dusk some scores of men came back from the front line, wounded or gassed. They had to cross the open at a run or a shamble, but I did not see any hit. Then the Brigade Major appeared and cheered us by promising a relief that night. It still rained shells, although not so hard as before dusk, and we did not feel capable of standing much more of it.

As time wore on the shelling became more fitful, although it never actually ceased. It was comparatively cool again and one could drink and even eat a little. My cap had gone in the general smash and I took another which happened to fit. No relief turned up, and about midnight two volunteers were asked for, to carry to the dressing station a boy prisoner, whose leg was smashed.

There was considerable competition for the job, as we were told that the men selected could go on to the rear afterwards. A Fusilier and I were the lucky ones. We managed to manufacture a sort of splint for the boy's leg and then tied his two legs together. The Fusilier got him on his back and I took his legs. It was a rotten job, as the poor wretch started screaming and screamed until he fainted. After hoisting him out of the trench, we had to cart him across the open, which was a wilderness of shell holes. To make matters worse, I found I was as weak as a rabbit and could hardly carry myself. Just as we left the trench, a long line of dark figures passed us. They wore the kilt and we concluded that they were the expected relief.

We managed to get the boy as far as the old front line, which was full of our own wounded, awaiting the doctor. There we found a hospital orderly and he suggested we should leave our burden with him. We were

> thankful enough to do so, as the dressing station was a full half-mile away. After that my only thought was to get out of shell fire as quickly as I could and I made for the road by the way we had come the night before. The field was dotted with small parties of men who had just been relieved. The ground was lower here and the stench of gas pervaded everything. Two small gas shells burst in the air above us, but I was too tired to worry about them. The road, when I reached it, was full of troops, bonnets and caps, kilts and putties, some alone, some in twos and threes, some even in sections or small platoons. These, however, soon lost whatever formation they had in the general rush. No one wanted to stay on the Menin Road longer than need be.

It was a grim journey and where a tree had fallen across the road there was chaos as men struggling to get around the obstacle but retain a footing on a stable surface. Clapham was behind a Scottish soldier who was struck down by a piece of white hot shrapnel. The Highlander cried, 'Gie us a hond, mate,' and Clapham and another half carried half dragged him to the dressing station at Hell Fire Corner.

There was no time to linger and wishing Jock 'Good-bye, and good luck', Clapham and his companions left him in the care of the RAMC and made their way down the railway line, always an uncomfortable route as they stumbled over the sleepers placed as ever at their inconvenient intervals. The route was littered with abandoned ammunition, equipment, food and clothing. Anything that was judged to be unwanted weight was jettisoned. The unsoldierly detritus was mute testament to the day's events. Clapham had been under shell fire for hours by now, but he observed that:

> The Hun shells seemed to follow us. One burst on the right of the line, the next on the left. The last one I saw that day, burst 100 yards away, as we came out on the main road, south of Ypres. Hereabouts some of the houses were still standing, and in one a light was shining. There was a rush for the door and in the ruined kitchen we found a pump which still worked. The water was of very doubtful quality, but no one had drunk for hours and its taste was sweet enough for anyone.
>
> When we left there it was quite light. Men were lying about, asleep all over the place. I saw an officer asleep on a pile of sacks just outside a ruined house and close by him three men lay in a ditch. I struggled on by myself and the further I went, the clearer became the road. I passed a dozen men of an Irish unit, who had stopped to eat, and there was a small crowd at a wayside watering place. Single men of all sorts shambled along, swaying from side to side, as if drunk or half asleep. A

> mounted transport man stopped me and offered me a mount, but I couldn't have mounted if I had tried, and if I could I am sure I should have fallen off at once.
>
> At one place I passed some artillery dug-outs. The men were all outside. They stared, asked questions and gave me a tot of rum. The story of the previous day had spread. I think we carried it on our faces.

Clapham struggled on and it took him five hours to reach the transport lines. He found a cook house and the cup of hot tea was nectar, he spread his 'wetter sheet' sat down but was asleep before he had time to remove his boots.

The long sleep helped and then a wash and shave completed Clapham's rejuvenation. He made enquiries and the news was mostly bad. Half the Battalion was reported to be lost, many officers had been killed and the Colonel and the Second-in-Command were both wounded. Clapham noted that his comrades looked 'Worn, old and our nerves are in tatters'. He recorded that shell bursts had everyone 'jumping out of their skins' and his own demeanour had changed because now, and uncharacteristically, he cursed anything and anybody. He wrote ruefully that he supposed that it was his nerves. Clapham had no heroic pretensions. He hated his time in the line but like so many of his peers he recognized that he had duty to fulfil. He noted that the following day:

> We had the Brigadier round. We were all lying about half asleep at the time, and with a consideration somewhat unusual in a brass-hat, he did not have us paraded. We were congratulated and patted on the back, and told that we had done very good work, and that next time we should have a chance on our own. What luck! He wound up by saying that troops that could stand that shelling could not be broken, and that he was afraid that we would have to go back into the trenches almost at once.
>
> These chaps cannot understand that we are not soldiers and that we don't want to be soldiers, and though we shall carry on as well as we can, we don't in the least like it and are not in the least degree pleased at the prospect of a 'brush with the Hun'. What we really like is the rest field after the 'brush' is over.
>
> One can have no idea of the blessed peace of rest after a bad time. To lie on one's back in the sun, to watch the sunset, to wallow in the dirty washing pool, to get a clean shave again, not to be tired all over, to feel against all expectation that one is still alive, to play a quiet game of poker again or to try and do in the 'Crown and Anchor merchant'.

Clapham's account has been recognized as an example of the best sort of war reporting. It is much admired and much quoted – not least here. Goold Walker, for example, used Clapham's words to illustrate the history of the

HAC[10] and Cave similarly quotes Clapham as illustrative of the experiences of an infantryman.[11]

Clapham is ruthlessly honest. He was not engaged in any sort of close order fighting, he claims no credit, admits readily to his fear and in this respect he was much more the typical British soldier than Alfred Pollard ever was. The latter was to play his part in another part of the field, and his account of the day is far less lucid and contrasts with the two that have preceded it.

To return to 0415hrs on 16 June, and to Pollard, who we left having been detailed off as a runner. By now an artillery barrage was being directed at the German line and the opposing artillery replied in kind. The noise was deafening, it numbed the senses when Pollard reported to Captain Spooner of the Lincolns. Spooner stood on the fire step looking up and down his section of trench. Just below him the two young HAC soldiers exchanged grins brimming with anticipation and excitement – any time now.

The two forms of employment with the highest mortality rate on the Western Front were signaller and runner. Often when communications were disrupted signallers acted as runners. Frank Richards, a regular soldier, from 1901, in the Royal Welch Fusiliers,[12] said:

> A runner's job was very dangerous: he might have to travel over ground from where the enemy had just been driven and which was now being heavily shelled. In shell holes here and there might be some of the enemy who had been missed by the mopping-up party or who had been shamming dead: they would pop up and commence sniping at him. I remember one show we were in later on, where extra runners had been detailed off for the day losing fifteen out of twenty.

Richards added that he could not understand why signallers (and runners) were not issued with revolvers because, although they expected to move quickly around the battlefield, they carried and wore the same weapons and equipment as everyone else.

Spooner mouthed the words, 'One minute to go', and along the trench men moved into action. Everywhere bolts pushed rounds into the chambers of rifles that already had bayonets fixed, short ladders were propped onto the forward wall of the trench, a Lincoln stood at the bottom of each ladder with others close behind. Some men fingered the tip of their bayonet. Other men's mouths moved in silent prayer. Spooner raised his arm, and then sprang up the ladder in front of him. Pollard and Springfield were close behind. All along the line a host of men in khaki scrambled above ground and advanced at a steady trot.

Although Pollard had been under artillery fire for months, on and off, the only infantry action he had seen was the abortive and bloody assault on Moulin Rouge and there he been a mere spectator. To his surprise, the hail of machine-gun fire he was expecting did not materialize. There was no response from the Germans at all. The absence of enemy fire was almost a disappointment to AOP and he observed, 'I never once dreamed or considered that I myself should be hit. Even in this first attack I had the extraordinary feeling of being myself exempt, though not to the same degree as later on.'

The shells shrieked overhead, HE shells burst upon the German position and great black gouts of earth flew into the air to mark each strike. The noise continued unabated in volume. Spooner ran on looking to his left and right to see that his company was in line with him. Pollard and Springfield were hard on his heels as they jogged toward their appointment. Pollard judged that there was still 400 yards to go; an insuperable distance if they came under fire, and if they did, then there was no turning back.

The Lincolns were just short of the opposing trenches and Pollard sprinted the last few yards, his rifle thrust out before him, bayonet point to the fore. There was no wire to impede them and both young men overtook the officer and jumped into the trench packed with grey-uniformed Germans. Pollard recalled that:

> The Germans soldiers had sightless eyes and waxen faces. Each man gripped his rifle and leaned against the side of the trench in an attitude of defence but all were dead. We were attacking a position held by corpses.

Pollard was nonplussed. He wondered momentarily if the figures were dummies - some sort of trick designed to trap the attackers. Then it dawned on him:

> This was unvarnished war: war with the gloves off. There was something ludicrous about that trench of dead men. One wanted to laugh at their comical appearance. There was also something fine: every man in his place with his face toward the enemy. Death must have come over them so suddenly without giving them a chance in their own defence. They certainly gave me a different reception from anything I had anticipated.

The absence of wire and the dead Germans were mute testament to the power of the artillery barrage. They must all have been killed by the blast of an exploding shell. Pollard retraced his steps back across no man's land to Captain Boyle to report that the Lincolns had taken the first line and were now assaulting the second German line. The message passed, Pollard once more traversed no man's land because, as he put it, 'I wanted to get back to the

Lincolns and see some of the fighting. I was still sure that there would be a hand-to-hand contest.'

The gap between British and German lines was, by Pollard's estimation something between 400-500 yards. For the third time he was to run over broken ground, laden with his pack and carrying his weapon. The artillery fire continued to be intense and now German machine-gun fire from their reserve trenches hissed across the shell hole-pitted landscape. He was certainly fit but whether he was up to bayonet fighting at the end was not put to the test. Pollard returned to the trench full of corpses, and following it, found a communication trench. It was here, that he said that he:

> Saw my first live Hun. He was laying half in and half out of a dug-out, pinned down by a beam of wood which prevented him moving the lower part of his body. All the same he was full of fight. He had a thin face, with an aquiline nose, on which were perched steel-rimmed glasses. He reminded me forcibly of a German master we had at preparatory school. In his hand he held an automatic with which he was taking pot shots at whoever passed. He had killed one man and wounded another. I arrived just in time to see a Tommy stick him with his bayonet.[13]

The German slumped back with a gasp and his weapon dropped from his lifeless fingers. The Tommy withdrew his bayonet and moved on; the warm, early morning sunshine glinted on the bright, fresh blood now coursing down the blade of his bayonet.

AOP had been a silent spectator to this minor drama, one of so many similar incidents being played out all around him. Pollard found Captain Spooner, but no Germans. It seemed that they had disengaged. Much to his chagrin, AOP was told that his function had been discharged and was told that he should return to his unit. An unhappy Pollard withdrew to a small wood, which had been the scene of savage fighting. Corpses carpeted the wood and Pollard noted the body of a Fusilier who had been armed with an axe – a weapon from a bygone age but effective nevertheless, as the blade of the axe was 'red with blood'. Pollard found himself, figuratively, in a rural charnel house. He could do nothing for the multitude of dead but helped where he could with some of the wounded. He reflected:

> One man I shall always remember. He was hit in one of the arteries just above the heart and the blood was pumping out in regular beats. He was a big Highlander with a gigantic chest and only his great physique prevented him from collapsing. I plugged his wound as well as I could, but I have often wondered since whether he survived.

The high probability is that the Scot did not survive. Early removal from the battlefield is the key to survival, a matter demonstrated frequently in wars of the late twentieth and early twenty-first centuries.

Pollard found that the body of a dead German had fallen and jammed the communication trench. He recorded that:

> I took him by the shoulders and another fellow by the feet with the intention of heaving him out of the way. We lifted all right, but a shell had taken away the top of his head which fell forward and poured the whole of his brains over my tunic. I was red from chin to ankle. From my appearance I might have been in the bloodiest of bloody encounters. And yet my bayonet was virgin: not one single round had been fired through my rifle.

Returning as bidden, AOP met Captain Holliday, who commanded the machine-guns of 1 HAC. Holliday promptly co-opted AOP to fill a gap in his ranks. Holliday placed his guns in the second German line on the edge of the wood. Soon after the position was established lines of grey-clad enemy launched a counter-attack and Holliday's guns inflicted great execution at long range. Pollard was not a gun number and so, as supernumerary, he amused himself by engaging targets with his rifle – although he confessed, 'I cannot say definitely whether I succeeded in hitting anybody.'

German artillery played over the battlefield and especially over the positions so recently taken by the British (as Clapham has already testified), but Holliday's position attracted no fire at all and it was 'a calm oasis in a desert of desolation'. AOP was re-employed as a runner and, in this role he had to brave constant shell fire to deliver his messages. As he roamed over the battlefield he picked up the news of the casualties suffered by 1 HAC. Lieutenant Colonel Treffry, the Commanding Officer, Major Ward, Captain Boyle and Lieutenant Davis were among the officers wounded. AOP's platoon had advanced as far as the fourth German trench but there were no reports from them.

It was clear that the day had not gone well for the HAC.

Everywhere Pollard went he found 'maimed and shattered bodies, many of them men with whom I had been laughing and joking the previous day'. Nightfall brought a diminution in enemy shelling and 'the welcome jingle of accoutrements. Following a hail in broad Scottish, the Gordons were arriving to take our place.'

Pollard's first attack was over and it had been a salutary experience. The war diary of 7 Brigade recorded that 'The result of these operations was the gain of 250 yards of ground on a front of 800 yards. Over 200 prisoners and three machine-guns were taken and the enemy suffered severe losses.'

The arithmetic is chilling. The nine battalions of 3rd Division that had taken part in the attack of 16 June lost a little under 4,000 men in an area about 1,000 yards square.[14] The HAC's share of this butcher's bill was fifteen officers and 200 men.

On 26 June a draft of replacement arrived led by Major HT Hanson who took over command of the Battalion, and Colonel Treffry, the wounded, highly respected and much loved CO, was repatriated. The whole Battalion was delighted when news arrived that he had been appointed a Companion of the Most Distinguished Order of St. Michael and St. George (CMG).[15]

Goold Walker summarized the attack in this brief and characteristically neutral tone by saying:

> An attack to straighten the line between Hooge Château and Railway Wood was ordered for 16 June and the task of the HAC was to follow up 1st Bn the Lincolnshire Regiment. This was carried out with great dash and gallantry but at a cost to the Battalion of fifteen officers and 200 men killed or wounded, a regrettable waste of potential officer material[16] which should never have happened; these casualties were replaced with another draft of over 300 men from 2nd Battalion.

Notes

1 See the photograph.
2 Ion Idriess, *The Australian Guerrilla, Book 2, Sniping,* quoted by Martin Pegler in *Out of Nowhere*, p222.
3 HS Clapham, *Mud and Khaki*, p136.
4 AO Pollard, *Fire-Eater*, p77.
5 HS Clapham, *Mud and Khaki*, p138.
6 Private Arthur Lincoln Springfield had joined the HAC two days after Pollard – on 10 August 1914. He was wounded on 16 June 1915, recovered and returned to duty five weeks later. He was commissioned in the Somerset LI and was killed in action on 9 April 1917.
7 Ernst Jünger, *Storm of Steel.*
8 Samuel Hynes, *The Soldier's Tale.*
9 G Goold Walker, *The Honourable Artillery Company in the Great War 1914-1919*, p40.
10 G Goold Walker, *The Honourable Artillery Company in the Great War 1914-1919.*
11 N Cave, *Sanctuary Wood and Hooge*, p29.
12 F Richards, *Old Soldiers Never Die.*
13 AO Pollard, *Fire-Eater*, p85.
14 N Cave, *Sanctuary Wood and Hooge*, p36.
15 An individual is usually appointed to this order for diplomatic services. There is a degree of irony in Treffry, a most undiplomatic officer, being so honoured. The only alternatives available at the time, for an officer of his rank, were the CBE or DSO, as he already had the OBE. A DSO would have been much more appropriate decoration for a lieutenant colonel in command.
16 This is a familiar refrain and a blindingly obvious fact. However, at the time no one had the wit or wisdom to use the HAC to best advantage.

Chapter 5

The Distinguished Conduct Medal

'Although severely wounded, Sergeant Pollard continued to throw bombs.'

July–October 1915

Pollard was scathing in his assessment of the battle. He opined that units did not understand their objectives, there was little or no attempt at consolidation once a position was taken, the artillery did not provide support where and when it was needed (because it had no knowledge of the whereabouts of friendly troops), that soldiers of different units became inextricably mixed and as a result, command and communication broke down. All of these judgements are perfectly sound however: they are not the musings of a lance corporal just after the event, but of an officer who had been privy to post-war examination of the operation.

Pollard mentioned in glowing terms the actions of Major Billy Congreve,[1] a staff officer from HQ 3rd Division, who had performed minor miracles during the long day. AOP did not come across him in the flesh he but must have learned about him later.

Percy Lewis survived the battle but was wounded in the process. He was shot through the thigh, left behind and captured. A glimmer of hope was snuffed out when he died in a German hospital on about 27 June. Ernest Chaland was 'missing' – he was one of many and, in due course, was notified as 'killed in action'. Although, he too died as a prisoner of war on 26 June. AOP was distressed at his death and thereafter he carried Ernest's razor strop in remembrance of a dear friend.

The Battalion mustered barely 350 men when it paraded a day later, the officer ranks were particularly thin. Command of 'C' Company passed to Captain FP Morphy, known to the soldiers as 'Bun'. Pollard avers that:

> He was a popular officer, an Irishman with a dry sense humour, never at

> a loss for a word or a quick riposte or repartee. He carried his name through the war with the magnificent record of always doing thoroughly the job that lay nearest.

Alfred Pollard was promoted to full corporal, a rank he believed to be ideal as he explained, 'On fatigues … the party is either large enough to need a sergeant in charge or small enough for a lance corporal. The full corporal misses it both ways.' Despite its heavy losses, 1 HAC was given very little time to re-organize, recover and replenish and it was sent back into the line. Pollard remarked that it was interesting to view the area over which they had fought in daylight. The wood was now reduced to a collection of stumps but the trenches had been repaired and new wire erected. An attack was to be delivered by 1 Wilts, on the right, the next night. The Company was to follow up the attack and hold the trench once 1 Wilts had done its business. The trench map showed:

> … that it was going to be ticklish spot. A barricade had to be built and manned in a German communication trench, forming a sap head in our new position. I at once volunteered myself and my section for the job. I wanted an opportunity to avenge Ernest, whose real fate we did not then know.

It was this night that AOP had a conversation that altered the manner in which he was to fight his war. Captain Holliday, who was in command, asked Pollard if he would like to take any bombs with him. Pollard had no acquaintance with 'bombs', the generic word for grenades of all types, and he eagerly agreed.

> I was equipped with a sort of waistcoat, which I tied in front of me, and a dozen bombs called Mark 6 and Mark 7 - light and heavy. One ignited a sort of glorified match by striking it against a brassard like the enlarged side of a match box tied on the arm. The match lit a fuse which would burn for five seconds. Having got the fuse underway one threw the bomb into the enemy trench where it exploded or else it did not. Added to my normal equipment I found the outfit damned heavy and uncomfortable.[2]

The bomb/grenade had been a weapon of war in some form or another since the invention of gunpowder and in 1914, the Army had smalls stocks of a very crude device that owed its origins to a Japanese design dating back to 1904/1905.[3]

This design was probably as lethal to the thrower as the receiver because it had a 16ft wooden handle. If, in the act of being thrown, the bomb hit the trench wall behind, the result was likely to be vastly inconvenient to anyone in close proximity.

The alternative means of delivery was to eschew the handle and cast it in the manner that one might play darts. The problem here was that the range was very considerably reduced – again with potentially lethal consequences for the thrower and his friends. All manner of experiments were carried out to improve the bomb, which was destined to become a very useful area weapon in a trench environment.

Necessity being the mother of invention, a crude jam tin bomb evolved. This was literally made with a tin from which the jam had been consumed. The tin was then stuffed with nails, broken glass, stones or any material that would inflict injury if and when it was propelled with explosive force. The down side was that once again, the jam tin had a fuse and that had to be lit. This presented difficulties in the rain or a high wind. Once thrown, the bomb would not necessarily explode if it, say, landed on its fuse on a muddy trench floor. Much more significantly and inconveniently, the opposition could re-light the fuse and throw it back from whence it came.

By 1915 there were twelve variants of the hand grenade in use – none of them satisfactory and even so, their supply was inadequate, and in August 1915, Field Marshal Sir John French called for a supply of 63,000 a week – the reality was that in October of that year, only 8,000 a week reached the front, to be spread very thinly indeed.

After lengthy development work a safe, relatively light and effective grenade was produced. This was the Mills bomb, a fragmentation grenade that first came into service in May 1915. It superseded the need for matches, fuses and wooden handles because it had 'a spring-loaded striker and percussion cap igniter within the body of the grenade'[4] and eventually it replaced all the other doubtful bombs in issue. The new weapon was known to generations of soldiers from 1915 until the late 1970s as the No. 36 grenade. It weighed 1lb 7oz (1lb 9oz in some variants) and most soldiers could hurl it about 30 yards. It transformed trench warfare and Alfred Pollard was to establish his reputation with it.

Pollard, now clad in his waistcoat, returned to his apprehensive section, which by now realized that their enthusiastic corporal could be a health hazard, and not just to the Germans. As it happened, the attack was called off and AOP did not have the chance to bomb anyone. He remarked:

> I was hoping to get to close quarters … the loss of Ernest fresh in my mind. My spirit all worked up with the determination to kill or be killed. These were all contributory factors which decided me later on to become a bomber.

The Salient had one characteristic that made it particularly unpleasant. The water table was naturally very high and passage made by wheels, feet or hooves quickly converted the top soil into thick, clinging mud. Shell fire compounded the problem. Water lay on the surface and all shell holes quickly filled almost to the rim with toxic water. These shell holes became a serious hazard and countless soldiers drowned in them; some were lost for ever as their bodies were buried under the silt. Trenches, by their very nature, were below the water table and they became waterlogged ditches. Life in the trench system of the Salient was highly unattractive.

The HAC was employed in the Salient all through the miserable wet summer of 1915. It marched up to the line, did its three-day tour and marched back out. Three days later, it did it all again. It did not take part in any set piece attacks nor did it repel any. However, the artillery of both sides continued to cause attrition on both sides. The lice were a constant, as was the incessant rain that added daily to the water that lay everywhere. Sleeping was difficult. AOP wrote to his mother and gave a flavour of trench life when he said:

> We are now in a wood, in dug-outs in reserve, and we go into the actual trenches tomorrow for nine days. … Incidentally, I have not washed for a fortnight as the only water near us was a duckweedy pond with a dead dog in it. And I don't want skin disease. Mrs. B sent out some excellent lice powder which managed to kill all of my menagerie. I think it is strong enough to kill elephants. Anyway it got into a cut and gave me slight blood poisoning in the leg: not enough to prevent me going into the village a mile away for some grub, but sufficient excuse for me (old soldier) not to attend any of the silly parades and route marches which we were pestered with during our so-called rest.

Pollard was due for home leave and he was busting to see his 'Lady'; even the news that he had been selected to command 'C' Company's bombing section, a group of sixteen soldiers, barely distracted him from his thoughts of home. He wrote to his mother in early August and said, 'I shall be in a position to turn anarchist after the war. Anyway, I know a good bit about bombs and grenades. They are very jolly things to play with. Would you like one as a souvenir?'

He had been at the front for almost eleven months and had been under artillery fire for lengthy periods throughout his stay in *La belle France*. He was very fortunate and one of the very few not to have suffered a scratch as, of the 800 original members of 1st Battalion, little over 100 remained.

Pollard went on leave, his thoughts entirely focussed on his 'Lady'. He arrived at the family home before it was astir. He threw a stone at his sister's window – and broke it. The stone was too big and the throw too vigorous. Breakfast with the family was a pleasure to all concerned but unable to contain himself, he rushed round to visit the family of his idol.

She was not at home and Alfred suffered the agony of acute disappointment. The lady in question had signed up as a nurse and Alfred arranged to meet her the following day. Closely chaperoned by her two sisters and his own, the five young people lunched at the Piccadilly Hotel. After lunch they all drove around Regent's Park in a taxi.

The frustration factor must have been sky high. Despite that, Pollard decided that this was, without question, the girl for him. He had raised her almost beyond mere mortality and in his own words:

> I was thrilled. To feel her sitting next to me: to hear her speak: to know that I was with her. Regent's Park was heaven and the taxi a golden chariot. I knew I loved her then. I would have done anything in the world she asked me. I was a knight fighting for her protection. I was a door mat at her feet.[5]

These painfully revealing words make the reader feel intrusive. They are far too personal to share but Alfred had not finished. In his book, *Fire-Eater,* he exposes his audience to a lot more of the same, in graphic detail. 'Besotted' is a word not nearly strong enough to describe his condition and certainly, rational thought was long gone. For example: 'If she wished me to go alone across no man's land in broad daylight I would have done it. She held my heart in the hollow of her hand.'

For four and a half days AOP frequented theatres, restaurants and shops. He spent money like water. He cheerfully admitted that 'eat drink and be merry for tomorrow may bring a bullet or a shell' was his creed. He got by on three hours' sleep a night in order to make best use of his leave. How much time, if any, he spent alone with his heart's desire we do not know.

Young Alfred Pollard ruminated on his leave during the long journey back to the front and at his age – he was still only twenty-two – he contemplated a serious issue. He explained that:

> I knew now what I wanted: for the first time in my life I began to think of marriage. Of course she was ever so much too good for me. I recognized that from the start. She was the most divine, glorious creature that ever breathed. Try as I would I knew I could never reach her standard but I must do my best.

Pollard's non-relationship with this girl, which, when seen at a distance of almost 100 years, seems to be seriously out of balance, but was nevertheless critical. It had the effect of motivating him to 'better' himself and he speculated that, were he to be commissioned, she would see him in a much more attractive light. 'Suppose I went to her as an officer covered in decorations?' he wrote, 'then perhaps she would deign to smile on me.' The lady had actually raised the matter of a commission and laughed at him for not having already applied. The suggestion, albeit lightly made, was sufficient. The seed had been planted.

It was enough.

Alfred Pollard returned to France a different man. He averred that 'I would apply for a commission. I would take every chance that came my way to earn distinction. Her knight would win his spurs. The following day I filled in my application form.'

Thomas Pryce, who had joined up with Alfred Pollard, beat him to the punch. He had been selected for a commission in the Gloucestershire Regiment and he left the Battalion in late September. He was commissioned in October and by June 1916, he had won two MCs. Pryce was one of very many to be plucked from the ranks of the HAC for service as an officer elsewhere.

Trench life had not changed but the Battalion was in reserve and there was time for bridge and *vingt-et-un*. Pollard was detailed to command a guard on a road through the 'C' Company trench line and at about the same time it was rumoured that a German spy, a tall man over 6 feet tall, was abroad wearing a British uniform.

The guard commander struck on the idea of stringing a cord across the road at exactly 6 feet from the ground. Any passer-by who disturbed the cord would be closely examined. Unfortunately, one of those stopped was a regular staff sergeant, a CQMS, from 3 Worcesters, hurrying on his way to catch the train that would take him home on leave. The altercation that followed between 22-year-old Corporal Pollard and a forty-year old senior, regular army NCO was spectacular. Captain Morphy was summoned. He rose, most unwillingly, from his bed, applied some common sense and the CQMS went on his way.

Corporal Pollard mused that he 'hoped the Quarter bloke caught his train.' He had distinguished himself after a fashion but 'did not write to tell My Lady about it.' Alfred Pollard had not the least doubt of his suitability to be an officer and, some twelve days after the incident with the CQMS, the Battalion moved back into the St. Julian area. He indulged himself by taking every opportunity to roam around in no man's land. The implication is that he went on these forays by himself and quite what he had in mind he did not explain. These were not the actions of a disciplined soldier and it is surprising that he was allowed to get away with it.

When he was not 'roaming' he and his comrades had to make their new position habitable. They took over a complete shambles. The trenches were:

> Half full of unburied corpses killed in some (earlier) action. We moved to a new trench dug just behind the old position. Even here all digging operations encountered bodies. The Huns were now 800 yards away and there was plenty to see in the intervening space. On one of (my) excursions I came across an excellent Burberry with only five small shrapnel holes in it. By it, in the bottom of the shell hole where I found it was a solitary head. It stood upright in the centre of the crater and there was no trace of the body to which it belonged. For some reason it fascinated me. It looked so droll and yet so pathetic. To whom had it belonged? Was he friend or foe? *Had death overtaken him whilst he was dashing forward in a charge full of the lust of battle or had he been cowering in sickening fear, his nerve shattered by the thunder of bursting shells? I hoped he was a fighter who had gone down with his face to the enemy, his courage high and his mouth set in grim determination. That was how I hoped to die if I had to: though I would have liked one second's warning so that I could breathe Her name. Afterwards, if my head remained to mark the spot I should like it to be pointing to the trenches I had never reached.*[6] [Author's italics.]

These latter sentiments were not contemporaneous with the event and one is able to detect here the work of a professional author who might be allowing his well-won reputation as a fire-eater to guide his pen, particularly so in the passage in italics.

Pollard had his first independent command when he was given charge of twelve men and told to occupy a listening post about 300 yards in front of the British line. The position was a ditch surrounded by corpses and Pollard was bursting to be attacked. He had about 100 'bombs' with which he intended to 'make a good show'. To his regret, the Germans did not attack, the bombs were not thrown and there was an anti-climactic end to the exercise when his party withdrew un-blooded.

Alfred Pollard wrote to his 'Lady' to mark her birthday in September 1915. He admitted that 'my pen ran away with me' and he declared his feelings for her. 'In for a penny in for a pound,' he went further and proposed that she marry him just as soon as the war was over. The letter concluded with a statement of his total devotion. He awaited her reply on tenterhooks.

Meanwhile, he was sent off for two weeks to attend a course at the 2nd Army Grenade School at Terdeghen, a blessedly quiet spot after the Salient. Pollard enjoyed the course and learned the characteristics and effectiveness of every grenade British and German then in use. He was taught the mechanics of trench clearing and admitted that 'Without the knowledge I gained I doubt very much if I would be alive today.' He explained that:

> A bombing party consisted of eight men. Two ordinary riflemen with fixed bayonets led the way. Their job was to protect the bomb-throwers from surprise and tackle any of the enemy they came across. Behind them came the first bomb-thrower followed by a man carrying a supply of bombs for him to throw. Then came another bomb-thrower and another carrier. Then the leader of the party and lastly a spare man who acted as an extra carrier or could be used to replace casualties.

Pollard heard the message but later, and in practice, he rejected it and subsequently arranged his bombing parties differently. The graduate of the bombing course hastened back to his battalion, in late September, to find that four officers of 1 HAC had all been killed by a shell that landed directly in their dug-out. Among the dead was the officer appointed to command the bombing platoon that had been formed in Pollard's absence. The death of four officers was a regimental disaster but it resulted in Corporal Pollard being presented with a rare opportunity. He was selected to take command of the bombing platoon. During the war, platoons were often commanded by senior NCOs but rarely by a corporal, other than in extreme circumstances – these were just those circumstances.

The platoon was composed of thirty-two men drawn from all four rifle companies and it was deployed in small groups of three or four men along the Battalion front. This made any sort of central control unnecessary, which was fortunate, as it was impractical anyway. The platoon was untrained but willing and AOP took great pride in leading them. He visited each group frequently, be they in a sap head or out in no man's land in a listening post. He had to traverse the Battalion front – a journey of perhaps ten minutes as an energetic crow might fly but the complexity of the trench system was such that his tour took about two hours.

A major assault was planned and Pollard was charged with establishing fourteen bomb shelters. This was quite beyond the capacity of his scattered platoon. Corporal Alfred Pollard took himself off to visit his CO 'to have a chat with the Colonel', to explain the problem. The CO issued an order to all officers commanding companies that Corporal Pollard was to employ as many of their men as were required. The shelters were duly constructed, at night, under AOP's supervision. He and his men had not slept for five nights and they were utterly exhausted. They withdrew from the line when the HAC were replaced by fresh troops who were to make the attack. On withdrawal, the bombing platoon halted for the routine 'ten-minute smoko' – they all fell asleep on the spot.

The next day Pollard was promoted to sergeant and clearly, his work had drawn attention because about a week later he received a 'stiffy' – it was a card from the GOC 3rd Division addressed to 1023 Corporal AO Pollard, and it said:

> Your Commanding Officer and Brigade Commander have informed me that you distinguished yourself in the field. I have read their report with much pleasure.

The card was signed by Major General J Haldane, who commanded the Division – it was the next best thing to a medal. Pollard had probably been put up for a Military Medal (MM) by his CO but in the order of things, recommendations were routinely downgraded and the GOC's commendation was the result. It has been thus for over 100 years. British soldiers who win gallantry decorations earn them and they do not come up with the rations. From the height of the GOC's commendation and promotion to sergeant came the bad news.

The very bad news.

The 'Lady' replied to Alfred's proposal in the most crushingly negative terms. She wrote to say that she was amazed that Alfred had ever considered the remote possibility that they had any sort of personal relationship. She went on to say that her actions in sending him chocolates and cigarettes were no indication that she had any greater regard for him than any other soldier. He was a friend of the family and merely one of the few men she knew personally serving in France. Her letter closed in the most uncompromising manner when she said that it was improbable that she would ever marry and that even if she did, Alfred Oliver Pollard was most certainly the last man whose proposal she would consider.

This was rejection with a capital 'R'. The Lady was implacable, inflexible and indomitable – she might have been one of Admiral Jackie Fisher's Dreadnoughts for all the compassion she displayed. AOP was utterly shattered. But still, as infatuated as he was, he was quick to admit that:

> She was right, dead right. In fact I never knew her to be anything else. Her logic was invariably unassailable. I had no right to assume that she might care for me. I was a sentimental, romantic, love-lorn fool whilst she was a clear-thinking, consistent materialist who considered things as they were and not as they might be.

Pollard took himself off to the village and failed miserably to get drunk and only succeeded in getting sufficiently tipsy to trip over every guy rope in France on his way back to his tent. Bruised, physically and mentally, he fell into his bed roll, soon to be roused by the call to 'stand to'. A bleary Pollard discovered that the Battalion was to move at once and the effort required to assemble his platoon served to take his mind off the 'Lady'. He found that his period in command had come to a swift and unheralded close, as it was bound to, when Lieutenant EWF Hammond[7] arrived to take over the platoon and Pollard, having fallen the men in, reported them as 'present' to the officer.

The Battalion was formed up in the dark and it set off on a 9-mile march to the Salient with the bombing platoon marching at the head of the Battalion and directly behind the Colonel and Adjutant. Pollard realized that, in his hung-over state and in the rush, he had failed to put on his puttees. Inevitably, dawn broke and in the light of early morning, the CO spied the incorrectly dressed and newly promoted Sergeant Pollard.

Pollard described it as a 'strafing' but in modern parlance, it was a king-size, imperial 'bollocking' that the CO administered. Sergeant Pollard was a rising star and a protégé of the CO. His public fall from grace was thus all the more painful for both parties. The rocket left its mark on AOP and he was distressed at the Colonel's displeasure. The dressing down did him no material harm and was probably good for his soul.

The route march 'halted for breakfast and bully beef and biscuits washed down with hot gripe' (tea?) made Pollard feel a deal better. He felt even better when a runner arrived and summoned Lieutenant Hammond to an orders group. Pollard reported that:

> Hammy returned about the middle of the morning full of tremendous news. Fritz had blown a mine under 4th Bn the Middlesex Regiment in the middle of the night, killing ninety men.[8] In the subsequent scrap they had succeeded in re-occupying the mine crater. We were to counter-attack them and turn them out. Only the bombing platoon would be employed. The rest of the Battalion would be in reserve.
>
> I mentally rubbed my hands. These were great tidings. It was the biggest opportunity I had had in the whole war to show what I could do. My bombers that I had trained would cover themselves with glory. The position was as good as taken.

To digress for a moment – it would be useful to put this crater, which was to be the site of a central event in Pollard's life, into its proper context.[9]

In June 1915, the British position at Hooge and Sanctuary Wood was unstable. The Germans held the higher ground and had line of sight across the British trenches. The High Command resolved that a redoubt, currently held by the Germans, and recently significantly reinforced and strongly manned, was a threat that had to be eliminated.

To this end, 175 Tunnelling Company, Royal Engineers, under the command of Lieutenant Geoffrey Cassels, was given the task of driving a mine under the German position. It was a daunting task; the water table was high and very quickly the sappers found themselves working in ankle-deep water. There was the constant threat of a cataclysmic flood. The Germans had suspended all mining activity in this area because of the water table. They mistakenly expected the British to do the same. It was serious mis-judgement that was to cost them dear.

After thirty-eight days of toil, the 65-yard long shaft was completed and at its end a chamber was hollowed out as a repository for about one and a half tons of explosives. Most of this was ammonal, but gun cotton and gun powder were also deployed.

4th Bn the Middlesex Regiment and 1st Bn the Gordon Highlanders were briefed and it was to be their task to seize the ground as soon as the mine was detonated at 1900hrs on 19 July 1915, the designated 'H' Hour.

Fuses were laid and the sappers withdrew. At the appointed time the mine exploded and high into the air went masses of rock, soil concrete and the remains of several hundred unfortunate Germans. As the spoil rained down on the 'Diehards' in their forward position, ten men were killed. Lieutenant Cassels was promptly placed in arrest but, when common sense took over, he was released and awarded the Military Cross.

The survivors rushed into the crater that had been formed. It was 40 yards wide, 20 feet deep and it had a lip about 15 feet high. The British took the far rim and then spread out into the German trenches that radiated from the crater. Early success did not last and eventually hampered by a lack of grenades only the crater was secure.

The fighting in and around the crater was intense and the ground changed hands several times. This was the setting on 30 September 1915 when Pollard recorded that he felt absolutely no fear and did not entertain the thought that he might be hit. He was just delighted that he and his men had been selected for the hazardous task that lay ahead. Pollard explained later that he saw the ensuing action to be some form of game. He said that he was resolved to reach the other side of the crater before 'Hammy'.

It was to be a lethal competition.

'H' Hour was set for 1500hrs and just ten minutes before that, five soldiers from the Royal Scots[10] presented themselves to supplement the bombing team led by Pollard. The five men were untrained, the HAC men were little better and although they understood the theory, they had never 'bombed' in practice.

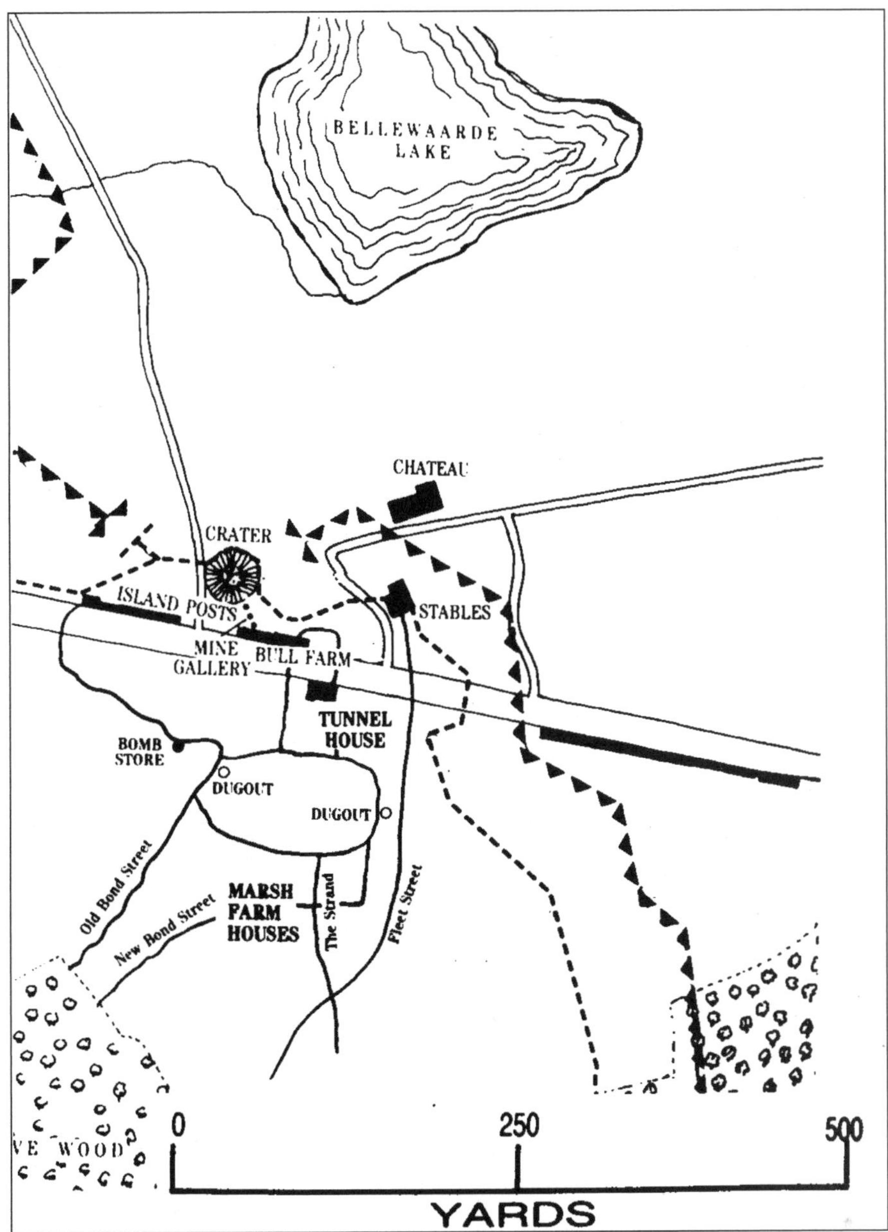

The Hooge Crater.

▲▲▲▲ *German line, after explosion.*

- - - - - - - *British front line.*

– – – – – – *British support trenches.*

From *Sanctuary Wood and Hooge*, p45. (N Cave)

Pollard was aware that for the first recorded occasion the senior Regular regiment and the senior Territorial regiment were to go into action side by side – and he was to lead them.

On the dot of 1500hrs, the preliminary barrage opened and Pollard was very dismissive saying that it was a 'travesty of the barrage of 16 June – shouted commands could be heard easily'.

Sanctuary Wood was reported to be 'a place of some beauty, its trees stood almost unshattered and the undergrowth was so thick in most parts it provided complete shelter from the view of the enemy.' The ramparts, on the other hand, told a different story '... in the autumn of 1915 when in the support trenches that ran through (the wood) one could frequently gather blackberries in the dead ground and those with a little condensed milk ...'

This was now the setting for a savage encounter. Pollard and his small band advanced down a communication trench in the prescribed formation, a bayonet man leading, but, after only 50 yards, they were halted by a barricade that blocked their passage. AOP signalled to the first of his bombers, who pulled the pin on a grenade and hurled it as far as he could over the obstruction. The bomb burst with 'a curious hollow sound, the explosion deadened by the tree trunks'.[11]

The Royal Scots were enthusiastically engaged and were throwing bombs as fast as the pins could be pulled. Initially the fusillade of bombs overwhelmed the enemy but the Huns re-grouped and soon responded in like manner.

A German grenade that looked as innocuous as a jam tin on a small stick dropped onto the parapet and hissed its short life away. It exploded but AOP and his men had ducked low and its vicious energy was expended wastefully. This bomb was the precursor and immediately afterwards, the German bombing increased in intensity.

It was evident that Pollard had a serious fight on his hands, although it was at a distance as the barricade kept the adversaries apart and out of sight of each other. Alfred Pollard determined that to take the fight to the enemy he had to get over or around the barricade.

It was going to be a very risky undertaking.

It was at this point that Pollard realized that he was as much at risk from his own team as the Germans. His men included in their mixed bag of bombs those stick grenades mentioned on page 68. He realized that at any moment one of his inexperienced men, swinging a stick grenade behind him, could knock the percussion head on the trench wall with a deleterious, inconvenient and uncomfortable effect upon the team. Pollard stopped operations, gathered up all the stick grenades and dumped them over the parapet. He decided to rely on what he called 'time bombs', that is to say, a grenade with a five-second fuse.

The barricade was still to the front, a major obstacle and the opposition was on the other side. At this critical place in the action, Pollard takes up the narrative:

> In the order of advance laid down at the Grenade School, the leader of the party occupied fifth place. I wonder if the man who instigated that order ever tried to urge five men across a 7-foot barricade in the teeth of the enemy before he tried it himself. I very much doubt it. My experience throughout the war was that you could lead men anywhere provided you yourself were prepared to go first and show the way. I went first round the barricade. Before I made the attempt I ordered the spare men to collect piles of the bombs in readiness. The throwers were to drop five bombs each over the barricade in quick succession and then concentrate on throwing as far as they could.
>
> Immediately my miniature barrage commenced I climbed out of the trench closely followed by half a dozen men. We were at once exposed to enfilading rifle fire from the Hun lines. I lost four men out of my six getting round the barricade, but I got round. Two dead Huns were lying in the trench, victims of my bomb attack. As I jumped down off the parapet I nearly joined them. A Hun bomb exploded right in front of me, hurling me back against the barricade from which I sank in a heap on the ground. My senses reeled and I believe that for a moment I was unconscious.
>
> 'Are you done in, Sergeant?'
>
> The urgency in the tone of one of my two followers who had successfully run the gauntlet of the barricade brought me to myself. I sat up and shook myself like a dog. All over my body were little prickles where splinters of the bomb had pieced my flesh.[12]
>
> 'I'm alright,' I cried. 'Get on up to the next traverse and keep guard!'
>
> We had driven Fritz back a little way and I wanted to renew contact with him whilst he was on the run. The two men kept guard whilst I called over the barricade for reinforcement. With the help of the rest of the party we pulled down the sand bags until they were only waist high so that more of my men could join us. But now Fritz was employing another device to hold us up. Unable to stop us with bombers he had posted a number of snipers in the branches of the trees. From a distance of 40 yards they were pouring shot after shot into my party with deadly accuracy. Casualties were coming much too fast for my liking. Still never a man shirked, either of our regiment or the Royal Scots. All were head up and heart up in the fight.
>
> I began to experience that curious sense of detachment to which I

have alluded before. It was just as though my spirit was detached from my body. My physical body became a machine doing the bidding coolly and accurately, which my spirit dictated. Something outside myself seemed to tell me what to do, so that I was never at a loss. At the same time I felt quite sure that I would pull through.

There was one curious incident which I shall never forget. I was giving orders to one of the Royal Scots. He was a little man of not more than 5 feet 4 inches. He was standing in front of me listening to what I had to say, when – whist! – a bullet took him through the throat and he fell dead at my feet. Now I am 6 feet 2 and was as much exposed to the enemy as he was. Ever since I have asked myself what caused the Hun sniper to select the little Scot for a target instead of me. The knowledge that some fate had spared me on that occasion helped me considerably in the later years of the war. I used to think, if not once why not twice?

There were plenty of chances to get hit in that scrap. We started with sixteen of our men and five Royal Scots. Only seven came out unscathed. I was not one of them.

We made better progress after we passed the barricade. Fritz did not like our hail of bombs and retreated steadily before us. Presently we came to a second barricade, though not as high as the first one. I think that this must have been part of the original British front line. Anyway, I was more than halfway round the side of the crater, although I could neither see nor hear signs of 'Hammy's' half of the platoon.

My blood was now thoroughly up. I was determined to take that crater or bust. We dealt with that barricade as we had done the first, this time without any casualties. Bombs were running short and I sent back a messenger for further supplies. I hopped back onto our side of the barricade to fetch a sack of bombs which was lying there. I picked them up and was in the act of handing them to a man who had turned to take them when he suddenly pitched forward on his face. At the same time my right arm fell to my side and the sack dropped to the ground.[13]

Pollard was not the target of a sniper; that was the man to whom AOP was handing the sack of bombs. The round went through the unfortunate man and he fell like a stone. That initial and fatal impact caused the round to 'tumble' once it had exited the dead man's body but with sufficient velocity to do very serious damage and it went on to hit Pollard in the shoulder - base first. He wavered and then he collapsed. A comrade put a water bottle to his lips and the content of rum and water was 'nectar'. He got unsteadily to his feet but did not remain erect for long. He fell again and lapsed briefly into unconsciousness.

AOP came to and, with the help of one of his men, managed to walk to a very busy dressing station that was dealing with the effects of shell fire on the battalion supporting the attack. Pollard was a stretcher case but he insisted on walking to the Casualty Clearing Station in the rear – it was a brave gesture but he fainted before he reached his goal. The following day he was evacuated further back and it was here that he formed his low, long maintained and absurd opinion of the RAMC.[14] This was because a soldier of that most excellent of Corps stole ninety francs that he had had on his person. Pollard had no money but the nurses came to his aid and sent a message to the Regiment. He was delighted when 'Hammy' arrived to visit him and bring him the news.

Pollard's half platoon had been severely depleted in the attack but Lieutenant Hammond's half was nearly wiped out and the officer had been lightly wounded. Despite an operation the bullet in Pollard's shoulder could not be found and he was further evacuated by hospital ship to Dover and then onto Manchester and Crumpsall Infirmary. Pollard was the only NCO in a ward of nineteen soldiers and he was accorded a degree of privilege that recognized his rank.

It was whilst recuperating in his hospital bed that he had a considerable shock when shown a copy of the *London Gazette*,[15] in which there was a citation that said:

> *Sergeant AO Pollard of the Honourable Artillery Company has been awarded the Distinguished Conduct Medal for conspicuous gallantry on September 30 at Sanctuary Wood during the bombing fight. Although severely wounded, Sergeant Pollard continued to throw bombs, at the same time issuing orders to and encouraging his men. By his example and gallant conduct he renewed confidence amongst the bombers when they were shaken owing to the enemy being in superior numbers and throwing many more bombs than were available to our side. He did not give up until he fell severely wounded for the second time.*

Two days later, Alfred Pollard received a letter from his CO, Lieutenant Colonel Harold Hanson, who wrote to congratulate him and went on to say, 'I was very pleased to learn that for your distinguished service on that date you have received the DCM,[16] but at the same time it was a matter of sincere regret to me and still is, that you were not awarded the higher recognition for which I strongly recommended you, and which I think you well earned.'

Colonel Hanson had recommended Alfred Pollard for the Victoria Cross, no less! Alfred was predictably surprised and delighted, and he had cause to be. A second operation found the offending bullet and within a couple of days

AOP was able to get out and about in Manchester, which he found much to his liking. Wounded, good-looking soldiers were very well treated, especially those sporting the maroon and blue ribbon of the DCM. Admission to all the theatres was free and lots of people wanted to buy a young soldier a drink. All in all, life was really quite sweet.

Pollard's parents came up to see him and his mother stayed on for a few days. She was grateful to have him at home, wounded or not. It transpired that just after Pollard was wounded, 1 HAC was withdrawn from the line, moved back to the area of GHQ at St. Omer and turned into an officers' training corps in order to give it some respite and to allow men to take leave.

Pollard had time to reflect on the war, his part in it and to consider what it was that motivated him and failed to motivate others. His philosophy was very simple. The country was at war, the survival of the nation was in question and every citizen had an absolute duty to serve in some capacity to defend the realm. In his autobiography Pollard waxes eloquent on the topic and his contempt for non-contributors is stark, not least for munitions workers striking for more pay. After the war Pollard was able to refine his views and he published several articles expressing them.

Pollard was now well on the road to a full recovery when a bombshell burst: he said, 'to my inexpressible horror I discovered I was marked permanently unfit for further active service.' Rather smugly he went on to comment that 'I suppose many men in my position would have been satisfied with the hospital verdict. They would have felt that they had done everything possible to satisfy their personal honour, as well as their duty to their country. In the idiom of the period they would "have done their bit".'

What Alfred says is certainly true but the impression he leaves behind is rather unattractive and it were better unsaid.

Notes

1 Major Billy Congreve, previously Brigade Major of 7 Brigade, won a VC, DSO and MC. He was killed on the Somme in 1916.

2 AO Pollard, *Fire-Eater*, p93.

3 Gordon Corrigan, *Mud, Blood and Poppycock*, p135.

4 Gordon Corrigan, *Mud, Blood and Poppycock*, p136.

5 AO Pollard, *Fire-Eater*, p98.

6 AO Pollard, *Fire-Eater*, p104.

7 Lieutenant Ernest William Frost Hammond joined the HAC in 1911. He was commissioned in August 1915 and wounded two months later. Later, he won an MC and was killed in action at Bullecourt in May 1917.

8 This is incorrect.

9 http://www.firstworldwar.com/today/hoogecrater.htm

10 The Royal Scots 'Pontius Pilate's bodyguard' was raised in 1633 by Sir John Hepburn and was designated the 1st of Foot. In World War I it raised thirty-five battalions and 100,000 men wore its cap badge. The contractions of the Army in the late 20th and early 21st centuries have, in combination, diluted the regimental line. Its descendants are now the Royal Scots Borderers, 1st Bn, The Royal Regiment of Scotland.

11 AO Pollard, *Fire-Eater*, p115.

12 These injuries would affect Pollard later in life.

13 AO Pollard, *Fire-Eater*, p119.

14 Royal Army Medical Corps.

15 *London Gazette*, 16 November 1915.

16 There were only three gallantry decorations available to soldiers in 1915. These were first, the Victoria Cross (VC), secondly, the Distinguished Conduct Medal (DCM) and thirdly, the Military Medal (MM). A soldier could also be 'Mentioned in Despatches (MID), in which case he wore an oak leaf on his campaign medal but had no post-nominal letters. The Meritorious Service Medal (MSM) came with post-nominal letters but it was not awarded for gallantry.

Chapter 6

Home Service – The King's Commission

'It was a higher honour than I had ever contemplated.'

November 1915–May 1916

In November 1915, Alfred Oliver Pollard had three clear objectives. First of these was to pursue 'Her' come what may and notwithstanding the comprehensive and highly unsympathetic rejection he had recently suffered. Secondly, to get past a medical board and, by hook or by crook, return to active service. Thirdly, to take up the commission that he now dearly coveted.

He was discharged from hospital at the end of November 1915, having taken Manchester and its people to his heart. He was granted two weeks' leave and he hurried home to his parents. 'One of my first acts after reaching London was to ring up My Lady at her hospital and ask her to meet me.' They met at Cannon Street Station and Pollard was consumed with anticipation.

Her arrival fed his wildest dreams because when she arrived she looked absolutely stunning in 'a purple costume with a small, close fitting hat of the same colour. Her face was framed in black fox fur and a wisp of golden hair which peeped coquettishly over one ear wound itself tightly around my heart.'

His dog-like devotion had not wavered, indeed if anything, it had strengthened. He had continued to endow her with every womanly virtue and believed that 'no woman who ever lived could compare with her.'

Poor Pollard had taken one beating and he was now going to get another, applied by a mistress of the cataclysmic 'put down'. They repaired to a tea shop and, just as soon as the tea was poured, she got straight to the point. She told Alfred that definitely and once and for all she would never marry him. Strictly no 'ifs' or 'buts' there was to be no sitting on the fence of legend here. She went even further and told him that if he made any further protestations of devotion she would never see him again. She was prepared to accept him as a friend but only if he gave his word never to refer to an engagement again.

He gave his word with a smile that 'hid a breaking heart'.

Things were not looking bright in the 'Objective One' department and a very chastened AOP moved on to 'Objectives Two and Three'. He reported to the 3rd or Reserve Battalion of the HAC, which was in billets in Richmond Park. He was made welcome by Captain Boyle, his mentor and hero. Boyle said that 'he was very proud of me, which meant considerably more to me than the greater effusion of lesser men.'

The CO of 3 HAC was a Lieutenant Colonel William Evans. Pollard remarked that he was 'a fine looking man with a long white moustache'. Evans was an old soldier and to his eternal regret, he was too old to serve overseas. The 3rd Battalion under his command was a well run and very large unit of over 1,000 men who were in the process of being trained before being sent out to supplement the two battalions on active service.

Pollard was routinely and formally interviewed by the CO on joining, and at that interview, Evans raised the matter of Pollard's application for a commission. Clearly, the administrative machine had been working and Evans was able to tell AOP that he had, in fact, been selected. What was more, Evans said, he was able to offer him a commission in the HAC. Pollard wrote later that 'no reward could have given me greater pleasure. It was a higher honour than I had ever contemplated. I accepted enthusiastically.'

This was Objective Three – a goal achieved.

There now remained the matter of Pollard's medical category and the key player in this area was the Battalion doctor. Dr. Instone (probably Captain RAMC) examined the significant scar in Pollard's shoulder and found it to be inflamed. He wondered why the scar should have the appearance of being 'stretched'. Pollard told him that he had been practicing bomb-throwing in the garden. The Doctor was amused, but appeared to be approachable and sympathetic; sufficiently so as to send his patient with 'the stretched scar', on another fortnight's sick leave. This, by happy chance, included the Christmas holiday.

The journey back to Richmond Park Camp from Wallington was easy. When AOP had unpacked in the sergeants' mess he quickly discovered that he would be moving to different accommodation very soon. This was because his commission was to date from 16 January 1916 – he was 'the proudest man in the world'.

Joining an officers' mess for the first time is a daunting experience. There are all manner of customs, social do's and don'ts, forms of dress, and significant adjustments to be made in personal relationships that are always led by the other, more senior party. Above all there is the need to conform to an ambiance that, although welcoming and amiable, is new. Hero he might have been, but for Alfred Pollard, Day One as an officer was as testing as any disputed German trench.

Pollard was made very welcome: he knew many of the officers already. It was the custom in the HAC (and still is) that all officers have to serve in the ranks before they are commissioned. As a result he had known about half the mess members as private men in France.

The newspapers were full of the unfortunate situation of 6th Indian Division, which under the command of Major General CVF Townshend CB DSO, was besieged in the desert town of Kut in Mesopotamia (now Iraq). Townshend had fought a brilliant campaign until he over-reached himself at Ctesiphon and was forced to retreat. The ongoing saga of Kut[1] stole some of the limelight from the Western Front.

Nearer to home, and in Richmond Park, 'Hammy' took AOP under his wing and guided him through the system. By the end of the first week Alfred felt at home – indeed, this was his home now. But not for long as he was sent off to Chelsea Barracks to attend a course for newly commissioned officers.

On completion of his course he returned not to Richmond Park but to the rather less convenient Blackheath, to where 3 HAC had been moved. He was despatched to Captain Ellis, who was in command of the Battalion Bombing School, and Pollard joined his team alongside 'Hammy' and Lieutenant Geoffrey Withers. There was hard training during the day and trips to London every evening with the two officers named. When young men gather together and drink is taken, sometimes common sense and good manners depart.

Pollard recorded that on one occasion the three officers went to the theatre to see a show called *Snowballs* as guests of the father of a brother officer. At the finale of the show the cast pelted the audience with 'snowballs' made largely of cotton wool. The audience threw them back and none more enthusiastically than the three bombers in the stalls.

Pollard, carried away by the moment, picked up and threw the hat of a fat gentlemen sitting in the row in front. One of the cast caught the hat and put it on, to great applause. The fat man did not see the funny side and when he asked Pollard if he had thrown his hat Pollard admitted that he had and then promptly threw the man's coat as well. An attendant was summoned and Pollard reported the conversation as follows:

> 'Wotcha mean by interfering with this gentleman's clothes?' he enquired truculently.
>
> 'I mean this,' I explained, and standing up I removed his hat and flung it after the other things. He was furious but as he did not like to tackle me by himself he retired for assistance. We decided that the moment had arrived to beat it.[2]

At one level this incident might be seen as high spirited fun by young officers in the middle of a world war and of no possible consequence. On the other hand, some might judge it to be yobbish behaviour.

Pollard was a big, aggressive man and on that evening, he physically intimidated those less well endowed who confronted him. He recounted the story with a deal of pride and it might have been better if he had not. This incident is, however, balanced by another.

Pollard and his contemporaries, with the impetuosity of youth, were swift to judgement. One officer was subject to a group judgement and was treated with ill-disguised contempt when he visited the mess. This officer had been a member of the HAC for some time before war broke out and he did not volunteer to sail for France. Nevertheless, he was commissioned and apparently given a soft job in the War Office. From time to time he visited HAC units, including 3 HAC, and because he was considered to be a 'shirker', he was treated accordingly. The officer appeared not to notice the manner in which Pollard and his peers ostracized him and that only served to exacerbate the situation.

Several years after the war Pollard was vastly embarrassed to discover that the object of all that derision, who was a fluent linguist, had been a member of the Secret Service and had, allegedly, spent periods of the war in Germany in the most hazardous of undercover operations. Pollard did not name him.

To his credit, AOP acknowledged that he had got it very wrong and said, 'He carried his life in his hands more than any of us. For any mean thought I ever held about him, I am most deeply repentant. He taught me never to judge any man's courage on outward appearances.'

The hope is that the officer concerned read Pollard's book. It would be agreeable to think that the two men took a glass in the Sutling Room[3] at Armoury House. If they ever did, we have no record of it.

Pollard enjoyed himself with 3 HAC; he was at ease with his fellow officers and included in their number was Dougie Davis, whose inadequate servant AOP had once been. However, by the nature of the unit's role, the population was constantly changing; Captain Boyle was among others who had departed to join the 1st Battalion and rumour had it that the Battalion would soon relinquish its officer training role and revert to a 'line' battalion.

Pollard was rightfully concerned about his brother Frank, allegedly serving as Guardsman Thompson JF, Grenadier Guards. As AOP reports it, the sequence of events was that Frank was granted leave and he visited Alfred, who took him to meet Colonel Evans. His extraordinary history was explained and Evans was persuaded that Frank Pollard's 'desertion' was only of a technical nature. Evans decided, probably correctly, that Frank's history was by far outweighed by his war service and he 'forgave' him his sins. He went further and invited him to accept a commission in his former regiment. AOP remarked, 'There was nothing to do but wait.'

This account, as it stands, strains credibility.

It all sounds far too easy, far too informal and simply not professional. The HAC is, in some ways, a law unto itself. Even so, there are some fundamental principles that apply even to the HAC. Frank was not arraigned, formally, on a charge of desertion, and even if he had been, it is not within the gift of a commanding officer to dismiss a charge other than for a soldier formally placed under his command. The Grenadier Guards would have had a view on all of this.

Colonel Evans was not in a position to acquiesce at the completion of application forms for a soldier not of his responsibility. The King's Commission is not granted lightly, even in wartime, and there was a multiplicity of issues to be resolved before Frank Pollard/Frank Thompson could sport a pip on his shoulder – no matter how worthy he might have been. AOP's glib summation of these events has simplified matters by apparently keeping it all in the family but nevertheless, the Grenadier Guards could not be ignored.

AOP was not versed in the administrative system operated by the Adjutant General for the wider Army and it may be that, in his ignorance, he has overly simplified the process. It is *just* possible that Colonel Evans took up the case and resolved to co-ordinate the application with the Grenadier Guards and the War Office. The matter of 'desertion' could have been dealt with administratively as part of Frank Pollard's rehabilitation. At this distance we may never know just who did what for whom and when. This was all in about April/May 1916.

On 28 April 1916, Kut fell to the Turks and General Townshend and his men went 'into the bag'. Many of these soldiers died in captivity but their general lived in great style, as 'an honoured guest'[4] of the Turks, for the remainder of the war and ruined his reputation in the process.

This reverse, following on from the debacle of Gallipoli, was a major reverse for British arms, only exceeded by the loss of Singapore in February 1942.

On the Western Front the war of attrition continued unabated, men went, died, and were replaced. The rumour mill was working flat out when it revealed that a further draft of officers was to be sent to 1 HAC and AOP, having sorted out his brother's fate, was determined to be in that draft. He was fortunate that 'Doc' Instone was one of the members of the mess with whom Pollard had struck up a friendship. AOP put his cards on the table with the Doctor, who promised to support him. Pollard volunteered and although

Colonel Evens demurred, the unequivocal medical report was compelling. Thus it was that Pollard's name eventually appeared on the list of eight officer replacements. They left Waterloo Station on 24 May 1916 in high good humour.

It had been supportive of the Doctor to help his friend but he probably did not know that the injury to Pollard's shoulder had affected the nerves in his right hand. The damage was sufficiently severe that he could not operate the trigger of his revolver. This would have been more than enough to cause him to be permanently downgraded. Alfred knew that and kept this little matter to himself. He concentrated on using his left hand. Every night before he went to bed he practised with his weapon, squeezing the trigger hundreds of times. It took time but eventually he was proficient with his left hand – a remarkable example of determination and very much in character for this extraordinary young man.

Notes

1 NS Nash, *Chitrál Charlie*, p220-271.
2 AO Pollard, *Fire-Eater*, p134.
3 The bar in Armoury House – at the top of the stairs on the left – is always called the Sutling Room.
4 CVF Townshend, *My Campaign in Mesopotamia*, p359-385.

Chapter 7

Return to the Fray – the 'Rum Jar' Incident

'Bombo! Put that thing down and come here at once.'

June–November 1916

Lieutenant Colonel Edward Treffry had returned to France having recovered from his wound and reassumed command of 1 HAC on 14 April 1916, 'To the joy of all who had served under him in the past'.[1] When Alfred Pollard[2] and his seven fellow officers arrived at the Hotel de France in Hesdin on 30 May 1916, they had not had time to unpack their kit when:

> We heard the clattering of hooves in the courtyard. Colonel Treffry and Captain, now Major, Boyle had called to welcome us. The Colonel's greeting was characteristically to the point. 'Well Bombo, you've arrived in the nick of time. I want a battalion bombing officer. Get going at once and train me a platoon of bombers.'

Pollard buckled down to the job on 5 June 1916 – he had been given a free hand and he was set on raising and training a platoon of specialists every bit the equal of that wiped out at Sanctuary Wood. Initially AOP saw this new platoon as his private fiefdom to be employed as an entity, but it was not to be like that and he was disappointed to find that his bombers were integrated into their company structure and would only be centralized when conditions so demanded. He accepted that 'I had no individual command. I was attached to Headquarters although I was also appointed to 'B' Company as a company officer.' Despite what was for him an unsatisfactory command structure, he got on with the training and in perfect summer weather he was able to implement his training programme. In less than a month, and by the end of June 1916, he created a platoon 'with a thorough knowledge of bombing and trench-clearing'.

On 31 May 1916 the Battle of Jutland was fought. It was a pyrrhic victory for the Royal Navy and although it was not appreciated at the time, the effect was to confine the German High Seas Fleet to its harbours and to allow the Royal Navy to impose a blockade that would eventually starve Germany into submission.

By November 1918, the German Navy was in a state of mutiny. Some historians would argue that it was sea power that won the war and that the gargantuan efforts on land were highly expensive, but ultimately inconclusive.

In France, matters at sea were of no concern to GHQ, which determined to launch a major assault to relieve the pressure on the French allies who were engaged in the attritional battle of Verdun.

The blackest day in the long history of the British Army was, without question, 1 July 1916. This was the day that 60,000 men were killed or wounded during the first, ghastly hours of the Battle of the Somme. By happy chance, 1 HAC was not committed to the ill-judged attack and so did not suffer the barbarous butchery of that ill-famed day. Had it been committed then it would probably have been obliterated and Pollard's chances of survival would have been very slim indeed. As it was, 1 HAC was billeted in Hesdin miles from the carnage, but hearing and reading about the unutterable catastrophe.

In contrast to the blood-letting further along the line, Hesdin was a quiet little place to relax and enjoy summer. But all good things come to an end and on 8 July, 1 HAC set off on a four-day march to join its new formation – 63rd Royal Naval Division (RND). This division had taken heavy casualties in the Dardanelles and after the evacuation of Gallipoli it moved to France, where it fought in the closing episodes of the Battle of the Somme.

The 63rd Division was one of the curious anomalies of World War I. It was originally formed with what was perceived to be surplus RN manpower that was under-employed. Initially the Navy had hoped that an admiral would be in command but that idea had no future and a major general took the job. Similarly, no generals were selected to command flotillas, squadrons or fleets.

Quite right, too.

Post Gallipoli, the remnants of the RND was formed into two RN brigades (188 and 189) supplemented by an Army brigade. This latter formation was designated 190 Brigade and was composed of 7th Bn the Royal Fusiliers, 4th Bedfordshire Regiment, 8th Bn the Dublin Fusiliers and 1st Bn Honourable Artillery Company.

The Divisional Commander, Major General Archibald Parris, was wounded and replaced by Major General CD Shute on 17 October 1916. It was whilst under the command of General Shute that the Division captured Beaumont Hamel. A depiction of the Division's prize, such as it was, is to be found overleaf.

A sketch of what remained of Beaumont Hamel railway station.
A sketch by Adrian Hill (HAC Archives)

General Shute had not volunteered for and did not welcome his appointment. He was not an admirer of RN customs and traditions and in a singularly short-sighted and provocative manner, sought to eradicate them from the *Royal Naval Division* [author's italics], a formation that was composed of 60% sailors and marines. Predictably, his actions made him highly unpopular. However, that all said, Shute was a capable and demanding commander. He was dissatisfied by the cleanliness of the trenches occupied by one of his Naval brigades and especially so about the state of the latrines when he inspected them. The fact that his sailors had inherited the ordure from the previous occupants of the trench was no excuse. The GOC made his displeasure well known, as was entirely his prerogative.

Alan Herbert,[3] who was to find fame through his pen in later life, was an officer in the 63rd RND and he wrote a poem that lives to this day. Long after Shute's's[4] death he is remembered – but usually, only because of these four verses:

The General inspecting the trenches
Exclaimed with a horrified shout
'I refuse to command a division
Which leaves its excreta about.'

But nobody took any notice
No one was prepared to refute,
That the presence of shit was congenial
Compared to the presence of Shute.

And certain responsible critics
Made haste to reply to his words
Observing that his staff advisors
Consisted entirely of turds.

For shit may be shot at odd corners
And paper supplied there to suit,
But a shit would be shot without mourners
If someone shot that shit Shute.

The re-organization of the Division took some time. It was not committed to the line for some weeks and during this lull AOP set out to train more bombers. Initially this was to produce a reserve of bombers as casualty replacements but eventually, and with commendable enthusiasm, Pollard arranged for every man in the Battalion to receive bomb training. He lectured to each company in turn and introduced them to the arcane arts of trench clearing.

By so doing he countered and then eradicated the natural caution with which every soldier approaches his first live grenade. AOP was able to report to Colonel Treffry that every man in 1 HAC had been trained and that all of them had thrown at least two grenades. Treffry pronounced himself to be 'delighted' and some days later when he was dining with the Brigade Commander, the Brigadier enquired if any of his men had any experience in handling bombs. 'All of them,' replied the Colonel expansively.

At this stage in the war the troops all wore soft hats whose function was to keep a chap's hair in place and provide a convenient platform for his cap badge. They provided not a whit of protection. Steel helmets were now being manufactured and issued but 1 HAC had not received any. An officer who had been attached to another unit returned with a 'tin hat' and presented it to Colonel Treffry, who was very proud of it. It was something of a prize and the Colonel 'hung it on a convenient nail behind the orderly room door.'

Alfred Pollard had been debating, with a brother officer, the worth or otherwise of these tin hats that were expected some day soon. Pollard asserted that the hat would stop a revolver bullet at close range. His companion stoutly said it would not. Neither of the officers had any evidence to support his position and the debate looked like coming to an inconclusive end. It was at this stage that Pollard recalled seeing a helmet in the orderly room and he suggested that they test its efficiency. The ownership of the helmet was not thought to be important and when Pollard fired at the helmet at the agreed 25 yards it spun around atop the post upon which it had been mounted and was found to have a dent the size of a man's fist. The round had, however, not penetrated the helmet. The now damaged tin hat was returned to its nail.

When the Colonel found that his prize helmet, the only one in 1 HAC, was no longer pristine, he was not best pleased. Pollard made himself scarce. Colonel Treffry blew for the Armourer and directed him to remove the offending dent. The hat was heated until it was red hot and then the Armourer tapped it with his hammer.

He tapped too hard – 'He put his hammer right through it.'

Eventually Pollard had to come clean and apologize to his CO. The situation was fraught at first, but the situation eased on 10 August, when crates of tin hats were delivered to 1 HAC and everyone was duly issued with his own – including Colonel Treffry.

The remaining summer months of 1916 passed without incident as 1 HAC was in a very quiet part of the line and not committed to any form of offensive action. The opportunity was taken to give the replacements a gentle introduction to trench life. The weather was pleasant and Pollard used to:

> Sleep out under a tree in preference to having my bed made up in a hut. One night I was awakened by having my face licked. I sat up and found two large dogs standing over me. One was a retriever and the other a sheepdog. They were homeless and promptly adopted me as their master.

Pollard became very attached to these two dogs, which did not always behave, and on occasions caused him some embarrassment, not least at a battalion church parade. The dogs and their affection had a softening effect on AOP; they gave him great pleasure and perhaps helped move the Lady out of the forefront of his mind. As the summer drew to a close so did the very agreeable lifestyle. On 3 September 1916, to the great regret of the whole Battalion, Lieutenant Colonel Treffry relinquished command; his old wounds had been causing him much suffering for some months and he could not continue. He had been an exceptional CO. His personal gallantry was matched by his moral courage and he would be sorely missed. Command of 1 HAC devolved on Captain, Acting Major, and (presumably) Local Lieutenant Colonel Ernest PC Boyle, Pollard's role model and mentor. Boyle was the right man at the right time. Goold Walker said:[5]

> It was no easy thing to take over from an officer of the experience and prestige of Col. Treffry, who left the unit, however, on good terms with

An observation post – very obvious and highly vulnerable.
A sketch by Adrian Hill (HAC Archives)

the authorities, with a thoroughly trained battalion and most excellent officers. The Battalion now formed a part of the 190th Infantry Brigade, 63rd (Royal Naval) Division.

Until the 17th of the month the Battalion remained in the Calonne sector, engaging in nightly patrols and doing good work in repairing the

> trenches they occupied. On the 9th, the 9.5" heavy trench mortar was brought into position at the mine shaft to knock out the enemy's rum-jar batteries. Unfortunately, their second shot landed on the centre company's headquarters' dug-out: 2nd Lieutenant H Link was killed,[6] Lieutenant GAT Darby was crushed, and 2nd Lieutenant Humphreys, who had just handed in his Company report and was sitting at the foot of the stairs sound asleep, escaped without damage - he had not heard the concussion.
>
> A relief of Mining Engineers was passing at the moment of the explosion and immediately dug down and saved these officers' lives. On the same evening, Lieutenant HW O'Brien, Sergeant Barris, Lance Corporal Holden and Private SD Payne, while on patrol in the German area, were sighted by enemy sentries, and Lance Corporal Holden[7] was mortally wounded.
>
> The patrol was subjected to a considerable amount of fire, but Lieutenant O'Brien succeeded in carrying Holden back to our lines, although repeatedly held up by barbed wire entanglements. The Commanding Officer sent his name in to the Division, and he was awarded the Military Cross.
>
> The snipers under 2nd Lieutenant Lamb had obtained complete ascendancy over the Bavarians opposite us, and throughout the period in the Calonne sector we had no casualties from their snipers: the average bag of our side was five *per diem*. The bombers under 2nd Lieutenant AO Pollard organized very efficient rifle-grenade batteries, and made it a point of honour to give the enemy ten rifle grenades for every pineapple.

The position at Calonne was held by three companies with one in support. It was a curious place as the left-hand company manned a trench that ran through a slag heap. The slag contained deep internal fires and the measure of the heat generated was that there was sufficient for the men to boil water by merely laying their mess tins on the surface. It must have been a very dangerous environment and the air must have been toxic. These slag heaps were considerable features in a flat landscape and to the rear of the HAC position one soared up almost 100 feet. The engineers cut a tunnel through it, which formed part of the communication trench.

It was at Calonne that AOP first came across the sophisticated deep dug-outs that were to become standard across the front where the water table permitted. These large holes were 40-50 feet deep and not only afforded complete protection against shelling but they were equipped with a degree of sophistication. Bunk beds and electric light provided some comfort. Pollard said that 'Those off duty could sleep in peace, secure in the knowledge that their shelters were shell-proof.'

Although the Calonne front was 'quiet' nevertheless, as Goold Walker said, above, there was intermittent shell fire. One of the most dangerous forms of shell fire was that of the German trench mortars, which fired two kinds of projectiles. The first, known as a 'rum-jar' was so called because it was constructed in a steel case shaped like a rum jar. It was packed with high explosives. The second type was known as a 'pineapple', partly because of its shape but more because of the heavy serrations on the body of the projectile. Both were devastatingly lethal if they landed in a trench. They were not high velocity weapons and the mortar shell could be easily spotted in flight. Pollard reported upon the manner that the Battalion responded to this particular threat. He said:

> To counter them each company posted a sentry provided with a whistle. Three blasts meant that the danger was to the right, two blasts to the left, one that it was coming straight over. When the warning sounded, the troops moved along the trench to another traverse. In this way we suffered very few casualties.

Pollard found the relative peace of Calonne not entirely to his liking and his ardour for offensive action was undimmed. His initiative in this respect was worthy of the attention of Goold Walker (above) and Pollard fleshes out the official historian's words by explaining:

> I found some rifle racks which took six rifles each. By tying all the triggers together with string I succeeded in firing them all at once. In each rifle I fixed a rifle grenade and pointed my engine of fearfulness toward where I had seen the 'pineapples' start. I provided each of the three companies with a similar machine and gave orders that the bombers were to fire not less than 200 rifle grenades per day per company. After a few tries we got the range: then we proceeded to send over two coveys of rifle grenades every time Fritz pitched one of his 'rum-jars' or 'pineapples'.
>
> 600 grenades a day! My requisitions to the Brigade Bombing Officer were terrific. After a few days he asked me to ease up. His supply was unequal to my demand.

Alfred Pollard had a desire to have a rum-jar as a souvenir and to this end found what he described as a 'dud', with which he proposed to have 'some fun'. His plan was unsophisticated - he intended to take out the detonator, empty the 60lbs of high explosive out and retain the empty and innocuous case. How he planned to get this extraordinary object home he did not explain. He bent to his task and whilst engrossed in his work heard the voice of his Commanding Officer, quite close but out of sight around a traverse. The CO was showing around the position the CO and Adjutant of a battalion that had been detailed to relieve 1 HAC. AOP heard the CO say: 'We are now coming to the part of the line held by 'C' Company.'[8]

At that point the little party rounded the traverse and saw Pollard sitting astride the rum-jar and presumably hitting the object of his affections with a hammer. The party swiftly went into reverse and backed behind the traverse. Over the parapet the Colonel's somewhat agitated voice was heard calling: 'Bombo! Put that thing down and come here at once.'

Pollard did as he was bidden and was interrogated by the Colonel as to what the hell he was doing. AOP explained that he was 'just taking the detonator out of a rum-jar …'

'Go back, pick it up and throw it over the parapet just as it is.'

'But Sir …'

'Do as I tell you. Do you want to blow us all to smithereens?'

Pollard said later that, having removed the detonator, the rum-jar was no more dangerous than a bottle of its namesake and he lamented that his CO really did not understand bombs and their inner workings.

It would seem that AOP was affectionately known as 'Bombo' and it was an appropriate sobriquet for a man who had become something of an expert in his chosen field.

Alfred Pollard was pleased to be back in France, pleased to be back with 1 HAC and even more pleased to be back in the line. His attitude was decidedly different to most of his peers and his love of Country was very strong motivation indeed. He also relished and thrived on the danger that the war provided. The words he used to express these thoughts were:

> One felt one was pulling one's weight for the Country, doing the right thing. I thoroughly enjoyed it. After a nine-month gap the knowledge that the Huns were just opposite waiting for an opportunity to kill me if I gave them a chance added a spice to life which I had missed.

AOP had already given the Germans ample opportunities to kill him but they had not seized the opportunities he presented to them. Particularly when he was perambulating in no man's land alongside his mentor EPC Boyle – but that was when he was a corporal. Now that he was an officer the initiative was his and he took it.

The first time he ventured forth, in command, he took a compass, Sergeant Harrison, a New Zealander, and Hughesdon, his runner. It was the latter's uncomfortable duty to accompany his officer wherever he went.

The trio left the British front line in single file, but prone, and they snaked very slowly, on their stomachs, across the detritus of the battlefield. Actually, in the twenty minutes or so that the expedition lasted, they crawled in a wide half-circle and ended up back at the British line – very wet and muddy but fortunate indeed not to have drawn fire from a watchful sentry as apparently, no password had been arranged. It was all something of a debacle and AOP blamed the copious wire for affecting his compass.

The following night he resolved to have another attempt and this time without a compass. The area to the British front was decorated with slag heaps and, in daylight, each of these was easy to identify as was their juxtaposition. At night, from a prone position, in low light, it was an entirely different matter. Soon after the expedition started Pollard realized that he did not know where he was, nor did he know where the enemy was. To his credit, he did not give up and with commendable determination, he and his two companions crawled on … and on. Their journey took about an hour and a half. It had been an exhausting, filthy business.

Finally they reached a line of wire. Perhaps it was German wire but there was no guarantee of that. The three men rose to their feet, surveyed the darkness and concluded that this wire had indeed been laid by the Germans. This judgement was confirmed when they were suddenly challenged by a stentorian voice shouting in German. They did not respond and inevitably, the sentry opened fire.

'Come on, you fellows,' commanded Pollard. The party turned on its heels and fled from whence they had come. By happy chance they were able to jump into a shell hole, just as the first flare illuminated the battlefield. From the shell hole they could see and hear the vigorous German reaction to their brief and uninvited visit. Grenades were thrown to explode where once they had stood and automatic fire hosed over their heads. They sat down with their heads below the rim of the crater and waited. Half an hour passed, the shooting petered out and flares no longer brightened the landscape.

The party turned for home and crawled back to the British line without mishap. It had been an exciting, hazardous evening and without material benefit. However, AOP commented that:

> I learned a number of things from that patrol: the necessity of arranging some signal so that I could easily find my way back, the difficulty the men experienced in crawling with their rifles and the ease with which one could approach an enemy position under cover of night. But mostly I realized how secure Fritz felt in his position. His wire entanglements were infinitely superior to ours. There had been no attack in this part of

> the line for over a year, and I suspect the Hun had grown careless through the absence of any particular threat against him. Could he have seen the mouth of a certain sinister opening in our trench he would have been considerably more uneasy. A shaft ran deep down into the earth. There was a miniature railway which carried down huge balks of timber and brought back loads of soil. Men toiled day and night like ants burrowing under the ground. They were a company of miners of the Royal Engineers and they were constructing a mine under the enemy's position.

There was almost a separate campaign fought under the Western Front by professional miners on both sides. The miners of the Royal Engineers were a formidable asset. They had to cope with protracted, hard physical work in a confined space, difficult soil conditions, flooding and energetic counter-mining by the enemy. Sometimes the two adversaries would meet in complete darkness in a narrow shaft and fight to the death with shovels and bayonets. On other occasions, miners would be buried when a counter-mine was exploded to thwart their efforts.

It took special men, blessed with calculated and consistent courage, to work as a miner. Their reward was the gratifying and awesome moment when a mine was completed, filled with explosives and detonated under the feet of an unsuspecting enemy. The result was a feature like the Hooge Crater – one of very many on the Western Front.

In 1740, when Sebastien de Vauban, Marshal of France, wrote his book *A Manual of Siegecraft*, he commented on his engineers, saying: 'Their science demands a great deal of courage and spirit, a solid genius, perpetual study and consummate experience in all the arts of war.' It seems that nothing changes.

Pollard was an intrepid man and he was able to recognize those who were similarly endowed. He admired the miners and their cold courage that was somewhat different to his own. Theirs was more clinical, more dogged, less intuitive. Pollard preferred to operate in the light of day – or at least, in the light of a Very light. The fear of mining was a constant companion to the infantry soldier manning a forward trench. Pollard remarked:

> I have often tried to picture what my feelings would be if I knew that the enemy was attempting to mine the trench underneath me. I suppose the answer is that one never does know until it is too late. Otherwise one would withdraw oneself and one's troops to another position. It is the one form of warfare to which there is no counter except by running a mine in opposition. The infantry are helpless.

Mines and mining was a form of warfare that he had to live with but he hoped not to be on the receiving end of German mining expertise. In *Fire-Eater* he commented upon the British mine that blew up Hill 60. This had been a major engineering feat and a tunnel a mile and a half long took two years to complete. This was in the face of German counter-mining that proved to be ineffective. The German position had been calculated with great accuracy and when the mine was detonated it went up in a cloud of earth, stones and enemy soldiers. In addition to the normal garrison, there was a 900-man strong German labour battalion at work on the hill at the time; every man was killed and many of them were atomized.

AOP recalled a counter-mine being blown in July 1915. He was in a trench in the Ypres Salient one night at about 2300hrs. Whilst standing on the fire step of the trench talking to one of the sentries, there was a cataclysmic and ear-splitting explosion. The parapet rocked violently and as AOP peered through the night he saw what appeared to be a black cloud rise slowly from the earth. The next instant, stones and dirt rained down all about him. He said that:

> Pandemonium broke loose in both lines of trenches. Every rifle and machine-gun opened fire simultaneously. I don't imagine that anyone knew quite what he was firing at. Everyone obeyed the common war instinct to loose off his rifle when in doubt of what was taking place. The shindy lasted for about half an hour and then died away. We did not stay at Calonne long enough to be in the fun when the mine was blown. We only did the one trip before we were withdrawn and entrained for an unknown destination.

On 18 September, the Battalion was withdrawn from Calonne and moved onto to La Conte, where 1 HAC was sufficiently well-known as to be welcomed by the inhabitants. War is not all 'muck and bullets' and in practice, a military unit is in a state of constant training. The training area for 63rd RND was at Marquay, and from 20 September, the Battalion was quickly absorbed into the divisional training program.

It was at around this time that Alfred Pollard heard of the death of his brother Frank, who was killed, in action, whilst serving with the Grenadier Guards. Frank was killed between10-12 September 1916. His death is recorded on the Thiepval Memorial[9] but before his demise, on 24 June 1916, he had reverted to his real name, JF Pollard. His demise was about five months after the interview with Colonel Evans, Commanding 3rd Bn HAC.

The HAC did some tidying up after the war and Frank Pollard's record shows him as having been 'discharged in September 1914'. This is patently untrue and is backdated window dressing that would never convince anyone. He was never other than a 'technical deserter' and then only briefly, but this is not a status recognized by the War Office then or the Ministry of Defence today.

Frank Pollard was a brave man and a patriot – he does not qualify for the odium accorded deserters because he left the ranks of the HAC not to avoid active service but to seek it.

Frank Pollard's name appeared in the list of members of the HAC published in June 1915. This is an unlikely entry if he was deemed to be a 'deserter', as that would have made him a pariah. The balance of probability is that by the spring of 1915, when the list was being prepared for the printers, the HAC was well aware that Frank was serving in the Grenadier Guards. AOP commented on his brother's death, sixteen years later, like this:

> It came especially hard in that his commission was gazetted within a few days of his death; had he lived another week he would have gone back to England for a six months' course at an officers' training school. I felt so deeply for my mother. Now my brother was gone all her worry would be concentrated on me.
>
> I was faced with a momentous decision. Ought I to rest on the laurels I had already earned and get a soft job which would keep me out of the danger of bullets and shells, or did my duty to my Country come before my respect for my mother's feelings? My own inclination went naturally towards staying at the front in order to revenge my brother's death. I felt that never again would I pity any of the enemy. Rather would I do my utmost to kill as many as possible. But one has sometimes to put one's own feelings on one side.
>
> My Country or my mother?
>
> In the end my Country won. I reasoned that, were we defeated, my mother's state would be infinitely worse. Therefore it behoved me to do my utmost to assure my Country's victory. In that way I would be serving both my Country and my mother. But I made a mental reservation that I would get leave to go home and see her as soon as possible.

Pollard's love of country is a constant and in these cynical days of the twenty-first century it is heart-warming to read what he wrote so disarmingly about an emotion that most of us keep very much to ourselves, even if we feel the same.

However, back in France, bereft at the death of Frank, AOP buckled down to winning the war. Two weeks later, by 2 October, the Battalion had 'developed a system of carrying messages in the field that proved to be so efficient that thereafter HAC runners always succeeded in reaching their objective.'[10] No details of this new system were provided. However, elsewhere, runners went about their hazardous business and ran greater risks than most of their comrades.

On 3 October, 1 HAC was moved overnight, by train, to Acheux, on the Somme. The Battalion arrived on the morning of 4 October. It was billeted briefly in Varennes 'in great discomfort but, notwithstanding, slept magnificently after our journey.'[11] Two days later, the command group went off to Mailly Maillet to reconnoitre the Battalion's proposed new position opposite Serre. This was a much more active area of operations and 'the neighbourhood was alive with artillery.'[12] The trenches were held temporarily by the 1st Bn King's Royal Rifle Corps. The trenches' egregious condition restricted the occupation to only seven men during the day. The Battalion had sight, for the first time, of the much vaunted tanks.

Lieutenant Colonel Boyle sent for Pollard as soon as the Battalion had occupied its new position and told him that that night he was to make a raid on the German lines and take a prisoner. Corps Headquarters wanted to identify the opposition. Pollard asked to see the map and on it the CO marked a section of German trench that curved out toward the British line and at the peak of the curve there was a sap head. That is to say, a spur that jutted further out from the German line and into no man's land.

'I shall want to go out and have a look at it,' said Pollard, flatly.

'There's no need for that,' said Colonel Boyle, 'it's all done for you. An officer from 1 KRRC made a reconnaissance last night.'

Pollard perused the report and noted that it read so convincingly that the officer who had drafted it might have actually occupied the sap head himself. The report was too good to be true and Pollard rejected it. He insisted on making his own initial reconnaissance. Colonel Boyle was unimpressed and gave the impression that Pollard's caution was a disappointment to him. He believed that there was a perfectly valid and up-to-date report to hand and Pollard was making more work and delaying the capture of a prisoner. With marked reluctance the CO acceded to Pollard's wishes.

AOP started to plan his foray and selected his team, of whom young Reggie Hughesdon was the first. He held his 19-year-old runner in very high regard and described him as being 'full of pluck and grit'. Hughesdon was a particularly good bomber and one who could throw further than most, and very accurately, too. AOP was able to trust Hughesdon to put a bomb just where it was most needed. His skills compensated, in part, for Pollard's inability to throw bombs because of his wounded shoulder.

The other two members of the team were Privates Fishbourne[13] and Marrs.[14] Fishbourne was an Australian and an extraordinary man who, at fifty-one, should not have been in the front line at all. He had had a hard life in the Australian bush and his experiences there had made him a very tough, tenacious individual, a brave man and a very good soldier.

Marrs, similarly, had spent his life outdoors, and had spent a large portion of his life in South America in the vast space of the pampas. There he had been employed as a 'wire rider'. This job entailed patrolling the hundreds of miles of wire fences of his employer that were designed to confine his large herds of cattle. It was a solitary job and it inculcated in Marrs a quality of self-sufficiency that served him well as a soldier. Pollard commented that 'A kick from a mule had knocked his nose on one side and badly scarred his face.' He added that Marrs 'had no conception whatever of what fear meant.'

Pollard had picked first-rate companions for his patrol and on the basis of his earlier Calonne experiences he realized that the short Lee Enfield rifle was not the weapon they needed for their form of business. He re-armed his team with revolvers and a brace of Mills bombs. They 'cammed up' by blackening their faces before they set off. That would be routine today but Pollard, when reporting this measure, implied that it was an innovative process. Pollard's mind set was revealed when he said:

> I was taking extra care over my precautions because I had not the slightest intention of confining my activities to a reconnaissance. The Colonel's attitude had stung me to a determination to go full out to capture a Hun that night. I had not said a word to a soul, not even the men who were going with me. I was going to have a look first, and if the situation was anything like the one outlined in the report, I meant to have a stab at laying out the machine-gun team, saving one alive for the Colonel.

The patrol was well briefed and very determined when AOP led it over the top. Hughesdon followed on and the other two moved over to either flank. The moon was up and it shed its cold light over the scene that had been a battlefield for months before. No man's land was pitted with shell holes that were a legacy of the recent fighting, most of these holes were filled with water and had to be skirted.

It was about 150 yards to the German line and in the strong moonlight, the line of wire could be seen clearly. The British trench line was similarly distinguishable by the presence of its wire. AOP moved forward cautiously and suddenly felt something 'scrunch under me'. He stooped to see what it was and gave a gasp as he realized that he was standing on a skeleton of a soldier – his bones picked clean by the some of the myriad rats that infested the front. The skeleton was complete but his uniform was not. It was torn to shreds, although there was sufficient of it for Pollard to identify the victim as a British soldier. His identity tags were missing and his pockets had been rifled. The unknown man had been robbed – not only of his worldly goods but of his identity, too.

The party paused and looked around. They were surrounded by small bundles of rags scattered all over the area. Each bundle was a British soldier and Pollard surmised later that they were all men killed in the savage fighting of early July. It was a depressing sight but Pollard and his team could do nothing for their compatriots and they moved on toward their objective. They were now over half way and Pollard recalled that 'I could make out the triangle at the top of which our objective was situated.'

Fishbourne, old enough to be Pollard's father, and on the left flank, suddenly gave a low signal to his young officer. Pollard moved to Fishbourne's side, who whispered, 'I can see something moving.' Pollard followed the line indicated and he too could see what appeared to be lines of men passing one way and then re-passing the other way. It was all very confusing, and the more so when Fishbourne added, 'There's a machine-gun, too.' Peering through the moonlight Pollard could see what Fishbourne had seen and it looked very menacing. The four of them were very close and any half-decent machine-gunner would scythe them down as soon as they were spotted. Pollard made his decision and told Fishbourne to:

> Make a slight detour and creep in from the left. Marrs will do the same on the right. Hughesdon and I will move straight forward. I'll fire one shot as a signal for us all to close in together.[15]

AOP crawled across to Marrs and then brought Hughesdon up on the flank. The party was now arraigned in a crescent and on a hand signal advanced on their target. All four had revolvers drawn and were ready to engage the enemy. Four revolvers against a machine-gun were absurd odds but turning back was never an option for AOP. The sap head got ever closer and still the machine-gun remained silent then, at no more than ten yards' range, Pollard realized that 'the men passing and re-passing' was an illusion. The movement was only that of tall grass dancing to the tune called by the breeze. As for the machine-gun - it was no more than a wooden post, uprooted and laying on its length. Life looked a little brighter and there was an added bonus.

The sap was deserted.

It was filled with barbed wire and beneath the wire lay the putrefying remains of a German soldier. His state of decomposition was an indication of how long the sap had been abandoned. Because the dead body had not been recovered the sap had presumably been evacuated in great haste. Pollard commented:

> I had vindicated my determination to reconnoitre the position before making the raid on another man's report. If I had organized the show and taken a dozen or so men over the top, we might easily have suffered several casualties from stray bullets and got nothing in return. Colonel Boyle was the first to agree with my point of view when I made my report on our return.
>
> 'It's a good job you insisted, Pollard,' he smiled. It was not much perhaps, but it was enough for me.[16]

The following night AOP took out the same party to find a focus for a raid. A message was passed down the line to the effect that a patrol was going out and the gunners of the Royal Artillery were among the recipients of the message.

After last light the small patrol made its way swiftly to the abandoned sap head. The patrol passed the sap head, still guarded only by its long-dead, sole tenant. It made its way down the left, ever closer to the German front line. Out in the wastes of no man's land it was very quiet, intermittently in the distance sporadic shelling could be heard and Very lights and their German equivalent provided brief intervals of vision. However, the patrol was close enough and visibility good enough for AOP to see that the artillery had played havoc with the German wire, which was in a very poor state. Pollard was experienced enough to know that Fritz rarely, if ever, neglected to repair his wire. He pondered the reason for the neglect. The gaps could have been left as easy exits for the Germans when they vacated their trenches to make a raid or perhaps they had been left to channel a British assault into carefully placed machine-guns.

Pollard crawled toward one of the gaps and cautiously made his way through. There was no response from the trench, now only a few yards to his front. Pollard signalled to his three men to join him and they too approached slowly and cautiously. The patrol spread out and Pollard moved ahead to the trench parapet. He took a deep breathe and put his head over the top.

The trench was deserted. 'Bombo' Pollard realized that this was:

> A stupendous discovery. In preparation for the big attack which everyone felt to be imminent, our artillery were daily sending over hundreds of shells with the dual idea of smashing the Hun wire entanglements and beating down the enemy morale …
>
> We searched along the trench for some distance, but we found no trace of any Hun whatsoever. The trench was full of mud and all falling to pieces. It had obviously not been occupied for some time. It is possible that we were deceived into thinking that the star-shells came from the front line when they really came from the second by the various twists

> and turns of the position. Anyway, I did not find Brother Hun that night or either of the two following, although I looked diligently for him.

At this stage in the proceedings Alfred Pollard said that he had a 'brainwave'. He decided not to withdraw – the sensible and safe option. Instead his patrol would stay in order to provoke the enemy into opening fire, thereby revealing their positions.

Fortuitously, close by and just short of the old German line, there were two large shell holes that were so close that they had merged into one vast crater. AOP ushered his men into this inadequate refuge and told them to lay out their Mills bombs on the lip of the crater. Whilst the men readied themselves, Pollard sketched the scene to his front, identifying such features as he could see. He told his men that, on his word, they were to throw their grenades as far and as widely as they could. The grenades were duly launched towards the empty German line and their bursts shattered the silence of the night.

As the sounds of the last grenade faded away a deep silence fell once more.

Not for long.

Suddenly, all along the German line the full orchestra of weapons burst into a discordant cacophony. It was an extraordinary over-reaction to the handful of grenades that had threatened no one and had exploded harmlessly near the abandoned trenches, a considerable distance from the nearest German. Small arms, machine-guns and various calibres of artillery all came to Pollard's party.

He sent his men to shelter as best they could in the maws of the crater whilst he sat with his head above ground marking on his sketch the location of apparent strong-points and machine-gun positions. It was now quite evident from the muzzle flashes that the front line had been completely abandoned.

So far his simple plan had worked but as he congratulated himself, things went awry. Clearly the message about his patrol had not reached the gunners because the Royal Artillery responded to the German artillery with a counter-bombardment. The gunners did not know that Pollard and his men were sheltering quite adjacent to what was now their pre-registered target.

The British shells fell all around the four men and continued to do so for about forty-five, very long, minutes. By extraordinary good luck the patrol survived unscathed and then, armed with valuable intelligence, it withdrew. Pollard's sketch was whisked up to Corps Headquarters, where it was used to co-ordinate future artillery stonks.

Alfred Pollard had still not captured his prisoner and cast around for a new plan. By late afternoon on 13 October he had the germ of an idea but for success, the plan depended upon others. The operation would hinge on a German-speaking member of the Battalion who had lived in Bavaria for fourteen years. AOP did not consult this man when he decided to use him as a decoy.

The plan was not very sophisticated. It would entail the decoy dressing in German uniform and playing the part of a wounded man in front of the German trenches. The individual was not vastly enthused and his lack of enthusiasm might have been because he knew he faced instant execution if captured in an enemy uniform.

Pollard briefed him and said that he was to groan, whine and call for help until such time as he attracted the attention of a sentry. Then he would be called upon to identify himself and at that point he was to claim to be a member of 82nd Prussian Regiment. He was to say that he had been wounded whilst on a patrol the previous evening. The 82nd was a regiment known to be in the locality and facing the unit on the left of 1 HAC. Pollard acknowledged that there was a possibility that the Germans might just shoot first, but he did not share this thought with his increasingly uneasy decoy.

Pollard calculated that, given the decoy's faultless German, 'the Huns would send out a stretcher party to carry him in. That would be my cue. I should be waiting in a convenient shell hole with my band of desperadoes and would fall on the stretcher party as they emerged from their trench.'

It was odds on that they would bag at least one of the stretcher party even if they had to kill the rest. Pollard arranged back-up in the shape of a full platoon that was to be positioned about halfway across no man's land. On the face of it, it was a simple and practical plan.

The decoy was dressed, rehearsed and reassured. The party assembled on the fire step and stood by for the signal to go over the top. However, just then German artillery fired an inconsequential barrage directed at a target somewhere to the rear of 1 HAC. The decoy, whose nerves were stretched tight, was undone by the shells passing over his head. It was too much for him and he displayed the symptoms of what is now called 'battle shock'.

Pollard said disgustedly that his teeth were chattering like castanets, he was shaking as if he had an ague and he was incapable of speech in either English or German. Pollard said, 'The show was a flop before it had started and I had wasted a double tot of rum on him too.' The following day, AOP's friend Percy Lewis[17] was killed by a shell in the fourth line.

Pollard wrote in *Fire-Eater* (page158) that:

> During the time I was home wounded he had been given a job in the orderly room as a clerk where he had been ever since. It was his turn to accompany the Battalion into the line or he would have been left safely in the transport field. My only consolation was that he was killed outright.

> I did not feel it as much as I had expected. I think my brother's death had hardened me. No one else seemed to matter now that he was gone. Never again would I feel such a sharp pang of infinite regret. My nature was becoming callous.

AOP's response to the death of Lewis – or rather his non-response, surprised him. It has also surprised those who have had occasion to examine Pollard's war service. It is appreciated that war and exposure to constant death will desensitize a man but it is unusual for even the toughest warrior to be unmoved by the death of a close friend.

Pollard made another foray that same day and whilst prowling around in the German barbed wire, he ran a piece of rusty wire into his knee. He returned to his own lines after an uneventful expedition. He slept for a few hours but when he woke his knee was very swollen and his leg was immoveable. The doctor thought that septicaemia was going to be a likely result and Alfred Pollard was removed to hospital.

Notes

1 G Goold Walker, *The Honourable Artillery Company in the Great War 1914-1919*, p59.

2 This is the first instance of Pollard being named in the Battalion war diary. His DCM was not recorded – indeed, the recording of decorations was sporadic, at best.

3 Sir Alan Patrick Herbert (1890-1971), usually known as AP Herbert, was a novelist and playwright, but above all else, a humorist of the first order. He was an Independent MP for Oxford University for fifteen years and although called to the Bar in 1919, he never practised law. He served in the RN in World War II, on the lower deck, whilst an MP.

4 Major General Shute commanded 63 RND for only four months, from 17 October 1916 until 19 February 1917. It was just long enough to ensure his undying fame.

5 G Goold Walker, *The Honourable Artillery Company in the Great War 1914-1919*, p60.

6 In the twenty-first century this would be termed 'friendly fire' – which it most definitely was not.

7 Lance Corporal Isaac Guy Holden was admitted to the HAC on 5 July 1915. Killed in action, Calonne, 9 September 1916.

8 This incident is recorded in the Battalion war diary and the entry is dated 2 September 1916.

9 Pier and face 8D. That he has no headstone indicates that his body was never found.

10 G Goold Walker, *The Honourable Artillery Company in the Great War 1914-1919*, p61.

11 G Goold Walker, *The Honourable Artillery Company in the Great War 1914-1919*, p61.

12 AO Pollard, *Fire-Eater*, p149.

13 Lance Corporal GW Fishbourne joined the HAC on 2 June 1915. He was killed in action at Beaucourt on 14 November 1916.

14 Corporal ES Marrs joined the HAC on 22 February 1915. He was killed in action at Bucquoy on 5 February 1917. Pollard consistently misspells his name as 'Mars'. It is corrected in this text.

15 AO Pollard, *Fire-Eater*, p153.

16 AO Pollard, *Fire-Eater*, p154.

17 Private PE Lewis joined the HAC on 19 April 1915. He was killed in action at Hebuterne, 14 October 1916.

Chapter 8

A Battle Missed, but a Coward?

'Soldiers don't have mothers.'

October 1916–January 1917

Pollard's incapacity spared him from involvement in one of the bloodiest actions fought by the HAC. He would consider himself cheated of an opportunity for close quarter battle and ample opportunities to close with and kill Germans.

AOP barely stopped at the field dressing station and he did not linger at the next level of medical care, the Casualty Clearing Station. He argued that he needed to be back with his company, but that cut no ice with the RAMC who, despite his low opinion of them, knew more about blood poisoning than Pollard did. He was removed back to a base hospital at Wimereux and he arrived by ambulance in the middle of the night. Tired and irritated he was put to bed only to be disturbed by a visit of the 'Night Matron'.

By the most extraordinary good fortune, this lady was the attractive sister he had met and befriended at Nantes back in 1914. It seems clear that these young people enjoyed some mutual chemistry and mindful of the proprieties, she could not merely sit by Pollard's bed and chat. She called by, but they had little chance for a lengthy conversation.

Three days later, and after treatment, the swelling in AOP's knee was subsiding and the pain was less acute. Thereafter, he made his way, aided by a stick, to the 'Night Matron's' office – this became a pattern for subsequent nights and he was entertained by the Sister/Matron and one of her friends for several hours. Later, when he was able, he could take short walks along the cliffs, enjoying the autumn seascape. The two ladies often accompanied AOP and on one such excursion he explained how worried he was about his mother. The Nursing Sister said that she could 'wangle some special leave' and initially, Pollard declined. However, concern for his mother overrode other considerations and he gratefully accepted the offer. The leave was duly granted.

The night before he was to leave for England the little party went on longer than usual – with great daring, Pollard had smuggled in a bottle of wine and the three of them managed to spin it out until about 0100hrs, although it was not exactly a 'boozy' party. Pollard made his way back to bed to find the Night Nurse waiting for him. She was furious and berated him saying: 'You've been away from your bed night after night. I haven't said anything before because I did not want to get you into trouble, but this is too much. I shall report you to Matron.'

The Nurse returned and following her was the lady with whom AOP had spent the previous three hours. 'Matron' duly administered a rocket and made Pollard promise not to transgress again. He solemnly agreed to mend his ways and said that he would sin no more.

It is a curious part of Pollard's make-up that, although he was clearly attracted to women, he did not seek any form of sexual favours from them. It is evident that the Night Matron was equally attracted to Pollard and had he pursued the relationship, it might have changed his life. He commented, sixteen years later, in *Fire-Eater*:

> She was a great sport. Unfortunately I have never seen her since. I must not give her name. She is a very famous personage. I wonder if she remembers me.[1]

All very intriguing.

At this distance, it is impossible to identify this nursing sister/night matron. She certainly remembered him because he too was a famous personage when those words were penned. At the time, however, his thoughts were less on the Nursing Sister and more upon his mother, and of course, the Lady. Mrs Pollard was bearing up after the death of Frank, and Alfred's presence was as good as a tonic to her. As soon as it was possible Alfred arranged to see that Lady and he reported that:

> She was very nice to me and once again I began to entertain foolish hopes. Not that I said a word to break our contract. Outwardly we were merely friends although she must have known my real feelings towards her were only kept in check by force of will.

There is absolutely no doubt that the Lady knew about Pollard's inner turmoil. She exploited it and he was played like a hungry trout rising to the fly. It was foolish of him to prolong the agony and cruel of her to allow it. As it was, Alfred took her out and about as often as he was able. One afternoon they had tickets for a matinee. After the final curtain as they emerged onto the street, the evening papers displayed banner headlines. 'Big British Push,' they screamed. Pollard was distraught. His battalion had gone into action and he was not with it. Reflecting on the event later, he concluded that it was unlikely that he could have got back to the unit even if he had forgone his leave.

As any soldier knows, getting into a military hospital is very much easier than getting out. All manner of esoteric rituals have to be satisfied before freedom is permitted and the health of the individual is not a consideration. As it happens, AOP returned to France on 14 November 1916, but it was still early December before he reached 1 HAC. He had been away for six weeks.

On 17 October, after Pollard's evacuation, the weather worsened. It got much colder and heavy persistent rain made life miserable for the Battalion as the roads deteriorated into mud slides. The Battalion moved into billets at Lealvillers and marched on to Puchevillers on the following day. The roads were in a terrible condition, and the problem was compounded by their being filled with troops in great numbers and all sorts of heavy traffic. There followed any number of further route marches as formations were manipulated into the desired juxtaposition - all conducted in appalling weather.

In addition to all of the *angst* associated with these constant moves there were fatigues to be carried out and to compound what the soldiers would have described as being 'mucked about', the command structure found it necessary to visit and inspect – on a regular basis. All the while and regardless of wind, weather or location, the Quartermaster, Captain GH Mayhew, 'with his usual foresight, made arrangements for supplying the men with hot food and completed all arrangements for their comfort.'[2]

On 20 October, the CO went to Mesnil to view the likely area of his battalion's operations and was slightly wounded on the nose by a fragment from a shell burst that ricocheted on the road. It could have been worse, especially as he was wearing spectacles. On the following day in a very severe white frost, the Battalion marched via Varennes to Hedauville. On the following day, the Divisional Commander, Major General C Shute CB, explained at a conference with Battalion commanders and seconds-in-command the objectives of the coming attack 'in a most masterly manner'.

On 10 November, the Brigade was inspected by the GOC again, this time at Puchevillers, when the Battalion was 'noticeably steady on parade'.[3] On 'X' day, the Battalion moved at 1300hrs and marched to Hedauville, and later the CO, seconds-in-command, company commanders and specialist officers attended a conference with the Brigadier at Varennes, when the final orders for the attack were issued.

At 0545hrs on 13 November, as Pollard was about to start his journey back to France, 1,000 British guns gave voice – 'the largest concentration of gun power per mile of front the war had at that time known'.[4] The assault up the Ancre Valley to the objective Beaucourt sur Ancre had started. This battle is of no direct relevance to this narrative as 'Bombo' was elsewhere at the time and the bloody events of 13 November 1916 are chronicled elsewhere. Suffice it to say that 1 HAC was in the thick of it and took heavy casualties. Eighty-one were killed and 184 wounded.

AOP knew none of this at the time. He eventually reached Le Havre and found himself enmeshed in all the typical rear area bureaucracy. Pollard took a degree of pride in 'doing as little work as possible' and this brought him to the attention of the Adjutant. That is the natural progression of these things. However, Pollard was aggrieved that the Adjutant did not take him to his bosom and seemed to be intent on catching him out. This should hardly have been a surprise.

AOP did, inevitably, find himself detailed as Orderly Officer. This routine, occasional and very undemanding job merely involved carrying out a series of checks during a twenty-four-hour period. There were armouries to be inspected, weapons to be accounted for, the sick to be visited. 'Soldiers under sentence' and those in close arrest were to be briefly interviewed, guards were to be 'called out', fire picquets to be exercised and meals to be seen.

It was this last element that caused a minor hiatus.

When he was Orderly Officer, Pollard had no doubt that the Adjutant would check up on him and so he was accordingly meticulous. One morning when on duty, Pollard rose early to visit the mens' breakfast, accompanied by his orderly sergeant. The latter, whom he did not know, led him down one of the many camp roads to a dining hall. Pollard fielded the usual complaints about the food: 'Not enough sugar in the tea, Sir'; 'The eggs are over/under cooked, Sir'; 'Why can't we have mushrooms?' There was nothing new there and Pollard, his report completed, went for his own breakfast, duty faithfully discharged.

The Adjutant sent for Pollard soon after and enquired why he had not inspected breakfast. Pollard, of course, averred that he had, and the Adjutant responded by saying that he had spoken to the Orderly Sergeant who said that he had never laid eyes on Mr Pollard. The atmosphere was getting unpleasant and AOP was affronted that the Adjutant should take the word of a sergeant over that of an officer.

The Orderly Sergeant was blown for and when he arrived Pollard said, 'I've never seen this NCO before!'

It transpired that in this vast base made up of several camps there were several orderly officers and a corresponding number of orderly sergeants. Somehow, the wrong sergeant and the wrong officer had teamed up and inspected the wrong breakfast.

Pollard recorded that 'The Adjutant was decent enough to apologize for his mistake.' He added, 'He treated me with considerably more respect afterwards.'

Pollard journeyed on and eventually rejoined the Battalion at Nouvion. Everyone who had survived was pleased to see him and he felt at ease with his 'family'. He noted that some already wore the splashes of colour on their breast that denoted a decoration. It was with a sense of anticipation that AOP went to report his presence and to see his hero and commanding officer, Lieutenant Colonel Boyle. The CO had been awarded a well deserved DSO on 4 December, to the acclamation of his entire battalion, including Alfred Pollard.

The meeting did not go as well as it might. The CO was tired and probably in the midst of writing letters to the next of kin of all of his men killed only days before. Initially he asked about Pollard's knee and Alfred replied cheerfully that it was now quite recovered. The atmosphere changed when Boyle enquired about Pollard's 'wangled' leave and the latter explained about his medical condition, the loss of his brother and the mental state of his mother. None of this cut any ice with Boyle and he replied coldly that 'Soldiers don't have mothers; your action was the action of a coward when you knew that there was a possibility of the Battalion going into action.'[5]

This criticism from a man old enough to be his father, whom he revered and sought to emulate, was a 'bitter pill to swallow'. Pollard was shattered and cast into a trough of misery. He already had qualms of conscience about missing the action in the Ancre Valley and Boyle's words cut him to the bone.

AOP was very conscious of his status. He expected 'respect' and bridled when he did not receive what he judged to be his due. Nevertheless, he felt free to disrespect others – indeed, he had a track record to prove it. Boyle's remark was ill-judged, unnecessarily harsh and overly blunt. To call a soldier a 'coward' would be extreme even in the worst of circumstances. Pollard patently was not a coward. He had a multiplicity of faults but cowardice was not amongst them. Boyle had personal experience of Pollard's courage and his unjustified charge hit at the core of AOP's very well developed feelings of self-worth.

Boyle had second thoughts about what he had said when he saw the catastrophic effect of his words. He realized that he had overstepped the mark and sought to correct the situation.

He invited Pollard to tea. What a remarkably British thing to do.

It helped. They had a cup of tea together and, during the process, the CO explained how well 1 HAC had done. Tea was drawing to a close when Boyle smiled and said, 'I think that it's as well you weren't with us, you'd most certainly have been killed and then I'd have had to find someone else to do my night

The aftermath of the battle of Beaucourt sur Ancre.
A sketch by Adrian Hill (HAC Archives)

patrols. You'll have plenty more opportunities to show what you are made of.'

It was not an apology but it was the next best thing. Pollard was mollified but he never, ever forgot the conversation.

Within the Battalion all the chat was about the recent engagement and Pollard could contribute nothing to the debate. His brush with the Adjutant at Le Havre was pretty small beer in comparison and he felt excluded. Worse was to follow when it was rumoured that 1 HAC was once more to be converted into an officers' training school. The rumour seemed to be soundly based given that there was already a 63rd Division School of Instruction and 1 HAC provided all the instructors – AOP was swiftly detailed off to join their ranks as the bombing expert and he started to impart his knowledge on 21 December 1916.

The school was attractively located in a large chateau standing in expansive and beautifully maintained grounds. It was an agreeable place to spend Christmas, if nothing else. Rumours multiplied and the latest to come down the wire was that 1 HAC was to return to the line – that was enough for Pollard and he promptly 'resigned' after six days' employment as an instructor. In wartime an officer goes where he is sent and the mechanics of how he managed to 'resign' his appointment are difficult to fathom.

An interesting insight into Pollard's standards is given by his description of a visit he made to Abbeville. He recorded that:

I visited a brothel in the street of the red lamps. It was the second and

> last time I was ever in one of these houses of iniquity. I heard that a young officer who had come down to the school for instruction had been fool enough to allow his desires to overcome his self-respect. I followed him into the place and dragged him out. It was quite simple. I asked him whether he had a girl at home who loved him. He said 'Yes'. So I said, 'How would you feel if she knew you had been in here?' He came away at once.

He was, by his own account, consistent and although his flight from the brothel in Nantes may in part have been a combination of embarrassment and lack of experience, here it was a question of moral rectitude. Who can criticize him for that?

In the first week of January 1917, Pollard's highly unsatisfactory tour as a bombing instructor fizzled out and he returned to the Battalion apparently with no loss of face. On arrival he was appointed to command No. 7 Platoon in 'B' Company. He recorded that his platoon sergeant was Sergeant HW Snoad, 'an extremely efficient soldier. His efficiency was no doubt due, in part, to the fact that before the war he was one of the private secretaries to the late Lord Northcliffe.'

Notes

1 AO Pollard, *Fire-Eater*, p162.
2 G Goold Walker, *The Honourable Artillery Company in the Great War 1914-1919*, p62.
3 G Goold Walker, *The Honourable Artillery Company in the Great War 1914-1919*, p63.
4 G Goold Walker, *The Honourable Artillery Company in the Great War 1914-1919*, p64.
5 AO Pollard, *Fire-Eater*, p164.

Chapter 9

The Military Cross

'For gallantry and devotion to duty …'

January–March 1917

Pollard might have had cause for regret at leaving that nice warm chateau when later in January 1917, the weather worsened and it became dreadfully cold. Snow fell heavily upon the frozen ground and digging was difficult, verging on impossible. 1 HAC moved forward and occupied old German trenches in front of Beaucourt. This was the setting of the Battalion's attack on 13-14 November. The Germans were the masters of dug-out construction and it was a bonus for Pollard and his comrades to be able to move into the very deep dug-outs and make themselves comfortable.

The Lady was out of sight but she was rarely out of mind and AOP placed extraordinary importance on the gift of a small doll from the youngest sister of the Lady. He christened it 'Billiken' and vowed to take it everywhere with him. Apparently, the small doll was carried in his pocket, both in and out of the line, for the remainder of the war.

The night of 29 January 1917 was bitterly cold, it was snowing hard and visibility was restricted to just a few yards. AOP's company was stationed in the support line about 400 yards behind the firing line when it received the order to 'stand to'. There was something, as yet unidentified, going on to the front.

It was standard operating procedure to establish listening posts in advance of the firing line in order to give warning of enemy activity and on this particular night, about 50 yards out in no man's land, 1 HAC had established four such posts. These were sizeable positions and were manned by an NCO and ten men. All four posts fell under the command of a subaltern.

The Company heard the brief rattle of automatic weapons but that was soon stilled and an ominous quiet took its place. The Company 'stood down' and AOP was only too happy to return to his relatively warm dug-out.

The next day it emerged that during the previous night, covered by the snow, a German fighting patrol about thirty strong and armed with clubs and bayonets advanced in complete silence and fell upon each of the HAC listening post in turn. It was a highly skilled, very well co-ordinated assault and the positions were all wiped out. There were only two survivors, both men badly wounded had been left for dead. Several men had been whisked away as prisoners.

The remainder were all killed.

The Officer had been in an adjacent shell hole and he suspected nothing until a Lewis gun opened fire. He ran the few yards to the scene but found that the engagement was all over. There was an empty drum from a Lewis gun, some cartridge cases, corpses and a great deal of blood. It was similar in all four posts. The Officer could only report back to Battalion Headquarters.

The Divisional Commander took a very dim view of the event and cast around for a scapegoat. The first step would be a board of enquiry and that could lead on to a court martial. When Bombo Pollard heard the story he allied himself very forcefully with the Officer. He was, of course, far too junior and not a credible witness, but he was able to relate to the practical difficulties faced by his comrade. He averred that if the GOC or any of his senior staff officers had spent a night in a shell hole, in driving snow and at constant risk of a violent death, their attitudes might be somewhat different. As it was, Pollard offered moral support to the Officer, who was, predictably, sorely aggrieved at the suggestion that he had failed in his duty.

'B' Company retired into reserve for a few days and in its absence one of the other battalions of 63 RND attacked, took ground and moved the front line some hundreds of yards forward. 'B' Company's position was on the crest of a hill in front of the Bois d' Hollande. To the right the hill ran down to the river Ancre, with Grandcourt on its opposite bank. No. 7 Platoon, commanded by Pollard, was placed on the right of the Company in shallow trenches that were difficult to deepen. AOP's men worked hard on the trenches, as he remarked, 'to help their circulation'.

Pollard had other things than digging in mind and he opted to make a reconnaissance of the German wire that he supposed they had placed to defend their front line. This was thought to be along the edge of a sunken road. He quickly discovered that the wire was minimal and what there was had been ineffectively laid. Pollard concluded that 'They were second-class troops or else the bitter cold was having an effect on their morale. In my experience Master Fritz very seldom failed to make himself as secure against attack as possible.'

On this latest foray into harm's way AOP took Reggie Hughesdon[1] on the patrol. Fishbourne, the gallant Australian, was no more, as he had been killed on 14 November. Marrs had been killed only very recently, on 5 February, by a British shell that had dropped short.

A patrol of two men could achieve just as much as a larger party,

'Tilbury', 2 Belmont Road, Wallington, Surrey. This is the handsome house in which Alfred Pollard and his siblings were brought up before the turn of the twentieth century. The house today looks rather down on its luck and it has been converted to flats. *(Author.)*

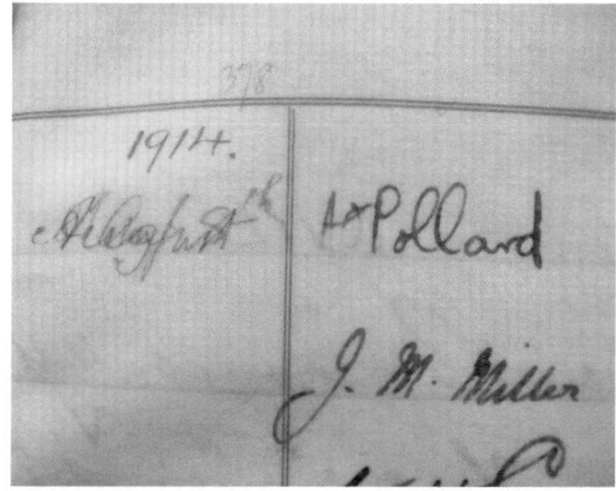

Alfred Pollard's signature in the Great Vellum Roll, dated 8 August 1914. JM Miller, who signed below him, survived the war. *(Author, from HAC Archives.)*

These gates of Armoury House had been closed to volunteers seeking to join up during the bank holiday of August 1914. When the gates reopened, Alfred Pollard ran through to enlist. *(Author.)*

Armoury House, the headquarters of the Honourable Artillery Company, 1914, pictured today. *(Author.)*

SS *Westmeath*, the ship in which AO Pollard and his 828 comrades of 1st Battalion HAC sailed to France in September 1914. *(HAC Archives.)*

The inspection, on 12 September 1914, of 1st Bn HAC, by King George V, the Captain-General. The officer accompanying the King is Lieut. Col. Edward Treffrey OBE, the much-loved Commanding Officer who took the Battalion to France. Immediately following this parade the Battalion was on its way to war. *(*HAC Journal *Vol. 7, 1930.)*

Pte. AO Pollard HAC 1914 (PF Wilson) and three officers who were to have a great influence upon him. These are, from left to right, CF Osmond, EPC Boyle and GH Mayhew. They are seen in a wider context in a later page in the group photograph from which this is taken. (HAC Journal *Vol. 7, 1930, p133.)*

The CSM and NCOs of Sgt. AO Pollard's company. He is pictured (front, left) sporting a moustache. He was promoted to sergeant on 26 September 1915. This photograph was taken at about that time although he has no DCM ribbon on his breast. The swagger sticks and clean boots are ample indication that the Company was behind the line and in reserve. (HAC Journal, *WJ Bradley.)*

Sgt. Dougie Davis, who, having been commissioned in 1915, made the rash decision to ask AOP to be his servant. Lieut. Davis died of pneumonia in January 1919. (HAC Journal *Vol. 2, 1924, p528.)*

The officers of No. 3 Company 1st Battalion HAC, 1915. Back row, left to right: 2nd Lieuts. WA Stone, DS Davis, VC Montague and LW MacArthur, NK. Front row, left to right: Capt. CF Osmond, Capt. EPC Boyle and Capt. CW Holliday. (HAC Journal *Vol. 3, 1926, p243.)*

German soldiers taken prisoner at St. Eloi. They seem to be happy to be spared further fighting. (War of Nations *Vol. VII, p299.)*

Officers of 1st Battalion HAC. Standing, left to right: Lieut. EL Samuel, Lieut. IH Mosley, Lieut. N Smith, Rev. ER Prance, Lieut. FB Garrard, Lieut. HF Kent, Lieut. AE Keech, Lieut. N Viney, Lieut. HW O'Brien, Lieut. AGF Osman, Lieut. HN Hall. Seated, left to right: Lieut. JH Lingwood, Lieut. GC Bailey, Capt. RC Hawkins, Major CF Osmond, Lieut. Col. EPC Boyle, Capt. GH Mayhew, Capt. JD Reid, Capt. R Spicer, Capt. RS Morshead. (HAC Journal *Vol. 5, 1928.)*

Flanders, after yet more heavy and persistent rain. (The War of Nations *Vol. VII, p41.)*

This photograph, taken at St. Eloi in August 1917, is further testimony to the frightful conditions in Flanders under which men lived, fought and died. It is little wonder that significant numbers of soldiers on both sides drowned. *(ET Archive, London.)*

Sanctuary Wood, 1915. The few remaining trees did not survive the bitter fighting in this area. *(*HAC Journal *Vol. 3, 1926, p215. See the sketch map by Adrian Hill on page XX.)*

This photograph taken just after the war shows the depth of a belt of wire. This one has been breached but more often than not they were not and the result is on the following photograph. *(*To Win a War*, p116.)*

This solder charged into a belt of uncut wire. He had no chance. In this particular case he was a Russian, but his fate was shared by tens of thousands of others of all nationalities. *(*The War of Nations *Vol. VI, p127.)*

The Hooge Crater, 1915. This was the scene of savage fighting and the setting for Sgt. Alfred Pollard's DCM. *(Internet sources.)*

Another view of the Hooge Crater, in September 1915. *(*Mud and Khaki*, p61.)*

Recce patrols deep into no man's land were always hazardous but for Alfred Pollard, a source of stimulation. This illustration depicts such a patrol and the three figures could well have been AOP, Hughesdon and either Fishbourne or Marrs. The artist has provided more light than would have normally been available. *(*The War of Nations *Vol. VII, p223.)*

Street scene, Ypres, 1915. (HAC Journal *Vol. 3, 1926, p108.)*

A depiction of bombers at work in the early days of the war, when the unsatisfactory stick grenade was in use. At close quarters it was, nevertheless, lethal – sometimes to either side. (The War of Nations *Vol. IV, p47.)*

Cellar billets in Ypres – not always the safest place to be. (Sanctuary Wood and Hooge, *p56.)*

An unknown 'Tommy Atkins' does what every soldier does, given the chance – he sleeps. (The War of Nations *Vol. V, p226.)*

The Cloth Hall in Ypres in flames. (The War of Nations *Vol. II, p108.)*

This photograph illustrates the level of sophistication of German dugouts. The shutters and doors on the accommodation make for comfort. Note the chimney. (The War of Nations *Vol. IV, p99.)*

A quiet moment in the line for 1 HAC. Trench P11, St. Eloi. This was rather less comfortable than the German trenches opposite. *(HAC Journal.)*

Second Lieut. WE 'Black' Scott the Wiltshire Regiment and Capt. EWE Hammond MC – 'Hammy', to AOP. *(Both images,* HAC Journal.*)*

Capt. EPC Boyle, who enjoyed Pollard's unqualified admiration, with 2nd Lieuts. BW Noble and DS Davis. They are grouped round a 'knife rest', upon which barbed wire was secured. (HAC Journal *Vol. 3, 1926, p245.)*

This photograph was taken at Armoury House on the day that Pollard and Haine were invested with their VCs. Here, AOP adjusts Haine's medal loop. Photographs of these two officers together are very few and the HAC Archive had only this one. Later in the day, the Artillery Garden was the venue for a major party. *(AO Pollard.)*

Alfred Pollard is decorated with the VC by King George V, his Captain-General, in the forecourt of Buckingham Palace. *(AO Pollard.)*

The much respected and admired Major George Mayhew MC. He was the exemplary Quartermaster of 1 HAC and a mentor and guide to Alfred Pollard. He maintained a meticulous record of the comings and goings of every soldier in 1 HAC throughout the war. This record is known as 'Uncle George's Book' and it is a treasured artefact in the Regiment's archive. He is pictured here after the war. (HAC Journal *Vol. 2, 1925, p765.)*

Below Left: 2nd Lieut. Reggie Hughesdon DCM MM. As a corporal he was in support of Alfred Pollard on numerous dangerous forays and was at his side when he won the VC. (HAC Journal.)

Below Right: Col. William Evans, the Commander of 3rd (Reserve) Bn HAC. It was this officer who offered 'a return to the fold' for James Frank Pollard in April 1916. (HAC Journal Vol *9, 1932, p181.)*

Far Left: Capt. RL Haine VC MC, chronologically and by a small margin he was the first HAC winner of the Victoria Cross. He was always known to Alfred Pollard as 'Bill' and is pictured after the war and wearing the badges of 35th Sikhs, with whom he won a Military Cross on the NW Frontier.

Above: Capt. TT Pryce VC MC* Grenadier Guards. He, Pollard and Haine all joined the HAC in August 1914. Tom Pryce won his VC posthumously on 13 April 1918. *(Both photographs, Goold Walker,* HAC in The Great War, 1914-1919.*)*

The two faces of Alfred Pollard. *Below Left:* 'Bombo' Pollard, as he was to be known, in 1st Bn HAC in about 1917. This is the photographic portrait that hangs above his decorations in the Medal Room at Armoury House. *(HAC Archives.)*
Below Right: As a middle-aged and successful author, in about 1953. This was a favourite family photograph. He was known to his family as 'Uncle Jumbo' and his demeanour in later life completely belied his ferocity as a soldier and his unwavering courage. *(Chown family.)*

PO AO Pollard VC MC* DCM RAF – a photograph taken in 1924, on the award of his RAF commission. *(Chown family.)*

Wedding Day, 5 September 1925. Standing, left to right: Lillian Chown (née Swarbrick), Alfred Pollard, Violet Pollard, Clement Chown. Sitting, left to right: James Pollard, Ada Pollard, Mrs Lillian Swarbrick, Mr Robert Swarbrick. *(Chown family.)*

Violet with the two Sealyhams, 'Soldier' and 'Sailor'. *(Chown family.)*

The Pollards greeting the Lord Mayor of London at a reception. *(Chown family.)*

Violet Pollard with her family. Left to right: Ray Chown, Daphne Chown (sister of Violet), Peter Chown, Dick Chown, Violet and 'Jumbo'. *(Chown family.)*

'Jumbo' Pollard and Brigadier Sir John Smythe VC at a gathering of VC and GC Association holders. *(Chown family.)*

The Pollards had a flat in this property at 18 Queen's Park Gardens, Bournemouth. It was here that 'Jumbo' Pollard died on 4 December 1960. *(Chown family.)*

Richard 'Dick' Chown, the nephew of 'Jumbo' Pollard. This book could not have been written without his support. *(Author.)*

particularly when there was no intention of engaging the enemy. The landscape was covered in snow and that made star shells and Very lights all the more effective. Pollard and Hughesdon moved cautiously, slowly, and they crossed no man's land without incident. When they returned to the HAC front line they were wet but exhilarated. The Commanding Officer was waiting for them in a state of great excitement. He did not wait for them to jump down into the trench but unwisely climbed up onto the parapet.

'I've got a magnificent job for you, Pollard,' boomed Ernest Patrick Charles Boyle. 'I want you to enter Grandcourt at all costs … At all costs,' he reiterated dramatically.

Pollard was less discommoded by his CO's orders than by his very loud voice, which rang out over no man's land, carrying well in the very cold night air. Any English-speaking German in earshot would have been delighted to share in Colonel Boyle's orders and would have been well able to prepare a reception for Pollard on his next foray.

The big issue was the matter of the river Ancre that flowed across the front of Grandcourt. It was an obstacle on a good day but on a freezing night, swimming or even wading across it was not a viable option. There were no bridges under British control. Not unreasonably, AOP asked his CO how he was to cross an un-bridged, defended river, under enemy observation. The Colonel replied airily, 'I must leave that to you, Pollard. I expect you'll find a way. Come and see me when you get back.' He continued encouragingly, 'The Air Force has reported that the Huns evacuated Grandcourt at dusk. I want you to confirm what they say before the Marines on the other side of the river find out. It'll be a feather in our caps if we're there first.'

There is no doubt that Boyle was a fine officer, an excellent and charismatic leader, but one questions the need for 1 HAC to get yet another feather in its cap.

Pollard had very little time to plan his patrol as it was already 0100hrs on 7 February. Nevertheless, refreshed and anxious to get on with the job, he briefed his team. He took with him Lance Corporal Freter and Lance Corporal Scharlach and, of course, Hughesdon. It was a clear night and the western front was bathed in moonlight that reflected off the snow. The moon was almost full and although it was an aid to navigation, it also made movement obvious and commensurately dangerous. The trio set off down the hill and after only 100 yards or so, they came upon a trench that had previously been occupied by another unit of 63rd Division. It had been a platoon position and the platoon was still in occupation – all were dead. They had been surprised at night, just as the four listening posts had been. Pollard concluded that:

> If the Huns had succeeded in surprising that trench they could only have done so from the flank. I tried to visualize what had happened. The British had probably considered themselves invulnerable from the river side. They had probably not bothered to place a sentry there. The Huns had simply crept up the hill and taken them, either in the flank or even in the rear. That meant that there was a way across the river. Well, if Fritz could find one I was damned sure I could, too.

The weather had continued to be very cold and the marsh land at the bottom of the hill that fringed the river was frozen solid. This was fortunate as in temperate weather the mud and water would have been a significant obstacle. AOP was able to follow the tracks left by the German raiding party and these led directly to a makeshift bridge across the Ancre formed by two railway lines.

There was every likelihood that the crossing was covered by a standing patrol but after pausing to listen and watch, there was no sigh of movement on the far bank. Pollard did not shirk his responsibility and, as ever, he went first. His revolver in hand he went forward and climbed onto the railway lines, which were encased in frost. His crossing was uneventful and he took immediate cover behind a conveniently placed, but ruined, wall.

The remainder of the patrol joined him, one by one, but Hughesdon, the last over, slipped on the ice-covered metal and fell into the freezing, waist-deep water, much to the amusement of his comrades. AOP moved forward a few more yards, he looked around and discovered just what his CO wanted to know.

Grandcourt was unoccupied.

Knowing where the enemy *was not* was useful, but equally important was to know where *he was*. [Author's italics.] AOP toured the ruined village; it was completely deserted. One of the patrol suddenly called attention to a man lying in the snow and they moved toward him to investigate. As it happens, it turned out to be a log. The significance of the log was that it drew Pollard out into the open and once there he looked up to see a group of men on the skyline. He did not know, at the time, whether they were friend or foe. There were a tense few minutes as he and his men approached the larger party with their hands in the air, although Pollard said that he had no intention of being taken alive and his apparent surrender was no more than a *ruse de guerre*.

In the event, the anonymous party turned out to be a patrol of the Royal Marine Light Infantry under the command of a corporal. This worthy was, at first, unconvinced of Pollard's *bona fides* and a whispered debate ensued in the snow, in no man's land and in the proximity of the enemy. A Marine officer appeared who, happily, knew Pollard, and soon all was well. Pollard guided the

Marines back to Grandcourt and then established the position of the new German front line by the simple expedient of inviting fire.

AOP did not, from choice, want to retrace his steps all the way to the railway lines. The small patrol hunted along the river bank and chanced upon a footbridge. Safely back on what was thought to be the 'British side of the river', Pollard confidently led his men back to the lines of 1 HAC. This routine matter was complicated by the sound of voices - speaking German. The fact was that somehow, they had contrived to get behind the German line. Pollard admitted that:

> I suppose I ought to have turned back and made a detour by way of the railway lines. But I had been out on patrol all night and I was tired. Also, it was getting on for dawn. Besides, I knew there was no wire in front of the Hun line to hold me up. I told my three men to follow me closely and do as I did. Then I crept silently forward. The voices came closer and closer. At last I could make out the spot where the Huns were congregated. They had no regular trench at this point but were disposed in a series of shell-holes.

Pollard led the way and, on his word, his patrol sprinted between the shell holes. The Germans were slow to react and their rifle fire was ineffective and increasingly so as the range increased. All four men reached their own lines, winded, exhilarated and unhurt. After the patrol Pollard had time to reflect and he observed:

> I took my mind back to the first time I saw a trench filled with dead men. That was on the 16th June 1915, when we attacked the Hun in Y Wood. What a lot of changes had taken place in my life since then. All my old friends were either killed or scattered and new ones had taken their places. Then the Battalion was fairly raw; now we were mostly seasoned veterans. But the chief change had taken place in myself. In June 1915 I was a mere boy looking on life with hopeful optimism, and on war as an interesting adventure. When I saw the Hun corpses killed by our shell-fire I was full of pity for the men so suddenly cut off in their prime. Now I was a man with no hope of the war ending for years. I looked at a trench full of corpses without any sensation whatever. *Neither pity nor fear* [author's italics] that I might soon be one myself, nor anger against their killers. Nothing stirred me. I was just a machine carrying out my appointed work to the best of my ability.

It was sentiments such as those above and in particular, an expression like '*Neither pity nor fear*' that have, over time, attracted the attention of analysts seeking to discover the secret of Pollard's single-minded and protracted performance in World War I.

Colonel Boyle was predictably 'tickled pink' with the report that Pollard gave him. He had returned with significant intelligence, had put one over the Royal Marines and presumably in the process had gained a feather for the corporate hat of the HAC.

The Germans may have evacuated Grandcourt but they still occupied shell holes on the top of the hill on the British side of the river, which gave them line of sight and allowed them to prevent the Marines advancing on the other side of the river. Boyle pronounced it to be an unsatisfactory situation and said he would discuss the matter with the Brigadier during the day.

It was now around breakfast time and soon after he had eaten, Pollard went to his bunk and slept solidly until past noon. It was a bitterly cold day as he rose and attended to his duties. Boyle too was about his business and among other things that afternoon he had arranged a meeting with the Brigade Commander.

Second Lieutenant Reg Haine recalled that day well and in a verbal recording, held by the Imperial War Museum, he recorded that:

> The gunners told us that there were forty degrees of frost. It made things almost impossible, because a shell bursting a quarter of a mile away could kill you. Now, usually if you were in luck, a shell could burst within a few yards of you and if your number wasn't on it you were all right. But at this time these shells just hit solid ice and they scattered (their shrapnel).
>
> We had our colonel killed … he was a wonderful chap; Ernest Boyle. He was fifty-six years old, which for a front-line soldier was very old … But he was one of the few real fire-eaters I ever met. There were a few; most were unintelligent people; they hadn't got the imagination. But Ernest Boyle was a complete and utter patriot and I remember he used to say, 'My ambition is that my bones shall be buried in Flanders,' – and they were, poor chap. He got just a thing from a shell which landed, oh two or three hundred yards away.[2]

Boyle had been hit by a splinter when he was just outside the Brigadier's bunker. He staggered a few paces and collapsed. He gasped to his second-in-command, 'I'm hit Osmond. Get particulars from Brigade about the attack tonight.' He died, moments later, at 1435hrs on 7 February 1917, mourned grievously by his entire battalion.

Pollard recorded: 'So passed the finest soldier we ever had in the Regiment. He was a man who never knew fear and inspired all with whom he came into contact with his own enthusiasm.'

Command of 1 HAC passed to the Second-in-Command, Major Charles

Osmond. He was known hitherto to the officers at every level as 'Ossy'. At a stroke he was now the CO and everything changed, he was now 'Colonel'.

Ernest Boyle's funeral was in Hamel Cemetery on 9 February and it was an event widely attended by as many officers and soldiers as could be spared. Many officers from other units were in attendance as were members of the staff, an indication of his standing. He was laid to rest alongside Corporal ES Marrs, who had been killed by that 'friendly fire' four days earlier. The burial of the two men was delayed because the frozen ground was rock hard and digging was impossible.

However, on 7 February, Pollard returned to his bed in the late afternoon and again he slept soundly until suddenly woken by his company commander, Captain Sherry Bryan. (Pollard refers to him as 'Sterry' in his book *Fire-Eater*.) As Pollard groped his way back into wakefulness, Bryan said excitedly, 'We've orders to attack, Alf.'

Pollard received the news with enthusiasm and said, 'Splendid, that'll keep the boys warm at any rate. When is it coming off?'

'At eleven o'clock tonight and it doesn't give us much time.'

The death of Colonel Boyle had disrupted the planning for 1 HAC but at this late stage, Bryan was able to say that the Battalion was to send two companies to clear the heights. 'A' Company would move to the right and 'B' Company was to advance on the left and cut off 300 yards of the sunken road. The left flank of 'B' Company was to rest on the communication trench known as 'Miraumont Alley'. What followed was a minor epic, in which Pollard played an important role. The events of 7/8 February 1917 are best explained by the man who was there:

> Sterry and I carefully discussed the dispositions for 'B' Company. I was to lead the assault with two platoons. Sterry would follow in support with the other two. Every man was to carry a parcel of sand bags and a couple of Mills bombs. I went down the trench to superintend the distribution of the bombs. Brigade had sent up a supply in boxes for our use.
>
> I opened the first box and examined one of the bombs to see it was in order. It was un-detonated.[3] A hasty search revealed the fact that none of them was detonated. Someone had blundered.
>
> Had I not been an old bomber they might have been given out and the troops gone into action with weapons as innocuous as tennis balls. I collected some men and we set to work to get them ready for action. We were ready at last. Five minutes to eleven found the two assaulting platoons lying out in front of the parapet in the snow. The moon was brilliant and it was nearly as light as day.
>
> The barrage opened punctually at eleven o'clock.

> At once I rose to my feet. In one hand I held my revolver ready for action, in the other a light walking cane. 'Billiken' reposed in the pocket of my fleece-lined Burberry alongside two Mills bombs. As I walked slowly forward, I glanced to right and left. Dark figures were rising from the ground at intervals of six paces.

Times had changed since 1914 and running across no man's land, to arrive exhausted at the enemy line, was now old hat. The creeping barrage had been introduced and an attack was now a carefully orchestrated exercise, calculated minute by minute. On this occasion AOP had nine minutes in which to cover 400 yards. There was no rush and he and his soldiers could take their time and proceed in a gentlemanly manner.

The British shells howled overhead and burst in front of the advance 'in a long irregular line'. Three minutes after the first shell had exploded the barrage lifted to a line just in front of the sunken road. AOP followed and his company was only 50 yards from its objective, 'with three minutes to spare'.

Pollard knelt and checked on his watch – it had stopped. He surmised that the concussions of the barrage were too much for it. He was going to have to play this one by ear because he knew that he had to be on and over the Hun parapet when the barrage lifted otherwise the Germans would be in a position to repel the attack. The problem was that notwithstanding the well planned timetable, he did not now have a watch. Alfred Pollard did not vacillate; he moved forward quickly, expecting his men to follow.

Later he thought that he must have started 'down the slope of the sunken road about thirty seconds before the barrage jumped'. One moment shells were bursting all around him and moments later, they were 50 yards ahead.[4] AOP realized that he was alone. He could not see any members of the Company. Had they not followed? He said:

> No enemy appeared to oppose me. Then all at once I saw two long flashes of light immediately in front of me.
>
> My eyes focused on two Huns about 10 yards away who had fired their rifles at me. In the excitement of the moment they both missed. I took careful aim and fired. One man collapsed in a heap. The other clapped his hands to his body and screamed wildly. I fired another shot. He pitched forward on his face.
>
> By now the road was full of our men. Sergeant Snoad was at my elbow calm and collected. We must find Miraumont Alley. With Snoad and half a dozen men at my heels, I ran forward along the road. Huns barred our passage. One instant they were there: the next they were swept away.

I fired my revolver.

Snoad got one with his bayonet.

The men were shooting and stabbing.

I fired again and again.

There was no resistance to my pull on the trigger. My magazine (sic) was empty. I must reload. I broke open my pistol and pulled out a handful of cartridges. I was so intent on reloading that I failed to notice a shell-hole in front of me. My foot stepped on air. I pitched forward on my face.

The men behind thought I was hit, and deprived of my leadership, formed a line and commenced firing over my prostrate figure. I was in the deuce of a position. I dare not sit up or I should have got one of our bullets through my head. I turned over on my back and started to shout.

Snoad was the first to realize I was unhurt. At once he stopped the men firing. I got to my feet, 'Bring a Lewis gun!' I ordered.

The Lewis gun effected a magical change as it hosed rounds down the road. In the face of its spitting fury German resistance melted away and without further opposition AOP located the opening into Miraumont Alley. Snoad returned with the platoon that had been earmarked to construct a barricade and he immediately organized the men for their task. Pollard was only too aware that it was a core German philosophy to counter-attack at the earliest possible moment with whatever force they could muster but before their adversary had had time to consolidate his new won position.

Pollard organized his defence and put in place measure to respond to the expected attack. He was delighted to note that morale was high with every man alert and ready for the next phase. The Lewis guns were sited to best effect and an added bonus was finding that two German machine-guns had been abandoned in the position. These too were moved and placed in the defensive arc; they were served by machine-gunners who knew how they functioned. These two guns added to what was, now, a formidable defence.

Sherry Bryan came forward, having established contact with 'A' Company, who had attacked on the right. They had occupied shell hole positions and were also consolidating and awaiting the inevitable counter-attack. Bryan and Pollard went to see how Snoad was getting on and it was clear that, excellent SNCO that he was, he had the matter well in hand and the barricade constructed of sand bags was growing quickly.

'D' Company should have filled the gap that 'B' Company had created between its old position and its new position. 'D' Company had been expected to fan out along the old German communication trench, Miraumont Alley, until they connected with 'B' Company. Later it transpired that the Company

Commander had misunderstood his orders and had failed to move.

There was now a dangerous gap to the left of 'B' Company.

Captain Bryan decided to move back to find 'D' Company and bring it into the line. He set off with his batman/runner and as they left the 'B' Company position the incoming German artillery signalled the long awaited counter-attack. Pollard gave his attention to matters of the moment and a shout of 'they're coming' brought him quickly to the parapet. He looked over and saw 'a long line of dark figures was moving rapidly toward us.' Over to the right a machine-gun chattered out its message and then a second gun joined the conversation. Individual riflemen were now selecting their targets as the line of grey-clad figures moved closer. Pollard snapped an order to his runner, who hared away to the *ad hoc* Company Headquarters, where the Company Sergeant-Major was awaiting an order to call in artillery support. The runner arrived and at once, the Sergeant-Major lit the fuses of three rockets that were waiting patiently in their housings. With a combined 'fizz' the three pyrotechnics soared into the sky. 'Red over Green and Red' was all that the Royal Artillery needed to see. It was the call for immediate support and before the rockets had fallen to earth, the first British shell was plunging down on the advancing German line.

The effect was devastating; the hurricane of fire swept the attacking force away and the defenders could only watch in awe as the 'Queen of the Battlefield' ruled supreme. The German counter-attack evaporated and for the moment, 'B' Company was safe.

Pollard took a moment to relax, but then a hand grabbed his arm roughly from behind. It was Captain Bryan's runner and he was 'white-faced and frightened'.[5] He was out of breath and had obviously been running hard. He turned to the rear and pointed towards Miraumont Alley.

'We're surrounded, Sir,' he cried. 'The Huns are behind us. They've killed Captain Bryan!' The runner had himself clearly just avoided the same fate as his officer and AOP was more that a little discommoded by this unwelcome news. He called Sergeant Burgess over to explain the situation. He told Burgess to take every third man and guard the parados. He added that they were not to open fire unless they were sure that they had Germans in their sights.

Pollard re-stocked with bombs and accompanied by his runner (probably Hughesdon) and Sergeant Sly, hastened to Miraumont Alley. On arrival he found evidence of the good work done on the barricade, which was, by now, almost 6 feet high and an effective obstacle.

Pollard and his two companions moved cautiously down the alley, prepared for instant confrontation. None came for the first 100 yards. Then German voices were heard, followed by the sound of a burning fuse as a bomb sailed over the heads of the small party. The bomb burst harmlessly, well behind them. Pollard motioned to his companions to proceed on their hands and knees, and in this manner they moved forward a few more yards. By now, German bombs, thrown with great gusto, were sailing overhead and bursting in the empty trench behind Pollard.

With ice-cold resolve, Pollard waited. The German bombing stopped, still Pollard waited. The clock ticked, about fifteen minutes passed. By this time, the Germans almost certainly believed that the threat had been eliminated. On Pollard's signal the party quietly laid out its stock of bombs and made ready.

Then, as one, they rose and threw three bombs each in rapid succession. The assault killed two of the enemy and the remainder moved swiftly to somewhere safer.

AOP despatched Sergeant Sly to call forward 'D' Company and very soon he saw the welcome face of Lieutenant Bill Finch, who was commanding the first of the 'D' Company platoons. Pollard told Finch to mount a patrol to ensure that there were no remnants of the enemy to the rear and then he set about consolidating the newly won position. Pollard wrote:

> I was now the only officer left in the Company. In addition to Sterry two subalterns had been wounded by shell-fire and gone down. Burgess and Snoad[6] were quite as good as any officers I could have had. With their assistance I knew I should pull through. Just now all my attention was concentrated on preparing for the big counter-attack which I knew would be launched very shortly.
>
> One of our Lewis guns was out of action. So was one of the German machine-guns which I had brought into use. A 5.9 had made a direct hit on it and it was no more. I examined the rest of our armament and made sure that the machine-gunners had plenty of ammunition handy. All the men were quite cheery and I had no misgivings about them making a good show when the time came.
>
> We had not very long to wait. The Hun put down a barrage ten times as great in intensity as before. It was a taste of what we might expect. Of course they had the range to an inch and a sunken road is a devilishly exposed place to be in during a bombardment. I waited as before until the attack had actually started before I sent up the SOS for the artillery. Again I sent my runner down to Company HQ with a message. Every second I expected the rockets to go up. Nothing happened. The Huns were coming steadily forward.
>
> I left the parapet and ran down to find out the cause of the delay. It was the simplest of human troubles. The Sergeant-Major could not get a match to light in the wind.

My runner tried.

I tried.

We all tried.

At last we got one red rocket to start. The others simply would not light. We kept on trying until we had exhausted all our matches and then gave it up. Fortunately someone was watching at Battalion HQ, and coupling the single rocket with the noise of the fight, had the sense to phone through for artillery support.

With the welcome sound of our counter-barrage in my ears I set out for the parapet. The Huns – what was left of them – were now within 100 yards. I wondered whether it was coming to a hand-to-hand scrap. Something hit me in the centre of my forehead and I went down like a log. For a moment I lay stunned, stars floated before my eyes. Then I picked myself up and recovered my steel helmet. There was a dent in the centre of it the size of an orange.

I was feeling deadly faint, but somebody told me the Huns were running. I think that helped to revive me. I went back into the road. A shell burst just behind me and a splinter hit me on the back of the head making a second dent, though not such a big one as the first. I had scarcely replaced my hat for the second time when something sharp pierced my back just below the shoulder blade. The air was raining shells.

Snoad came along and dragged me to the side of the road. I was still too dazed to think clearly and was standing in the most exposed spot in the road. Men were falling like ninepins. I could have wept with the maddening impotence of my position. We had come over the top with 150 men and four officers. I was now the only officer left, and I was wounded slightly, and I had about sixty men.

Would they attack again at dawn? That was the leading question. I waited until their artillery hall slackened down and then once again made a tour of the position. The men were marvellous considering the ordeal they had been through. Down on the right, where the Miraumont-Beaucourt road ran through our trench, there was an endless procession of stretchers taking away the wounded. We could not evacuate all the cases before the morning. Only the worst ones could be dealt with. We should have to make the rest of them as comfortable as possible until the next night.

At last came the dawn. We stood to and waited, grimy and weary, but no attack materialized. Fritz had had enough of us. The sunken road at Bailleseourt Farm was ours.

I crept into a dug-out which Fritz had started in the parados.

Someone put some iodine and a field-dressing on the slight wound in my back made by the shrapnel. My servant supplied a hot drink with a large sized tot of rum in it. I lay me down. Almost before my head touched the ground I was asleep.

That is a remarkably graphic account of an engagement that was summarized in the official history in the following, scant 100 words. 'Two companies attacked "A" on the right "B" on the left. The former had for their objective Bailleseourt Farm and the latter the sunken road. "C" and "D" Companies were held in reserve. Thirty-five minutes later all objectives were reported to be reached, the success of the operation being largely due to the magnificent creeping barrage put down by our artillery, Miraumont Alley was the scene of final resistance, and Captain SJ Bryan , a very brave soul, lost his life. Eighty-six prisoners in all were captured and our men soon got to work consolidating the new position.'

Thousands of men died in minor battles like this throughout the war and often the event went almost un-noticed and unrecorded. To those involved, these skirmishes were literally a matter of life and death - the deaths of the two anonymous Germans that Pollard shot would merely be two lines on a casualty return. How they died would be unknown to their CO or their families. Their bodies may or may not have been recovered. The action by 1 HAC on 7/8 February was one such action reduced, above, to just one paragraph.

Any British casualties were not recorded in Goold Walker other than the loss of Captain Bryan. Such was the conflict in which AOP was engaged. Later he could take a degree of pride in the fact that his patrol found official favour and he and Lance Corporal Freter were drawn to official notice. A week later, on 15 February, the Brigade Commander publicly congratulated them. It might well have been that in his last morning, Colonel Boyle wrote the citation that would result in the first of Pollard's Military Crosses.[7] The decoration was promulgated the following month. The citation, when published, was very thin indeed and it is surprising that it reaped a reward. The words published in the *London Gazette* said:

... has been awarded the Military Cross for gallantry and devotion to duty in the field. Lieutenant Pollard led a patrol and carried out a dangerous reconnaissance. Later he assumed command of a company and repulsed two strong enemy counter-attacks.

The extreme weather conditions were having a deleterious effect on the mens' feet. On sick parade in mid-February, the Medical Officer had to deal with 220 men – in many cases their feet had turned black. The Battalion was issued with gumboots around 17 February, but these were a mixed blessing.

Pollard wrote to his mother on 16 February and in his letter described the recent battle in terms more appropriate for a game. He said, 'I was the first man over the Hun parapet and landed right on top of two Huns who tried to do me in, but fortunately I managed to finish them off with my jolly old revolver. Hand-to-hand fighting was rather fun but we soon cleared them out.' Not wishing to disturb his mother he went on to describe the two strikes on his tin helmet as being of no great significance, although either was within inches of killing him.

Notes

1 Corporal Reginald Hughesdon DCM MM joined the HAC on 16 August 1915. He was commissioned in the HAC in January 1918 and served on until late 1919. In 1947 he was re-admitted to the HAC in the rank of major.
2 *Lest we Forget*, p84.
3 Mills grenades had to have a detonator inserted into the body of the grenade before use. For obvious reasons the grenades were packed and transported with the detonator uninstalled.
4 Any one of the thousands of splinters from these shells could have killed AOP, who was exposed in the open.
5 AO Pollard, *Fire-Eater*, p183.
6 HW Snoad joined the HAC in June 1915. He was commissioned and post-war he resigned his commission and returned to the ranks. This extraordinary step is not unusual in the HAC but is proscribed in the rest of the Army. He died in 1971.
7 The *London Gazette*, 26 March 1917.

Chapter 10

The Victoria Cross and a Bar to the Military Cross

'Throughout these operations the officer's superb courage, quick decision, and sound judgment were beyond praise …'

'A splendid example of courage and determination.'

March–April 1917

On 25 February, 1 HAC was ordered to advance on Beauregarde Alley and Beauregarde Dovecote. 'B' Company was, once more, leading on the left. There was a thick mist, snow muffled the sound of movement, and command and control were difficult. However, in combination, the weather conditions probably saved some casualties. Pollard sent out a patrol, which reported[1] that 'Gudgeon Trench was still held by the enemy who were on both sides of the road and they were supported by a machine-gun. The patrol was unmolested until it had almost got back, when it was fired on by this machine-gun, which later made any movement almost impossible.'

Enemy machine-guns frustrated forward movement and it was only when heavy artillery was employed that the trench was taken. 1 HAC had suffered thirty-nine dead and 100 wounded during its February operations.

A number of Germans surrendered during the month of bitter weather. All of the dispirited enemy soldiers were cold and very hungry. One sad case was a man, known afterwards as 'The Poet', who ran towards the British line and ignored the sentry's call to 'Halt'. The sentry challenged a second time but the man continued to run inwards.

The sentry cut him down with his Lewis gun.

His body was searched and a book of his poetry was found in his pocket. The last poem, to his mother, was unfinished. It spoke of how he intended to give himself up to the English because he was so cold. Had he walked he might well have survived to live out the war in a warm POW camp. Pollard recounted how, on another occasion, a drunken German was returning to his unit and somehow contrived to walk down the road into the British lines and captivity. He sobered up as a very confused soldier.

Lance Corporal Freter was a player in yet another incident on a misty morning in which visibility was down to a few yards. Suddenly, Freter jumped up onto the fire step and over the parapet. He disappeared into the mist but promptly reappeared with two Germans at the end of his rifle. One was a Prussian lieutenant and the other a sergeant-major. Both were sporting the air of a man who was having a bad day. It seems that each was in command of a company and the Lieutenant's company had been detailed to relieve that of the Sergeant-Major. The outgoing Sergeant-Major was showing the incoming Lieutenant the layout of the trenches when both got disoriented in the fog. Whilst milling about in no man's land the aggressive Freter emerged from the gloom and invited them to come and join 1 HAC. It is a cliché perhaps, but 'for them the war was over'. They ended up being interrogated by 'Ossy' whilst both German companies waited in the fog for someone in command to say something – anything. Later, an alternative version of events emerged, which was that the two company commanders had decided to surrender, but for appearances sake, cooked up the 'lost in the fog' story.

Pollard had a very relaxed relationship with his new CO. One evening he went to have his wound dressed and 'Ossy' called him into his dug-out. They chatted in the most informal way about everything except the war, the recent engagement or the egregious weather. The conversation went on all evening. Captain, Acting Lieutenant Colonel Osmond was a shrewd and very kind man. He spent time in making the young officer relax and Pollard commented, 'He said it would give my mind a rest and it certainly did. I went back to my job feeling very cheery.' Osmond had joined the HAC in 1896, he was just about old enough to be Pollard's father and his approach was paternal – and effective.

The casualties suffered in the recent actions were still on the ration roll and so 1 HAC was receiving rations for 139 men who were either dead or eating somewhere else. The result was that there was an 'ample sufficiency' of food. Pollard was wise enough to harbour the rum issue because he couldn't afford for his 'tiny garrison to be half tight'.

The winter of 1917 seemed to be endless. When it stopped snowing it was only because it was raining. 'B' Company was now situated in a part of the line that ran through chalk. This allowed easy and dry digging although there were already deep dug-outs for the Company to use. Where the water did lie – it was knee-deep. The measure of the misery endured by troops on both sides during that dire winter was illustrated by the case of a company sergeant-major of the Royal Marines who had lost his way and stumbled into a sentry. He was delivered to AOP, who gave him some hot food and a tot of rum. The Sergeant-Major shared his opinion of trench warfare with an audience of HAC soldiers:

> Give me the bleeding North Sea every time,' he said tersely. 'That's where I spent last winter and it was a picnic compared with this. Even if it was a bit cold on watch it was nice and warm when you turned in below. Here, you stands up to your waist in water while you're on duty. Then when you're relieved, you go down into a blinkin' deep dug-out like some blasted rabbit, and the rain comes pouring down the stairs after you and you has to sleep in a puddle of water. You can't get away from it.

It was only a small comfort to Pollard to know that he and his men were enduring more extreme hardship than other servicemen. As he said, 'It gives one a glow of inward righteousness.' In Pollard's view the worst job during the war was that of the Gunners who were subject to counter-bombardment and never saw the effect of their own fire. In addition the Royal Regiment of Artillery had his sympathy because 'the infantryman had the fun of going over the top and the chance of getting some of his own back in a hand-to-hand contest.' A source of enormous fun and stimulation denied to the unfortunate Gunners!

Colonel Osmond had slipped seamlessly into Colonel Boyle's place and the war had to go on. He detailed AOP and 'B' Company to take possession of a ruined farm called Beauregard Dovecot, which was located on a hilltop. The CO told Pollard that his company, which was now reduced to platoon strength of thirty-five, would lead as a reward for its sterling performance in the battle of Miraumont Alley. This was the military equivalent of a 'hospital pass' in rugby. The survivors of the savage fight a few days before would now be exposed again – as a reward.

Pollard welcomed the opportunity but the probability is that the rest of his company did not actively share his enthusiasm. That said, of his thirty-five men, eight were sick or incapacitated in some form and had every good reason to be 'left out of battle'. Pollard said, with a justifiable note of pride, that all eight of them 'volunteered to accompany me.' This speaks volumes for the loyalty of these eight men to their comrades as it has little to do with 'King and Country' and there are countless other examples of this sort of selfless behaviour. Pollard himself agonized at being absent from the line when he was wounded, wanting to share in the experiences of his fellows. It is the very essence of 'comradeship', an emotion, a mind set or even a guiding principle that Pollard retained for the rest of his life.

Field Marshal Montgomery, who fought in the trenches as a junior officer, had this to say on 'comradeship':[2]

> Why does the soldier leave the protection of his trench or hole in the ground and go forward in the face of shot and shell? It is because of the

> leader who is in front of him and his comrades who are around him. Comradeship makes a man feel warm and courageous when his instincts tend to make him cold and afraid.

On the selection of 'B' Company, AOP observed, 'That was Ossy's attitude. To him honour was more than life. The tradition of the Regiment meant everything to him.' Quite what the tradition of the Regiment had to do with it is unclear. For some these were quixotic days and it is evident that Pollard and Colonel Osmond were well matched.

When Pollard's severely depleted Company formed up in the early light of dawn it was misty and visibility was much reduced. The Company had the sunken road to its rear and to the front the ground was less battle scarred than any landscape that they had seen since very early in 1915. The young Company Commander, engrossed with his map and casting anxious glances at his watch, did not pay attention to his immediate surroundings and he fell over backwards into a shell hole that was, as normal, filled with freezing water. It was a very cold day, he was wet through and the chances of drying out were in the distant future.

Pollard waved to his company to advance. Laden with personal kit, entrenching tools, ammunition and water, the men of 'B' Company stepped off into the mist. Navigation was difficult. None of the features on Pollard's map could be discerned although he knew that the farm was about a mile ahead … somewhere. Progress was steady and not challenged. After about half a mile, a body of men were to be seen cutting across the front of 'B' Company. These men were anonymous and the first impression was that they might be Germans. It transpired that it was 'D' Company, which should have been heading toward the same objective. 'D 'Company seemed to have a predilection for being in the wrong place, this time it was heading there again.

Someone was wrong.

Pollard did not think that it was him. A brief discussion with the 'D' Company officer resolved nothing and so both companies continued on their now rapidly diverging courses. The 'D' Company officer was marching on a compass bearing whilst Pollard was steering by way of the contours marked on the map. He remarked that he had 'had experience of the deflections that barbed wire could have on a compass.' Some ten minutes later, one of the Company scouts emerged, like a wraith, from the fog to say that he had walked straight onto the location of the farm and that it was unoccupied.

Pollard dispersed his meagre assets in some of the scattered shell holes that pitted the green grass and sent a runner back to report the situation. It must have crossed his mind that it was not so long ago that he had been acting as a runner himself – bereft of responsibility other than to deliver a message. Now he was responsible for a portion of the British front line.

There was no sign of 'D' Company. And that was probably not a surprise. The portion of the line for which he was responsible got very much bigger when the runner returned with orders for him to:

> Extend my front to the outskirts of Miraumont. I was also to patrol the road as far as the top of the ridge overlooking Puisieux. It meant that I was responsible for 1,000 yards of front and I had thirty-five men with which to do it.

The men were grouped in pairs 50-100 yards apart. It was an absurd situation and everyone knew that any form of attack would overwhelm them with comparative ease. Things looked up when another group of British soldiers emerged from the murk. These worthies were from the Machine Gun Corps (MGC) and they had with them that most priceless of weapons, the Vickers machine-gun – they had four of them. The young officer in command 'did not know the ropes very well'[3] and he was but putty in Pollard's crisp and assertive hands. Pollard absorbed the Vickers into his plan.

It was late morning when the mist started to clear. 'B' Company and the detachment of the MGC discovered that they were positioned on a road that traversed a ridge. From their position they could see that the ground ran down into a shallow valley and then rose up again to a ridge in the distance. The map showed that the far ridge was enemy territory and that along that ridge was the trench known as 'Gudgeon Trench'. The Germans were now aware of the British presence and they exercised the machine-guns, which covered the valley with enfilade fire. Pollard realized how fortunate he had been to establish his position under the cloak of the mist.

Pollard now had ample opportunity to relish his wet clothes. He was unable to walk about, it was a cold day and he was chilled to the marrow. 'B' Company sat fast throughout the day. With nightfall came the all enveloping frost and, covered by darkness, Pollard strode up and down the road trying to get warm. He was not alone and although he could not leave his men, other officers came forward to visit him. From them he learned that 'D' Company had not reached its designated support position until the previous afternoon. The next day passed without any offensive action by either side. It was no warmer but Pollard's clothes were now merely damp.

Just after dark on the second night, 'B' Company was relieved by a company of a Yorkshire battalion of the 65th Division. The incoming Company Commander asked how many men he was replacing and when told that it was thirty-five he commented that his 250 men would not fit. Pollard put his mind at rest by telling him, 'Never mind, you've got 1,200 yards for them to spread out in.'

A tired, very cold 'B' Company climbed out of the shell holes, hoisted their kit onto their shoulders and withdrew. On the way back Pollard reported that:

> We passed gun-teams toiling to get their guns forward to new positions in pursuit of the enemy. Cursing men and sweating horses; a wheel embedded in the mud at the bottom of a shell hole. Poor devils of gunners. How lucky we were to be in the infantry.

The Battalion was sent to the rear to rest and it was billeted in Nissen huts. The weather turned for the better and 1 HAC was 'able to laze about until nearly the end of March.' Just as the lazing was coming to an end Pollard fell into a trench and sprained his ankle. The Battalion moved off without him and he was left as the sole occupant of the camp. This isolation was efficacious in hastening his determination to be back on his feet as soon as he was able.

The account above is based upon the memoirs of Alfred Pollard and it is at variance with the official version written by Goold Walker two years before. He recorded that:

> At 7.30 am on the 25th the Battalion began the advance. 'D' Company, in artillery formation, was on the right and 'B' Company on the left, with 'A' and 'C' Companies forming strong left flank guards. The assembly position was reached by 9.30 am, and after some delay the advance was made at 11.50 am in perfect order, but in a thick mist, which probably saved many casualties, though company commanders had difficulty in keeping direction. By 12.40 pm all objectives had been reached and consolidation had begun, when a patrol sent out by 'B' Company reported that Gudgeon Trench was still held by the enemy. Any effort to advance on this line was frustrated by enemy machine-gun fire and finally, on the 26th (February 1917), after a bombardment of the trench by our heavies, the patrol went out and secured its objective.[4] On the 28th, the Battalion was relieved by the 2/5th Bn West Yorks, and returned to tents[5] near Mesnil.

Pollard was not left alone with his sprained ankle for too long because the medical officer had made arrangements for him to be evacuated at least as far back as the Casualty Clearing Station. AOP asked to be allowed to rest his ankle for a few days there but 'once again the hospital authorities defeated me. They had a certain routine and they refused to depart from it by one jot or tittle.'

Pollard found himself once more in the Base Hospital but this time there was no attractive nursing sister to lighten his apparently endless and boring

What remained of the village was sketched by Adrian Hill. The snow could not conceal the destruction.

(HAC Archives)

days. It took eight days in bed before he could hobble about and he was discharged a fortnight after his tumble into the trench. He then reversed the process with which he was now familiar. He returned to 'the wretched camp at Havre where I was before. My friend, the Adjutant, mindful of the second ribbon that adorned my tunic, was considerably more friendly and respectful.'

Once more, Pollard uses the word 'respect'. It is evident that, for him, unspoken approbation was not in itself sufficient. He required there to be more than that, preferably an overt demonstration of approval. This is not a deficiency, but it is a character trait that, when viewed at close quarters, might come across as arrogance.

Pollard pressed the Adjutant to accelerate his return to his battalion. The Adjutant was 'vastly astonished that anyone should want to hasten back to the trenches when he had a chance of 'miking'[6] at the base.'

There then followed a tale that Pollard – ever an honest man – told against himself. It appeared that he was one of twenty HAC in the base and they were all to move up to 1 HAC as a formed draft. The draft consisted of a corporal and a private man, both of whom had already served in France, and seventeen replacements straight out from England. Pollard detailed off the private soldier as his servant and the Corporal as the Draft NCO. The draft 'en-trained' and the following morning their train was shunted into a siding at Abbeville.

Pollard went to find a Railway Transport Officer (RTO) and, by chance, the one he found was an 'Old Merchant Taylor', an officer from the same public school as AOP, whose name was 'Artie' Barrett. Barrett smoothed the path of the draft. He found out where 1 HAC was located and moved the HAC men to an appropriate train.

At 1700hrs on 12 April 1917, after twenty-four hours *en route*, this train ground to a halt and once more Pollard decided to commune with an RTO. This one advised him that their current transport was going nowhere near the post code of 1 HAC and that Pollard would be advised to switch to the hissing, growling train at the opposite platform.

Pollard was told that time was short and he issued hurried orders to his charges. The replacements were slow to gather all their kit and only Pollard, the Corporal and the soldier servant arrived at the terminus. The other seventeen men had evaporated into the maws of rural France.

AOP swallowed his chagrin and reported to his commanding officer. Colonel Osmond was only too pleased to welcome him back and said, 'Well played Alf. You're in the nick of time. We're leaving on motor buses at six tomorrow morning to follow up the attack on the Vimy Ridge.'[7]

The Adjutant cast a shadow on the meeting when he enquired as to the whereabouts of the draft that AOP was leading. 'I've lost them,' replied Pollard, with commendable honesty. The Adjutant was appalled, as he had every right to be. It appears that the draft then wandered across France for six weeks and, by the time they arrived, they had caused consternation and distress to countless RTOs and Town Majors – the members of the draft were now old soldiers and had probably already qualified for a medal.

The United States of America entered the war on 6 April 1917 and one week later, a message was sent from the 1st Battalion to the Ancient and Honourable Artillery Company of Boston,[8] Massachusetts, welcoming the HAC's younger cousin into the fray.

A brief explanation of the background to the events that were to follow appeared in the paper[9] prepared by James Colquhoun, and published in the *HAC Journal* in 2007. He explained that:

> The Somme campaign had finally come to a muddy halt in the second half of November 1916. Thus during the winter of 1916/17 the Germans decided to curtail their activities on the Western Front by shortening their line and to withdraw their troops to prepared positions about 20 miles from the Somme, which became known as the Hindenburg Line. At the same time they decided to rely on unrestricted submarine warfare to bring Britain to her knees. The Allies, though,

considered various plans and finally decided to rely on the French to launch a knock-out blow between Soissons and Rheims in April 1917 under their new charismatic, English-speaking commander, General Robert Nivelle. It was considered vital to this plan that the British Army should make a substantial attack to help draw the German Army's attention from the French offensive. In order to do this Haig instructed General Horne's 1st Army and General Allenby's 3rd Army to attack east of Arras. The opening day of battle, Easter Monday, 9 April 1917 was hugely successful and the Canadian Corps captured Vimy Ridge in a snow storm in one of the most successful operations of the war. Whilst this was going on, Allenby's Army attacked further south. Some of the units had debouched safely from tunnels which had started underneath Arras and, assisted by a massive barrage, they broke through the first two lines of defences. By the end of the day they had advanced 3½ miles. But after these successes the attack became bogged down by three days of the worst snow of the winter. It was at this juncture that that 1 HAC came into the picture.

1 HAC was still a component of 190 Brigade and part of 63rd Royal Naval Division. The Division was in 'Army reserve' during the first part of the battle.

On 17 April 1917, Private ES Simmons[10] joined 'B' Company as a replacement: he was no doubt somewhat in awe of the redoubtable Pollard, who exuded all the self-confidence that any young replacement lacked.

On 25 April 1917, Alfred Pollard wrote to his mother. They were very close and he often addressed her as 'Ladybird', as he did on this occasion. She preserved his letters and this one he reproduced in *Fire-Eater*. He wrote:

Dearest Ladybird,

Here we are again, out once more. I have had some most interesting and exciting times since last writing, including going over the top again. I am once more in charge of the Company as the man senior to me got laid out with a bullet. I shall probably be a Captain again in a day or two, but one never knows as somebody else senior may be sent along.

You see the present arrangement of the government is that all promotions arc by seniority irrespective of fighting qualities, so really one has no chance of being more than a Second Lieutenant whatever one does. However, I don't care a bit what rank I am.

I had a most exciting adventure in a Hun trench the other day. I cut through their wire and got into their trench thinking it was unoccupied, but soon discovered it was full of Huns and consequently had to beat a hasty retreat. I got out all right fortunately. I hear a rumour that the Brigadier has recommended me for a bar to my MC in consequence of this little business so if you keep your eyes glued on the paper you may shortly see my name in it. Don't think I have been taking any unnecessary risks because I have not. I have merely done what I have been asked to do.

Well, dear old lady, although out of the line we are still away from civilization. By the way I have received another box of new records but cannot play the wretched gramophone until those governor springs arrive so please hurry them up.

Best of spirits and having a good time. By the way, I have killed another Hun. Hurrah!

Well, cheerioh!

The letter gives a revealing glimpse of the young Alfred. He reflected on that letter after the war and decided to reproduce it in his text because, as he explained:

I have included this letter because it throws such a clear light on my attitude towards war at this time. I thoroughly enjoyed going into action and was never happier than when there was something doing. People tell me I must have a kink in my nature; that my zest to be in the forefront of the battle was unnatural. I do not agree with them. I have often thought about it since the war and the conclusion I have reached is that my condition of mind was simply a keen desire to win. I wanted the British to be victorious and was prepared to strain every nerve to attain that end. True, I wanted to be in at the death myself, but I think that was a natural rather than an unnatural wish. At this time also, I was convinced that it only needed a little extra effort for us to break through the Germans' last line of defence. I was bitterly disappointed when we failed to do so.

The 'jolly hockey sticks' flavour of Alfred's letter may have comforted his mother and led her to believe that life in France was all just a jolly jape but of course, the reality was very different. Pollard's command of 'B' Company had been a mere expedient on the death of Sherry Bryan and he got the job from a shortlist of one. His temporary/local captaincy came and went at fairly regular intervals hereafter. He was a substantive[11] second lieutenant and never rose above the rank of lieutenant during the war other than for brief and temporary periods.

Lieutenant George Thorpe[12] was transferred from 'A' Company, and as he was five months senior to Pollard, he assumed command. It was and is the way the system works. Pollard was philosophical about it and, giving a shrug, he remarked, 'I got on very well with old George and I felt quite sure we should pull together which was the great thing.'

The HAC advancing at Gavrelle. One of Adrian Hill's best known sketches of 1st Bn HAC in action. The battle around Gavrelle was to yield the Company two Victoria Crosses.
(HAC Archives)

The Battalion moved in stages through Arras to the village of Bailleul, which was the British front line and over a mile from the Boche. The Germans were presumed to have withdrawn to a strongly entrenched position in the next valley, a part of the Hindenburg Line. To test this presumption patrols were to be sent out at intervals of 500 yards. Orders were issued specifying that each patrol was to consist of an officer and twelve men. The aim of each patrol was to approach and examine a section of the Hindenburg Line. If the line was found to be unoccupied the patrol was to occupy it. The patrol commander was to send a message back to his parent unit telling it to move forward to his patrol's position.

1 HAC was to provide two patrols, of which Pollard was selected to command one. He asked if he might be permitted to amend the composition of the patrol and limit its size to four men. He was experienced in operations of this type and he believed that a group of twelve was far too

unwieldy to control in the darkness. He was overruled and so it was with a corporal and eleven men that he embarked on his patrol soon after it was dark in light rain.

It was a moonless night and accordingly, visibility was severely limited and control of his party just as difficult as AOP had predicted. The German guns were firing sporadically and in a random defensive pattern. This was presumably in the hope that somewhere, they might just hit something. The intermittent shelling did have the effect of unsettling some members of Pollard's patrol who were inexperienced - and it showed.

Pollard observed, 'I had not gone very far before I began to seriously think of dumping two thirds of them in a shell-hole and picking them up on my return. Many times since I have wished to goodness that I had, but at the time I carried on with them.'

Despite the dark night, initially navigation was simple because Pollard followed the railway line that ran from Arras to Gavrelle. The railway made a sharp turn to the south to avoid the ridge ahead. This was the spot at which Pollard had decided to leave the track and strike out uphill and across open country. He continued onto the higher ground and observed that:

> Two or three hundred yards to the north was a small clump of trees, which, standing on the crest of the ridge, gave me a landmark from which to take my bearings. At least I had intended to use it for that purpose had the night been sufficiently light for me to see it at a distance. As it was I had to search about until I found it.
>
> We were now about 400 yards from the Hun position which stretched along the bottom of the valley. Standing facing it, Oppy Wood was about forty-five degrees to my left hand whilst Gavrelle village was about the same angle to the right. Even though I could not see I knew I could not very well lose my way with these well-defined boundaries to limit my wanderings.

The patrol, led by AOP, advanced cautiously down the slope unable to discern any sign of the Germans in the stygian darkness. Somewhat unusually for the Western Front in 1917 the night was not being illuminated by star shells fired by either side. The party had made its way about halfway down the hill when it stumbled across a substantial hole in the ground. It must have been a German hole at some stage but it was empty and inviting. Pollard dropped off two of his men to occupy the hole 'with instructions that if they heard a shindy in front and a lot of firing and none of us came back, they were to return to Headquarters with the news of what had happened.' Moving further forward Pollard came across the first of two belts of thick German barbed wire

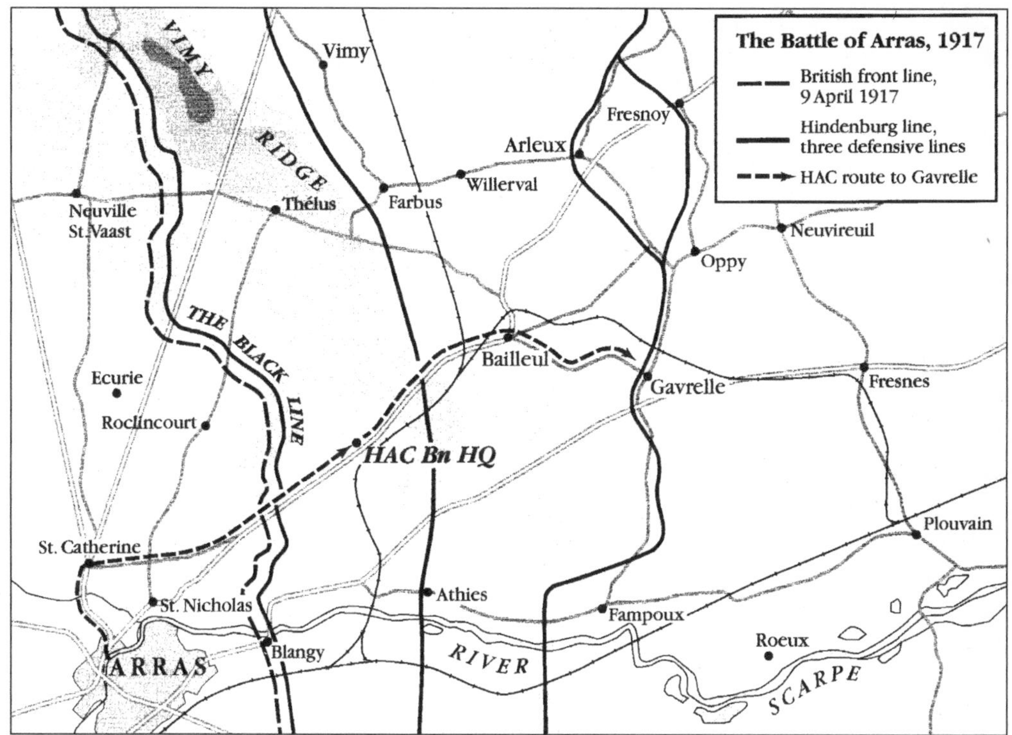

The Battle of Arras, 1917.
J Colquhoun, (*HAC Journal*, spring 2007)

entanglements. His men cut their way through but in the cutting made a great deal of noise. Incredibly, they attracted no fire and the obvious conclusion was that there were no Germans to hear them. Pollard left a man at each gap to act as a guide for the return journey.

They were, by now, standing on the parapet of a trench, which Pollard had felt for with the cane he was carrying. He was beset with doubts; his orders were to occupy the position and then send for the rest of the Battalion. However, he could not be sure that this trench line was completely unoccupied nor that it was indeed the right trench. He decided that he had to determine the exact position of his adversaries. As he recounted:

> The question in my mind was answered by the flash from a Very pistol some two or three hundred yards to my right. Someone was in the trench at any rate. Standing quite still from force of habit, I watched the light describe its parabola in the sky. It cast a shadow at my feet and I idly poked my cane at it. To my surprise my cane went through the shadow and revealed a crack of light.

> My heart leapt in a sudden acceleration of beats.
>
> This was very, very interesting. I dropped onto my hands and knees and bent my ear to the crack. I could hear voices talking in German: there was an occasional burst of laughter. We were standing over the entrance to a Hun dug-out.
>
> I got hastily to my feet. If there was one dug-out there would be others. The Huns were apparently sheltering from the rain which was now coming down fairly fast. All the same there would be some sentries in the trench somewhere. Either they were shirking their work or one would pass this way very shortly.

Bombo Pollard had to think quickly – there was a thick band of wire between him and any reinforcement and it was unthinkable to try to occupy the position with his slender recourses. Withdrawal was the only option. Pollard gave whispered instructions to Corporal Larssen-Nils,[13] who responded calmly and efficiently. Pollard later described the back-up provided by this NCO as 'magnificent'.

The retirement was not without its moments. Some of the inexperienced soldiers were too anxious to get away from the current danger and some mild panic started to show. This was manifested in the noise that they made re-crossing the belts of wire. Nevertheless, and by happy chance, they were not heard and drew no fire. Larssen-Nils assembled the men on the far side of the wire and counted them.

One was missing.

Allowing for the two men that had been posted in the shell hole there should have been nine. There were only eight accounted for. Pollard recognized his responsibility and realized that he would have to go back and find the missing man. In his words:

> I gave Larssen instructions to take the rest of the patrol back to the clump of trees and wait for me behind the shelter of the ridge. Then my runner, Reggie Hughesdon, and I climbed back through the wire. Our man was nowhere between the first and second belts so we went on to the parapet. I thought the missing one might be the man I had left in charge of one of the gaps.
>
> I emerged from the second line of barbed wire and turned to help Reggie. Someone challenged me sharply from the trench. I spun round in time to see the flash of his rifle. I fired two shots and heard him yell as I hit him.
>
> The firing gave the alarm. Men were appearing in the trench like magic. Reggie and I were caught like rats in a trap. It would have been

impossible to have broken our way out through the wire without offering a sitting target to the enemy.

There was only one thing to do. I seized Reggie by the arm and ran. Down the parapet we flew as fast as our legs would take us. Star shells were going up in all directions. By their light I could see that the trench was of a pattern known as 'island traversed'. That meant that there were two trenches parallel with one another joined at short intervals by cross-cuts. At intervals along the parapet were squares of concrete which I knew to be machine-gun emplacements. I realized it was a position that would take a lot of capturing.

We must have covered well over 100 yards before I spotted it. It was a miracle that I saw it at all – just a narrow gap in the wire entanglement left so that the holders of the trench could get out easily if they wished to. I darted into it with Reggie close on my heels. It zigzagged through both lines of wire. In a moment we were free of our cage and down on our hands and knees behind the shelter of the wire.

We had scarcely dropped before rifles and machine-guns opened up behind us. I prayed that Larssen had got the patrol safely over the top of the ridge. Reggie and I were as safe as if we were out of range. No bullets could pierce that doubly thick screen of wire[14] which protected us from our assailants.

We were safe from bullets but there was another menace which threatened us. I guessed it would be only a question of minutes before Fritz organized a patrol to look for us. We must get clear of his gateway. We crawled along behind our cover in the direction from which we had come. Five minutes later a sudden cessation of fire warned me they were coming. Reggie and I sank motionless to the ground whilst a long line of dark figures dashed out through the zigzag path. There must have been at least twenty of them. If they had searched along the front of the wire they would have found us, but I had banked on that being the one place they would overlook.

We stayed where we were for half an hour until the Huns had returned to their trench and all the excitement had died away. Then we rejoined Larssen on the ridge and made a startling discovery. In the rush of getting the patrol back into safety we had neglected to pick up the two men I had posted in the hole in the ground. Reggie and I went down to look for them but they had disappeared. We sent the patrol home and continued our search until daylight. No trace could be found of them. We learned afterwards that the Hun patrol had run into them, killing one and taking the other prisoner.

Of the first missing man, the reason for Pollard's retracing of his steps, there is no mention – Pollard did not name or could not name him and his fate is unknown. This first patrol earned AOP a bar to his MC and in his book he quoted the citation as:

> *Sec. Lt. Alfred Oliver Pollard, MC, HAC. He carried out a dangerous reconnaissance of the enemy's front line under very heavy fire, and obtained most valuable information. He set a splendid example of courage and determination.*

This is another very thin citation upon which to base a decoration. It must be presumed that Pollard's CO had lobbied his case beforehand. This is not in any way to deny the value of Pollard's patrol or the value that it had.[15]

There was no doubt that once again Alfred Pollard had demonstrated his determination and raw courage. He risked his life (and that of Reggie Hughesdon) in going back for his lost man. He could have abandoned that individual and no one would have thought any the worse of him. He acted like a brave man and a splendid leader. His was the only patrol that came close to the German line and the information that he brought back was used in mounting the operation that followed. Next morning 63rd RND was ordered 'to advance and dig in 200 yards in front of the German line.'

1 HAC 'A' and 'B' Companies led with 'C' and 'D' Companies in support. Colonel Osmond put Pollard in temporary command of 'B' Company, not least because he knew the ground. At nightfall Pollard set off with the two companies following in his footsteps. It was as dark as the previous night but at least it was not raining. Pollard strode out, found the bend in the railway line, mounted the ridge, moved down the far slope and then with an awful shock realized that he had come too far.

Much too far.

He had led his men right into the German wire that fronted the enemy position. Pollard described the situation, with masterly understatement, as 'a pretty predicament'. How right he was. If the Germans were alerted then the two companies, lying in no man's land, in the open, only yards from the muzzles of enemy weapons, would be wiped out.

Pollard kept his nerve.

He sent his sergeant-major to the rear of the column and told him to supervise a withdrawal, starting from the rear to the far side of the ridge. It says a lot for the discipline of 'A and 'B' Companies that this manoeuvre was accomplished in silence. No credit to the Germans who, for the second night, were not alert. However, the night's exercise did not end there and Pollard wrote that:

> When the last section was safely back, my runner Reggie and I paced a distance of exactly 200 yards from the German entanglements. Then we brought the men forward by sections and set them to work. We laboured all night to entrench ourselves. Fritz did not tumble to the fact that there was anything unusual going on until we had been working for nearly an hour. Then he began spasmodic bursts of machine-gun fire. His guns were firing high, however, which coupled with the fact that we were throwing up earthwork in front of us, prevented more than a few casualties.

It seems to be extraordinary that about 150 men could start digging a trench 200 yards in front of their enemy without active opposition. Star shells would have illuminated the diggers and star shells would have allowed the machine-guns to be properly aligned. As the night wore on Pollard waited, expecting to be joined by the battalion on his left. It was a long wait and the other battalion never did appear. 'A' Company was similarly isolated and Alf Hawes, who was in command, had no support on his right. Came dawn's early light and to the astonishment and bewilderment of both Pollard and Hawes they found that they commanded the only British troops in sight. On the whole slope there was not another British soldier to be seen. The two HAC Companies 'were opposing the whole of the Hindenburg Line by themselves.' Pollard confessed to being:

> Rather worried by the situation. The Huns could not do very much during the day except shell us because they were unable to pass their own compact wire entanglements. But when night fell, I could visualize a strong force emerging through their pathway in the wire and surrounding us. I must make some provision against surprise.

The position dug during the night was about 200 yards below the crest of the ridge. It made any rearward movement very hazardous as it was in plain sight of the enemy. Well knowing the risk, Pollard decided to get back to his CO and acquaint 'Ossy' with the facts. There was only one way and that was straight up the slope. He launched himself over the parados and sprinted upwards. He immediately drew fire but it was ill-directed and he made it up to the top of the reverse slope unscathed. Colonel Osmond did not vacillate and dispatched Pollard straight to Brigade headquarters. At Brigade they told Pollard to cool his heels as:

> The Brigadier-General was engaged with the Commanding Officer of the battalion who should have come up on my left. I decided to take the bull by the horns and burst into their presence. The Colonel was just reporting that his unit had dug in according to orders.

'Excuse me, Sir,' I interrupted him, 'your front line Companies may be dug in but they are not in sight of the enemy.'

'Are yours?' asked the Brigadier succinctly.

'Yes, Sir, both our Companies are dug in according to orders – 200 yards from the enemy front line.'

'How do you know they are 200 yards from the enemy?' asked the Colonel, sarcastically. He did not dream that I had come out of the front line trench in broad daylight.

'Because I paced the distance myself,' I replied crushingly.

The Brigadier roared with laughter and made me tell him the whole story. The Colonel was the first to agree that his men were at fault. He was a magnificent fellow, for whom I always had the greatest respect. It was not his fault that he had received an erroneous report from the officers under him. It turned out that they had encountered the entanglements of an abandoned trench and had mistaken it in the dark for their objective.

The Brigadier promised that we should be properly supported that night and I returned to the trench (by running back down the exposed slope). [Author's note.] Soon after dusk I placed a Lewis gun in a shell-hole about 200 yards on my flank and arranged for Alf Hawes to do the same on the right. It would probably be some hours before the troops moved forward to fill up the gap and I wanted to be prepared.

My anticipation that the Huns would make an attempt to surround us proved to be correct. Some half an hour later the gun on my flank opened fire. I at once went out to see what target they had found. A strong party of Huns had emerged from the wire almost in front of them. They were able to disperse that assault before it materialized. Shortly afterwards long lines of troops joined up with us and we were safe.

It is worth remembering that, in April 1917, Alfred Pollard was still not twenty-four years of age. Nevertheless, he had frequently accepted responsibility far greater than would normally be given to an officer of his age and so far, he had unfailingly acquitted himself with distinction. His maturity and judgement under stress, even by his own understated account, is remarkable. Many of his men will have been older but none were more skilled in the ruthless business of trench warfare. He had MC and bar and a DCM; these ribbons alone provided testament to his extraordinary courage, resolve and initiative. He should be forgiven for brief flashes of conceit and arrogance.

1 HAC stayed in the front line for a further two days and then were withdrawn while the artillery softened up the Hindenburg line prior to a major

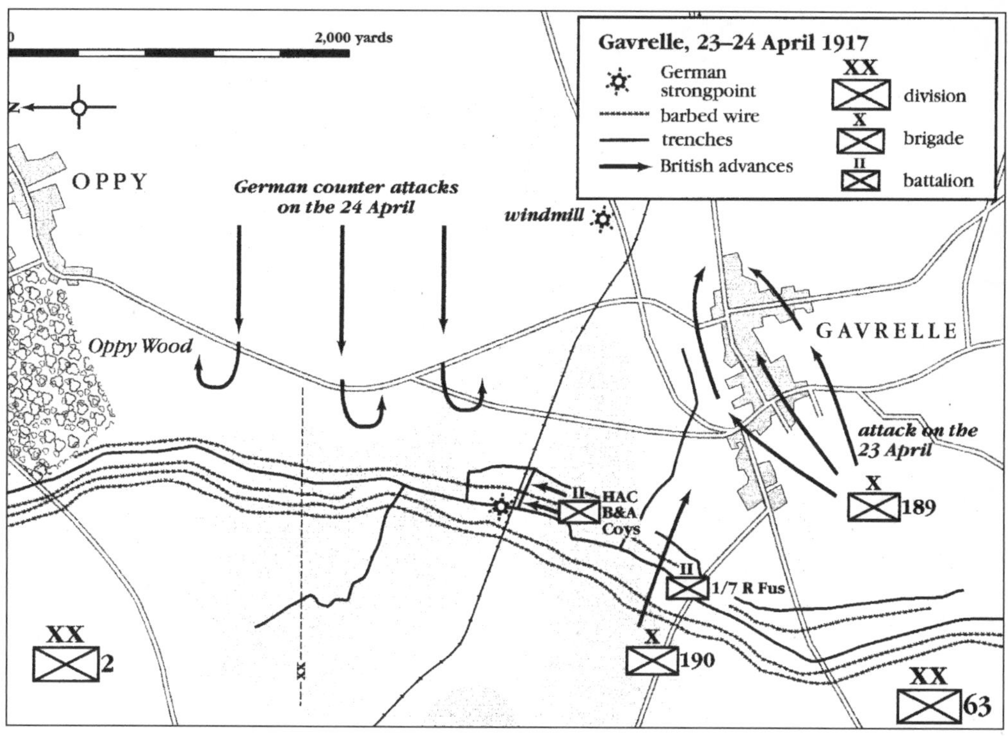

Gavrelle 23-24 April 1917.
J Colquhoun, (*HAC Journal*, spring 2007)

assault. The German wire was thickly strewn in deep belts – cutting it was vital if the attack was to succeed on 23 April 1917, St. George's Day.

'B' Company was to be held in reserve and was told that it probably would not be required. Pollard was not best pleased at this news but was cheered when 'Ossy' detailed him to take command. This may have made one officer happy but George Thorpe, having been superseded, will have been irritated at the very least. It is the CO's prerogative to make such decisions and Thorpe had no option but bite on the bullet.

The assault was duly launched and the wire was found to be still intact in places. In addition, the 5th Bn of the Prussian Guard offered very stern resistance. 'B' Company was called forward and as it advanced Pollard said, 'I could see the long lines of uncut wire with dead fusiliers hanging across it like pearls where the Hun machine-guns had caught them.'

Pollard led his usual charmed life and led 'B' Company through gaps in the wire and the enemy counter-bombardment. He passed through 'A' Company and took the position as far forward as the railway line. Resistance crumbled and 'the few Huns we encountered surrendered instantly.' A counter-attack was bound to follow and the situation was complicated because the complexity of the German trench system had allowed pockets of enemy to remain in place. They would be a factor when the attack came in. The regimental history had this summary:[16]

> The Battalion moved up during the night and arrived in position near Bailleul, in a sunken road lined with German dug-outs, just as the barrage opened at 4.45 am. At first the attack was a costly failure, the Fusiliers being reduced to about seventy men. The Bedfords, however, though suffering heavy casualties, managed eventually to secure a footing in the village. Consequently, 'A' Company, under Lieutenant AW Hawes, was at once sent forward to support the Fusiliers. The enemy garrison at this point, the 66th Wurtemburger Fusiliers, were good troops and defended stubbornly, but 'A' Company, after severe fighting, secured a footing in the German front line. 'B' Company, under Lieutenant AO Pollard, was then sent forward, and successfully cleared the enemy support trench, the whole of the first line trench system being then in our hands.

Looking over to 'B' Company's right was the town of Gavrelle and the British line extended almost to the village. However, the division that had attacked on 'B' Company's left had been held up and this failure prevented a modest success being a crashing victory. Douai church could be seen about 8 miles away and there was not a German between Pollard and that church. The ground was there for the taking but for the lack of support on the left.

The counter-attack came in the next morning and AOP said that in fact the Germans came over in waves all day long. The execution was awful as 'time after time long lines of men in field grey appeared over the crest of the ridge only to be swept away before they had descended halfway down the slope … never once did they get within 100 yards of us.' The German wounded lying on the exposed slope could be heard - some of the grey-clad figures called for help, others for their mothers, but many more lay quite, quite still.

Captain George Thorpe came forward on that morning, the 24th, to relieve AOP as soon as 'B' Company's position was consolidated. Having re-assumed command, inexplicably he apparently decided to recover a machine-gun that the enemy had abandoned in no man's land, about 200 yards in front of the British line. The gun was a significant asset to the Germans and to deny them the use of it was a laudable aim. However, Thorpe must have known that the gun was heavy and an awkward burden when carried in the upright position; to drag it 200 yards across broken, muddy ground would be a daunting task.

Without any explanation Thorpe crawled out, in daylight, toward the gun. Eventually, and having made good progress, he attracted the attention of a sniper and from that moment his fate was sealed. Watchers in the HAC trench heard a single shot and saw that Thorpe was hit. He slumped into the mud and lay still. He was severely wounded, but he lay out in no man's land all day. It was only when night cloaked the battlefield that a group of 'B' Company men slipped over the top and brought their company commander in. It was too late and George Thorpe died of his wounds. What had motivated Thorpe will never be known. He had no need to prove his courage as he had already been 'Mentioned in Despatches'. It was a wasted life and his needless death cast a pall over 'B' Company.

Perhaps he felt overshadowed by Alfred Pollard and saw a need to assert his position in the leadership stakes. Whatever it was that drove him, he now entered the world of casualty statistics and sole possession of an engraved headstone.

Pollard reassumed command of 'B' Company.

Colonel Osmond briefed AOP and confirmed that the initial attack had not been an overall success. Oppy Wood was a German strong-point and the division on the left flank had been unable to take it. There were similar difficulties on the right flank where the unattractive chemical works at Monchy were also strongly fortified. To compound the situation aerial photographs showed that the Germans were constructing fresh trenches in the open fields in front of Douai. Pollard reflected, 'If only we could have gone on, to be so near and yet so far.' Goold Walker takes up the narrative saying:

> During the night of the 23/24, 'C' and 'D' Companies, under Lieutenant RL Haine and Captain HW O'Brien respectively, moved up and took over the captured position from 'A' and 'B', 'C' Company relieving 'B' on the exposed left flank. The relief was carried out successfully, but when dawn broke a small party under 2nd Lieutenant J Newton (of 'B' Company, temporarily attached to 'D'), occupying an advanced post in a demolished trench, came under fire from enemy snipers. Lieutenant Newton and Sergeant Nicole were both killed, and the whole of their detachment became casualties.
>
> It was intended to make an attempt early on the morning of the 24th to carry the strong-point north of the railway, but this plan was rendered abortive by a general counter-attack on the part of the enemy, which was launched in something approaching mass formation against the village of Gavrelle with the evident object of recapturing the ground lost by them on the previous day. It was a determined effort, wave after wave of the enemy advancing with the greatest gallantry, led by two battalions of the Prussian Guard, but the deadly fire of our artillery in the early stages of the attack broke up the advance, which failed

> completely before the machine-gun, Lewis-gun and rifle fire from our trenches. The few Germans who came through unscathed were ready enough to put up their hands, and not a yard of ground was regained. As a counterstroke it failed signally and disastrously, though it was afterwards stated that nearly 10,000 men took part in the attack. The German casualties were estimated to be over 3,000. The position then remained unchanged until the night of the 24th when the Battalion was relieved by the 2nd Battalion, Royal Marines. It is significant to note that, after this severe fighting, each company of the HAC was reduced to about forty effectives.

1 HAC was pulled back and into reserve at the so-called 'black line' until 27 April and 'A' Company even managed to get a bath in Arras. In the absence of the Battalion the front remained static with both sides strengthening their positions. Haig opted to straighten his line and remove the bulge around the small village of Arleux, which is about 3 miles north of Gavrelle (see map on page 143). On 27 April, 1 HAC moved forward. It had been told that the division on its left was going to make another attempt to take Oppy Wood. In tandem with this assault there was first to be the routine wire cutting barrage and then 'C' Company under command of Lieutenant RL Haine was to 'bomb out' that same enemy strong-point on the railway line 'by working along the trench'. This latter phrase is obscure and difficult to place in its correct context without a trench map.

The trenches in this sector all had names with the initial letter 'F' – thus, 'Fatty', 'Faulty', 'Fable', 'Flurry', 'Fabric' et al.

The wire that protected the German line had withstood the artillery barrage. The attacking troops of 2nd Division and the 1st Battalion, Royal Marines, had not only to contend with the obstacle but also a formidable foe sheltering just behind it. These were the Prussian Guards, who were well-trained and obdurate.

AOP gave a very simplistic description of a 'C' Company exploit that morning when he wrote that 'Bill Haine[17] (Lieutenant RL Haine) charged forward under cover of the barrage, took an enemy strong-point, fifty prisoners and two machine-guns. The prisoners revealed that they were all Prussian Guards, most were recruited from Berlin University and spoke perfect English.' Pollard observed that they 'were rather a fine crowd of men.' He went onto recount how:

> Bill found one of them lying wounded in a dug-out in the strong-point. He said he was hungry, so tender-hearted William gave him a meal. Shortly afterwards, Bill and his party were forced to retire

through a strong counter-attack. Bill retook the strong-point the following morning. The wounded man was still there. He remarked naively that his compatriots were so busy keeping Bill from recapturing the position that they had not found time to give him anything to eat since their arrival. This appealed to Bill's sense of humour. He gave the fellow another meal and sent him to hospital on a stretcher.

It was not quite like that and AOP got his account out of synch with events. He would have been well advised to read the war diary of 1 HAC before he wrote *Fire-Eater.* The core of his account is correct but the context is inaccurate. In fact, the failure of the artillery to cut the wire and the slow progress of the attacking force impacted on 'C' Company, which discovered that a key point on the railway line was still in German hands and from this position the Germans were employing machine-guns that:

> … had inflicted severe casualties on the Marines. Without any hesitation, Lieutenant Haine decided to attack it and he and Lieutenant N Baines[18] led no less than three successive attempts to capture the position, but without success, and 'C' Company suffered heavily in their valiant efforts. Haine then decided that further assistance was essential, and sent back for a Stokes mortar with which to put up a barrage to cover the next assault. Meanwhile, 'D' Company, under Captain O'Brien and Lieutenant GS Barrow, had bombed up the German support trench to a point some distance north of the railway, and were in a position to afford some help to 'C' Company by engaging the obstinate strong-point from the rear with rifle fire and rifle grenades.
>
> Time was now a most important factor, and there could be no question of waiting long for Stokes mortars, heavy artillery or tanks, all or any of which would have been most useful, and so, with the slight assistance which' D' Company could give him, Lieutenant Haine attacked for a fourth time, and on this occasion carried the barricade and captured the post with several survivors[19] and two machine-guns.
>
> It was at once quite apparent why the position had given so much trouble, as it proved to be a very strongly defended post, capable of holding more than 100 men and several machine-guns. With the small force Haine had at his disposal, it was quite impossible for him to hold on to the position, and a strong counter-attack by the Huns from the direction of Oppy Wood forced the remains of 'C' Company to retire once more south of the railway line. Corporal I Young showed great gallantry and skill in covering this retreat with Lewis gunfire.[20]

Both sides had recognized the importance of this strong-point (see map on this page), which was the key to the whole position. Having retaken the post the Germans were able to use it as a base from which to launch flank attacks using the cover provided by the trenches that ran south from it. If these attacks were successful the Germans would be able to isolate the village of Gavrelle and overwhelm the small group of British soldiers holding it.

The Prussian Guards, 'fine crowd of men' although they might have been, were doughty opponents and they now followed up their success in regaining the strong-point by launching a series of attacks on 1 HAC, on 'C' Company in particular, that continued throughout the remainder of the day. The two sides were so closely engaged that neither could call for supporting artillery support. The salvation of 1 HAC was the Lewis gun and well disciplined and effective rifle fire. Supporting fire was provided by machine-guns of other RND units. It was a savage close quarter business and the regimental history records with justifiable pride:

> The rifle and Lewis gunfire of the Battalion was magnificent, and there was at least one case of a wounded man, unable to fire himself, sitting on

Trenches at Gavrelle, 28–29 April 1917.
J Colquhoun, (*HAC Journal*, spring 2007)

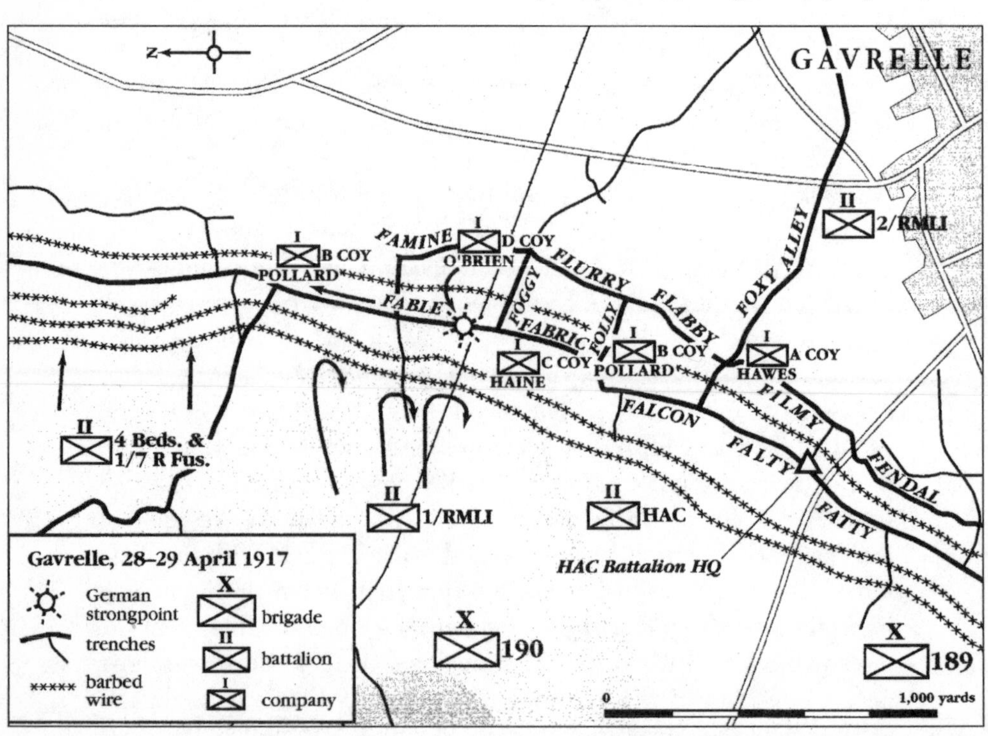

the fire-step recharging rifles with ten more rounds ready to pass up to his friend. Seven definite attacks were driven off in this way, and at the end of the day the Battalion had not lost a yard of trench.

Darkness fell and although the intensity of the fighting slowed, harassing fire and the use of grenades by both sides ensured that no one in 'C' Company slept. It was the foil to German plans and the Company had bourne the brunt of the fighting for thirty hours. Food was brought up by the CQMS, wounded were evacuated and where possible the dead were moved to a temporary rest place. Ammunition was replenished, weapons cleaned and preparations made for the bloody day that would soon follow.

All this time 'B' Company was in reserve and in support of 1RMLI. As he did not anticipate being called on, Pollard did what a soldier should always do given the chance. AOP cheerfully recalled that, knowing the fight was not his, he made himself comfortable, and slept.

The night wore on and Haine did not sleep. He was still only twenty years of age and clearly a very special young man. He had already shown exceptional powers of leadership and soon after dawn he underscored that quality when he gathered the remnants of 'C' Company around him. He spoke to his soldiers and tried to imbue in them his determination and the absolute conviction that the strong-point could and must be taken. It is extraordinary that even after the casualties inflicted on 'C' Company, it was not defeated.

On the young officer's signal 'C' Company, now barely at platoon strength, climbed out of their trench and stormed across the bullet-swept gap of torn earth that separated them from the enemy. The speed of this final attack overwhelmed the Prussians. Those who were not shot dead, or bombed, surrendered – fifty of them together with two more of their lethal machine-guns. Pollard had been correct in part, but it was the sixth assault.

Haine's amazing personal courage and his leadership over a protracted period, whilst bearing responsibility far beyond that expected of a very junior officer, was recognized by Lieutenant Colonel Osmond, who reported it in glowing terms. In due course, Haine was awarded the Victoria Cross. Never was the decoration more richly deserved. The entry in the *London Gazette*[21] read:

> Reginald Leonard Haine, Second Lieutenant, Honourable Artillery Company. For most conspicuous bravery and determination when our troops, occupying a pronounced salient, were repeatedly counter-attacked. There was an ever-present danger that, if the enemy attack succeeded, the garrison of the salient would be surrounded. Second Lieut. Haine organized and led with the utmost gallantry six bombing attacks against a strong-point which dangerously threatened our communications, capturing the position, together with fifty prisoners

and two machine-guns. The enemy then counter-attacked with a battalion of the Guard, succeeded in regaining his position, and the situation appeared critical. Second Lieut. Haine at once formed a block in his trench, and for the whole of the following night maintained his position against determined attacks. Reorganizing his men on the following morning, he again attacked and captured the strong-point, pressing the enemy back for several hundred yards, and thus relieving the situation. Throughout these operations the officer's superb courage, quick decision, and sound judgment were beyond praise, and it was his splendid personal example which inspired his men to continue their efforts during more than thirty hours of continuous fighting.

Notes

1 War diary, 1st Bn HAC, 25 February 1917.
2 FM Viscount Montgomery, *A History of Warfare*, quoted in *The Greenhill Dictionary of Military Quotations*, p104.
3 AO Pollard, *Fire-Eater*, p196.
4 Pollard made no mention either of artillery support nor did he claim to have taken the defended Gudgeon trench, 700 yards away and up a slope. Someone's memory is at fault. Pollard was there – Goold Walker was not, but the latter did have access to the war diaries. Goold Walker recorded that a Lieutenant N Baines was awarded a Military Cross for his conduct in the operations at Gudgeon Trench. This officer was not of 'B' Company.
5 It is a small point, but Pollard specifically mentioned Nissen huts.
6 'Miking' was slang for shirking.
7 Vimy Ridge was a formidable German position taken by the Canadian Corps in a three-day battle over 9-12 April 1917. They suffered 10,602 casualties in the process. The battle of Vimy Ridge is central to Canada's sense of nationhood and in that respect the battle has significance far greater than the tactical success achieved.
8 The A& HAC was founded in 1637 by Robert Keayne, a member of the HAC, and since that date the two Companies have enjoyed close and fraternal links.
9 James Colquhoun, *Two VCs*, published in the *HAC Journal, Spring 2007.*
10 It is to ES Simons that this book is dedicated. See Appendix 2.
11 Permanent.
12 George Robert Thorpe enlisted in the HAC on 21 September 1914 and was commissioned on 21 July 1915.
13 Lance Corporal Carl Larssen – Nils was later killed in action, on 19 April 1917, at Oppy Wood.
14 An indication of just how formidable these wire barriers were.
15 The *London Gazette,* 18 June 1917.
16 G Goold Walker, *The Honourable Artillery Company in the Great War 1914-1919*, p88.
17 Haine's Christian names were Reginald Laine. Nevertheless, Pollard and most others referred to him as 'Bill'.
18 Noel Baines had enlisted at Armoury House on the same day as Alfred Pollard. He won the MC.
19 No mention here of fifty prisoners.
20 G Goold Walker, *The Honourable Artillery Company in the Great War 1914-1919*, p90.
21 The *London Gazette*, 8 June 1917.

Chapter 11

The Second Victoria Cross and a Lady's Hand

'With only four men he started a counter-attack with bombs and pressed it home till he had broken the enemy attack...'

April 1917

It was now the turn of Pollard and 'B' Company. He led his men as they passed through the 'C' Company position, leaving Haine to consolidate the strong-point, reposition the German machine-guns and thereafter, perhaps, make a swift brew.

AOP pushed ahead and occupied a trench a short distance ahead. There was no doubt in anyone's mind – a counter-attack would be coming in at any moment. The most likely axis of that attack would be under cover of one of the recently vacated German trenches.

Pollard gave instructions to his second-in-command, Ernest Samuel, to deploy the Company into a series of shell holes that ran diagonally across the trench. Pollard was now able to present a wider front and bring to bear more weapons on the line of any German advance.

AOP, accompanied by Lance Corporal Hughesdon, who had no choice in the matter, and Lance Corporal Scharlach, who did, moved cautiously down the trench toward the enemy. It was ominously empty, save for the dead. Pollard was aware that of a lull in the fighting, there was a marked absence of shell and small arms fire. It seemed to be the still in the eye of the storm. The sun shone; there was quiet, and a curious feeling of peace. Although 'peace' was not quite what Pollard had in mind.

He said that he could see the Royal Marines on their objective and the unit on the left of 'B' Company had reached a trench line that was not quite contiguous with that of the Marines. Pollard pressed on to the end of the trench when artillery fire started to rain down on Oppy Wood. The bombardment was furious for several minutes and directed at a target about a mile from where Pollard was observing. Suddenly and inexplicably, without having been the object of the artillery strikes, the troops between Pollard and Oppy Wood left their trenches and started to stream to the rear and by so doing giving up the ground so dearly won the day before. This sort of panic is contagious and desperately dangerous. This was a critical time. It was evident to the enemy that they had no immediate opposition and could now roll up the British position from the left. Pollard wrote that the fleeing troops had an effect on him:

> I felt my knees knocking together under me. I was obliged to clutch at the parapet to prevent myself from falling. Then the thought fired my brain that with all the troops having cleared out between me and the enemy, in a few minutes my own company would be assailed, and if we failed to stem the victorious torrent of Huns, the whole of the left of our division would crumple up like a leaf. How long I remained there shaking I cannot say. It seemed like minutes; actually it could not have been more than a few seconds.
>
> Then the curious feeling came to me which I have described before, that I was no longer acting under my own volition. Something outside me, greater than I, seemed to take charge of me. Acting under this mysterious influence I ran forward.
>
> Already officers of the terrorized troops were attempting to rally them. I found a handful who were still in possession of their senses. I arranged as many as I encountered in shell-holes to right and left of the trench and ordered them to fire their rifles. I did not care a damn whether or not they hit anything. There is nothing so soothing to the nerves as to be doing something. My antidote to their panic was to make them shoot. Encouraged by the example of the few I had rallied, others joined them. Soon I had a moderate force spread out in an arc. They were steady now and I had no further fear of a fresh withdrawal. The British Tommy does not do that sort of thing twice in a morning.
>
> With the defence organized and the knowledge that my own stalwart company was in support to back them up, I turned my attention to finding out how far the Hun attack had been successful. The bombing had now ceased, from which I inferred that Fritz had overcome the resistance in his path.
>
> Two of my own men had followed me down the trench. My runner, Reggie Hughesdon, as in duty bound, and Lance Corporal Scharlach. Why he had accompanied me I do not know to this day. At the time I did not stop to enquire. I was only too thankful to have two men on whom I could rely implicitly. Both were trained bombers.
>
> My instructions to them before I started were very simple. Each had a Mills bomb in his hand with the safety pin out. I told them that if I

fired my pistol they were to throw their bombs immediately to pitch about 15 yards in front of me. This would land them in the next traverse in front of where we were. They only had two bombs each and at the time, I gave no thought as to where we might find a further supply.

These preparations only took a few seconds and we were on the move almost at once. The trench was quite empty and we were able to move forward fairly rapidly. Round traverse after traverse we dodged, I with my revolver held ready for instant action. In the first 100 yards we encountered nobody. We were now well in advance of all British troops, and the noise of my improvised defence was receding in the distance. I could hear them still firing, but only one of them had followed me. He was a private in one of the battalions of the Royal Fusiliers, and he made the fourth member of my little army.

We covered another 100 yards without resistance.

Then suddenly, as I entered one end of a stretch of trench between two traverses, a big Hun entered the other, rifle and bayonet in his hand. I fired; he dropped his rifle and clapped both his hands to his stomach. Almost instantaneously with my shot I heard the whizz of Reggie's bomb as it passed over my head. A second man appeared behind the first; I fired again and he dropped like a stone.

Bang! Bang! The two bombs thrown by my followers exploded one after the other. The third man saw the fate of his two predecessors and turned to go back. Those behind, not knowing what had happened, tried to come forward. I fired again. Bang! Zunk! went the remaining bombs of our small store. That was enough. The next instant the Hun attack was in full retreat.

We followed as fast as we could. Discretion had gone to the winds or I should have realized the utter foolishness of running as fast as I could into the enemy's territory with only three men to support me. But my blood was up. I felt a thrill only comparable to running through the opposition at rugger to score a try.

In and out we went round traverse after traverse.

Every now and again I caught a glimpse of field grey disappearing round the corner ahead. Twice I fired, but I was running too hard to take careful aim. At last I came to a place where a shell had blown the parapet right across the trench, forming a natural barricade. My brain told me we had come far enough. I stopped.

Knowing the Hun's little ways I expected to be counter-attacked as soon as he had rallied his troops. I at once started putting my strong-point in a condition of defence. The fusilier knew nothing of bombs so I stationed him on the look-out beside the barricade. We furnished him with seven rifles, some Hun and some British, all fully loaded. Even then, I could not help thinking of Robinson Crusoe's similar preparations.

The rest of us collected all the bombs we could find.

Fortunately the trench was well provided, though, of course, all the bombs were German. Strange though it may seem I was glad of this. One can throw a German bomb farther than a British.

The reason for this is quite a simple one. The Hun bomb is a canister full of high explosive on the end of a short stick … it weighs one pound. The Mills bomb on the other hand is designed to do considerable damage when it bursts. It consists of a serrated cast-iron body filled with two and a half ounces of ammonal. It weighs a pound and a half. One can throw a pound weight with a stick to act as a lever very much farther than one can throw a pound and a half of dead weight. Certainly the Mills bomb is a much superior weapon when it happens to explode in a trench, but in the excitement of a bombing attack the vast majority fall on the top or outside the parapet. The greater noise of the Hun canister when exploding has a far greater effect in the long run than the few more dangerous Mills bombs which fall on their objective.

It was less than ten minutes before the Huns returned. When they came they were determined to retrieve the ground they had lost. I could tell that by the vigour of their attack. Right from the first, bombs fell thick and fast. We three replied with as good as we received.

I threw off my tin hat to give my arms better play for throwing. Next went my gas mask. Bang! Bang! Bang! Bang! The air was thick with bombs going and coming. Those that fell in the trench we flung over the parapet before they had time to explode. My two companions were magnificent. Our fusilier friend protected our front. Reggie suddenly drew my attention to our fast failing supply of missiles. 'Hadn't we better retire?' he suggested.

'I'm not going back one foot, Reggie,' I cried. 'If we run out of bombs, we'll keep them out with rifles.'

Fortunately we did not have to resort to such a desperate measure. The Hun attack ceased as suddenly as it had started. We were still undefeated, but we only had six bombs left. If Fritz had only known. For that matter if he had known we were only four he would have undoubtedly rushed us over the top. That was the tremendous luck of the whole affair. He did not know. He failed to take a chance. His failure cost him the position.

Not that I thought he had given up trying. Our respite was only a breathing space. We employed it in going back along the trench and collecting more ammunition. We were once more ready for him when a welcome face appeared round the traverse behind us.

'Hallo, Alf!' cried Sammy. 'I thought I had better bring the Company along to lend you a hand.'

'Have you brought any bombs?' I asked quickly.

Sammy laughed. 'As many as we could carry,' he chuckled. 'I knew you would want them.' Good old Sammy! His cool brain never failed in an emergency. He is one of the finest fellows I have ever known. He hated war, mud, discomfort, but he served throughout the whole campaign with the greatest cheerfulness, always ready to carry out his orders to the letter. If his ancestors amongst the fighting tribes of Israel[1] were able to watch their child conduct himself during the greatest conflict the world has ever known they must have rattled their ghostly spears in pride of their worthy descendant.

I quickly made my dispositions. I placed Lewis guns in shell-holes 50 yards on either side of the trench with instructions to fire ahead of us across the trench. Scharlach was provided with rifle grenades which would fire about 60 yards ahead. I arranged another corporal with another type of rifle-grenade to drop about 120 yards ahead. Reggie and I would throw hand grenades.

We had not very long to wait for the second attack but it only lasted about five minutes. The rifle grenades bothered the Hun line of communications and the Lewis guns prevented them from getting out over the top. They soon had enough of us.

I left Sammy in charge of the strong-point and went back to rally the battalions who should have been occupying the position. When I was assured that their temper was now sufficiently strong for them to be left I handed over the position to them and withdrew my Company to their former trench.

The Brigadier sent me a telegram during the day, placing me in command of the trench and bidding any officers concerned to carry out my orders. I sent out patrols to occupy shell-holes some 200 yards in front of the position and generally made the position quite secure. But Fritz left us severely alone.

The three men with me were given Distinguished Conduct Medals.[2] Unfortunately the Fusilier was killed by a shell on the following day so his was awarded posthumously.

It is unfortunate that Pollard did not name that gallant fusilier who had shared in his exploit. The fact is he had either forgotten it or did not bother to look it up. It was Corporal John McCarthy,[3] of 13th Battalion, Royal Fusiliers, and he was awarded an MM, not the DCM he so richly deserved.

There was another member of the Royal Fusiliers who played an important part and whilst AOP had been bombing his way north, 2nd Lieutenant SF Jeffcote of 22nd Battalion, Royal Fusiliers 'performed a magnificent feat dividing his little party into two, one to work north and one – under his personal command southward. Lieutenant Jeffcote bombed his way down some 400 yards south of the divisional position until he came in touch with men of 4 Bedfordshires and 1 HAC of the 63rd Division …'[4]

Jeffcote sent a message to his CO and asked for reinforcement and a company of 23rd Battalion made its way forward into the Oppy line by the railway. Jeffcote briefed the commander of the incoming company, but was then mortally wounded and died the following day. Jeffcote's gallantry and tactical sense were key factors in the successes of the day but sadly, and unlike Alfred Pollard, he gained scant recognition. Pollard's account is much more stirring than that in the regimental history that summarized the event in much more prosaic and precise terms, as follows:

> A counter-attack down the trench was expected at any time, so Pollard, with a handful of men and some bombs, placed himself at a point nearest the enemy. In due course the attack started, the Germans bombing their way down the trench towards Pollard and his few men. But they were up against a strong proposition. Pollard was an excellent bomber, and before the attackers got within range of him he was able to reach them with his Mills bombs. Thus he held up the attack with such success that the Huns actually retreated back a traverse or two to get out of range of his deadly accurate throwing.
>
> Pollard at once seized this opportunity to advance, and once he started he never stopped. Bombs were passed up to him and carried by his thrice stalwart supporters, and by this means he cleared no less than 300 yards of trench. As he advanced he collected what men he could to man the trench he was capturing, including men from the units of the division on our left, while 'A' Company and 'D' Company spread out to occupy the increased front. Thus Pollard achieved the remarkable feat of capturing and holding a system of trenches which had held up a whole brigade assaulting from the front.
>
> When the Battalion was relieved by an East Yorks battalion of the 31st Division on the night of the 29th, it handed over to the incoming

battalion over 2,000 yards of trench, which was being held with about 120 men, the survivors of the desperate fighting of the past 48 hours.

When Pollard and his company trudged out of the line to St. Nicholas,[5] a small village outside Arras, it was mentally and physically exhausted. Pollard still had adrenaline coursing through his blood and he had several whiskies in the mess tent before he stripped off all his clothes. His servant had made up his bed but his pyjamas were not to be seen. Naked as the day he was born he lay down and covered himself in his blankets. However many men he had killed that day certainly did not cause him any undue concern. The Scotch probably helped and he slept soundly.

The following day, 30 April 1917, got off to an unusual start when the second-in–command of 1 HAC burst into his tent at 1000hrs and shook the somnambulant Pollard into wakefulness.[6] 'Get up Pollard,' Major Bun Morphy ordered, in his Irish brogue, 'the Divisional Commander wants to see you – right now!'

Pollard demurred, pointing out that he was stark naked and in no condition to entertain generals. He said that when he had found his pyjamas he would attend on the general at once. The debate with Morphy was in full swing when Major General Lawrie[7] resolved the issue by appearing at Pollard's tent flap. He was accompanied by his GSO1, Lieutenant Colonel Aspinall.[8]

Pollard had something of a dilemma – how does one acknowledge a general when one is naked. Morphy said apologetically, 'This is Pollard, sor.' Pollard hugged the blankets to his chin. Colonel Aspinall fitted his monocle to his eye and Pollard recorded that 'The General held out his hand and said, "I'm proud to meet you Pollard. I've been hearing about what you and Haine did yesterday and I want to tell you that I am recommending both of you for the Victoria Cross."'

Pollard, who said that he always stammered in moments of great excitement, took a moment to collect himself. He replied, 'Er, er, it's most awfully g, g, good of you, bu, bu, but I'm frightfully so, so sorry I can't stand up, sir. As a mat, matter of fact I couldn't find my pyjamas last night and er .... Major General Lawrie was a very tactful man. He appreciated my embarrassment. "I quite understand," he interposed. "You've not had time to dress. Have a bath and we'll chat later." He turned to leave the tent. Colonel Aspinall's eye glass dropped with a faint click. I felt he was smiling. I was alone with my thoughts. 'The VC!'

The Battalion, or what was left of it, had marched back to the tented camp at Roclincourt. Here the men licked their wounds and buried their dead. They were visited on 1 May by the Commander of XIII Corps, Sir Walter Congreve

VC KCB MVO. He congratulated the 1st Battalion warmly upon its exemplary performance during the recent operations. When he spoke to the Battalion, he had this to say:

> The fighting recently has been very severe, and, sitting behind as I have to do, I admit that at times on the 28th April I was anxious as it appeared that our position might possibly be worse than it was in the beginning.
>
> Then word came through that the Honourable Artillery Company were bombing up the Hun trench to their north, and afterwards that the Honourable Artillery Company had driven the enemy out of his front line. This was a very great relief to me.
>
> Nobody hates the Boche more than I do, but I admire him as a very fine soldier. You had against you the finest troops of the German Army - the Prussian Guard and you beat him.
>
> That is enough.
>
> Your regiment has a very fine record in history, and you have indeed added a page which is worthy of any previous page in that history.
>
> We have a long way to go before the Boche is beaten, and the only way to do it is to go on training and making yourselves ever better than you are, and passing on the knowledge you have gained to those who come out.[9]
>
> To thank you and congratulate you, and to tell you how proud I am of you, is what I have come here for today.

General Congreve's words were much to the liking of the Battalion, which spent a little over a week at Roclincourt enjoying early summer sunshine. It was employed on routine fatigues of a completely non-hazardous nature. The HAC was much visited during this period. One of the visitors was the Commander, 63rd RND, General Lawrie.

The Battle of Arras had cost the HAC two officers and forty-two men killed and five officers and 130 men wounded. These 179 represented about 44% of the strength of the Battalion at the time. The ferocity of the fighting can be measured by the daily casualty rate. The arithmetic is shocking. The Somme cost 2,943, 3rd Ypres 2,323 and the final offensive in 1918, 3,645.[10] The battle of Arras cost 4,076 casualties per day until its cessation on 17 May 1917. The battle had been hugely expensive in human terms and although the British Army had advanced 7 miles at the furthest point on a front of 20 miles it had, nevertheless, failed to break through the Hindenburg defence system. The only tangible gain was the village of Arleux.

It was by now an open secret that both Haine and Pollard had been nominated for the VC and, given the laudatory words coming from the officers who would have to endorse Osmond's citations, the prospects looked to be extremely rosy. In passing, there cannot be many generals who have the pleasure of endorsing the nomination of two of his subordinates for this decoration.[11]

After the parade for General Lawrie it was 'a joyous company' that returned to the mess. Mutual congratulations were offered all round, although Haine and Pollard came in for the lion's share. The General, who was clearly 'on side', stayed for lunch and in the course of the meal he unbent more than a little and enjoyed himself in the company of the survivors of the recent battle. They, in turn, basked in the mild euphoria of just being alive.

On 4 May, it was to be AOP's twenty-fourth birthday. Egged on by his mess mates, he was encouraged to ask General Lawrie if he would agree to the band of the Royal Marines coming to play on that afternoon. It was 'with the run of the play' and given the GOC's sunny demeanour it was no surprise when the request was readily agreed. Accordingly, three days later, the highly professional band from Chatham arrived and entertained, not just the officers, but anyone in earshot. The band had a full diary of engagements and was due to play that evening in the Divisional Headquarters Mess. Throughout the afternoon the band was plied with both grape and grain and unfortunately, so too was their driver.

The band left in reasonable order but the excesses of the afternoon told on the driver and he drove his bus and the band into a ditch in the middle of nowhere.

The band did not appear at the Divisional Mess that evening. History does not tell us of the fate of the driver but the probability is that his advancement to lance corporal was somewhat delayed.

It got worse because Pollard, having heard of the debacle, wrote a thank you letter. In the circumstances he decided that it might be better addressed to the GSO1 and not the GOC. Colonel Aspinall was a busy and important man in the military firmament. Alfred Pollard dropped his simple note of thanks into the orderly room post box and thought no more of it. Once the note was in the system it was given a degree of priority the content did not deserve. 'A bright spark at Brigade headquarters fished it out of the usual post bag and despatched it by special runner.' It was 0200hrs when the runner arrived at his destination and they woke Colonel Aspinall to deliver it. This was the same Colonel Aspinall who had not had the benefit of a band in his mess a couple of days before.

Fortunately for Pollard it was his turn for leave and on his return to the UK, his life underwent a dramatic turn. The particular event that made this leave special as well as being different from all others, was that he broke his promise to his Lady. He explained in the most disarming and honest way how he felt about her:

> How it came about I cannot say. Thinking it over since, I have decided that the impulse that moved me must have been a sudden overflow of pent-up emotion. For more than a year I had been harbouring a passion that possessed my whole being. Possibly because I had had very little opportunity of mixing with the opposite sex in the meantime the pedestal I had erected in my heart had reached abnormal proportions. The excitement of leave, the expectation of receiving the highest honour I could attain, the reputation I had earned as a fighter, the knowledge that I stood high in the regard of my comrades in the Battalion all had their part in carrying me away.
>
> She and her two sisters were staying in my mother's house. I was due to return to France in a couple of days. It was late at night. Most of the party had gone to bed. Somehow 'She' and I were left alone together. Something welled up within me. I took her in my arms. In a rush of half coherent phrases I told her how much I loved her, how badly I wanted her, that I couldn't live without her.
>
> She was bewildered by the suddenness of my attack.
>
> Even so she did not repulse me. Neither did she embrace me. She suggested quite sensibly that we had better sleep the night on it and talk it over quietly in the morning.
>
> Morning came at last. After breakfast we went for a country walk. There was ample opportunity for discussion. I expounded the simple fact that I had never loved anyone in my life but Her. She, for her part, declared quite frankly that she did not love me or anyone else for that matter; that she really had not had any intention whatever of getting married, but that she would think it over very carefully and let me know her decision.
>
> She told me she liked me as much as any man she knew, that she trusted me, and that as I loved her as much as I did, it hardly seemed fair to disappoint me. No doubt if we did marry, she would learn to love me afterwards.
>
> We kissed once.
>
> The following day I went back to France.

It is evident from this entry that AOP and his intended did not have much in the way of sexual chemistry. 'We kissed once' is a sad little phrase and it makes clear that ardour, passion, affection and love were not on the menu.

Certainly not love.

This tough, athletic and courageous young man had been 'worshipping', and that is not too strong a word, worshipping this young woman for years. His immature and unbalanced emotions had been, hitherto, anathema to the object of his worship. Nevertheless, she now agreed to consider marrying Alfred. This is, in itself, an extraordinary decision and in her way, she was just as unbalanced as he was.

This was not a sound basis for selecting a mixed foursome's partner for the summer knockout at the golf club, let alone a partner for life. If ever there was a recipe for a failed marriage and great unhappiness they are all there in the passage from *Fire-Eater,* quoted above.

When AOP returned to 1 HAC he found that 63rd Division was still resting and there was no immediate prospect of returning to the line. The endless round of fatigues had to be satisfied, although the officers were not involved in any sort of drudgery that involved humping and dumping. Roclincourt is just outside Arras, and there 6th Corps had established an officers' club. This facility attracted the attention of the officers of 1 HAC who, though they were members of XIII Corps, still made good use of the club, and the bar in particular. Pollard was in a fever of impatience. 'I had two things on my mind. Would I receive a VC? What would be Her decision? I speculated for hours on both.'

The Battalion was paraded on 6 June 1917 and after all the normal preliminaries conducted by the RSM the officers took post and the AA & QMG[12] of 63rd RND, Lieutenant Colonel Foster, announced the award of the VC to Lieutenants Alfred Pollard and Reginald Haine – the first two VCs the Regiment had ever been awarded.

It was a momentous day.

The whole Battalion rejoiced as did the members of the HAC serving elsewhere in the world. At the major party that followed most of the Brigade and Divisional staff attended. Goold Walker commented dryly that 'It was a source of intense gratification to members of the Company to find that their comrades in the Brigade seemed almost as pleased as if their own units had received the honours.' Goold Walker's comment was the only 'dry' thing about that day and judging by the biblical amount that was drunk, his phrase 'intense gratification' was entirely apt.

It seems that amply pre-warned, the Mess Secretary had been into Arras and AOP said, 'He bought up every drink he could lay hands on. The result was a glorious binge. Everyone got tight from the Commanding Officer downwards. It was a most thorough business.'

Pollard's citation was published, two days later, in the *London Gazette*.[13] It read as follows:

> *Alfred Oliver Pollard,* MC,[14] *Second Lieut., Honourable Artillery Company. For most conspicuous bravery and determination. The troops of various units on the left of this officer's battalion had become disorganized owing to the heavy casualties from shell fire: and a subsequent determined enemy attack with very strong force caused further confusion and retirement, closely pressed by hostile forces. Second Lieut. Pollard at once realized the seriousness of the situation and dashed up to stop the retirement. With only four men he started a counter-attack with bombs and pressed it home till he had broken the enemy attack and regained all that had been lost and much ground in addition. The enemy retired in disorder, sustaining many casualties. By his force of will, dash and splendid example, coupled with an utter contempt of danger, this officer, who has already won the DCM and MC, infused courage into every man who saw him.*

Pollard enjoyed the party, savoured the 'respect' that was accorded him and developed a personal relationship with 'Bill' Haine. He savoured his success and said that:

> A few days later I received my other answer.
>
> She would marry me.
>
> We were engaged.
>
> I had the VC and now I was engaged to the most glorious girl in the world. Did ever a man's cup of happiness brim fuller? I did not think so then.

This was probably the high spot of Pollard's life. He sought nothing else and as it happens, during the rest of his life there was no single day that ever matched this one.

Lord Denbigh wrote to the Captain-General to tell him of the awards and in reply the Personal Secretary to King George V replied saying, 'His Majesty was immensely gratified at reading of the way in which the Regiment had been adding to its already glorious records and considers that all ranks may well be proud of what they have achieved and will continue through the splendid fighting spirit that animates them …'

The War Office, in its characteristic fashion, did not allow Captain, acting Lieutenant Colonel CF Osmond very much time to savour the victory that had been achieved by the Battalion under his command. The much loved 'Ossy' was replaced by Major (soon to be Lieutenant Colonel) PC Cooper, who arrived from 2nd Battalion to take over command on 4 May 1917. Some small compensation was the DSO awarded to Osmond – an award that found favour with every member of the Company. Nevertheless, it was not a happy period and Colonel Cooper must have found it difficult. AOP commented as follows:

> But although I myself was as happy as the day was long a cloud had settled on the Battalion. 'Ossy' was superseded by an officer sent out from home, Lieutenant Colonel PC Cooper. It was a most unfortunate happening.
>
> Looking at the whole affair with an impartial mind from the distance of time, I do not see how any blame can be attached to PC. He was merely a very senior officer who, although he crossed the water with us in 1914, was invalided home before we got into action and was kept at home right up to May 1917. That he was senior to our beloved 'Ossy' was a matter of chance and the fault of the system which insists on promotion in time of war by seniority instead of by merit. Not that I am questioning PC's merit. He was very capable in some directions. No one can judge of his ability in the line. He was never in it when an action was in progress and only for a short time in ordinary trench routine.
>
> His fault was that he arrived to supersede 'Ossy'. Had he been any other man, with the single exception of Colonel Treffry, the result would have been the same. We wanted 'Ossy' and we were not prepared to transfer our loyalty. Nevertheless in spite of all our fuming, 'Ossy' went down to Major; Bun Morphy returned to the command of 'C' Company and PC took control.
>
> Bill and I went on leave shortly afterwards. That I went was a miracle, or shall I more truthfully write, a wangle. I had only been back from my other leave three weeks. But the authorities decided that as Bill would probably receive his decoration I ought to be with him. I was in the seventh heaven. I was going to see my fiancée so much sooner than I had anticipated. We had so much to say to one another: so many plans to make: a ring to buy.
>
> Life was marvellous.

Notes

1 Pollard's remarks about Lieutenant Ernest Samuel are bordering on patronising and they seem to be out of kilter with the rest of his narrative. It was not necessary to point out that Samuel was Jewish and if the reference was intended to demonstrate Pollard's lack of anti-Semitism it had the effect of begging the question.

2 This is not the case. Lance Corporal Scharlach was awarded the MM. Hughesdon, who already had an MM, now received the DCM.

3 McCarthy was born in Bromley and enlisted at Hounslow. He was listed as 'killed in action', 28 April 1917.

4 HMSO, *Official History World War I.*

5 The regimental history identifies the location as Roclincourt, the two places are only two miles apart and the names are probably interchangeable in this context.
6 AO Pollard, *Fire-Eater*, p19.
7 Major General C Lawrie took over command of 63rd Division from General Shute on 19 February 1917.
8 General Staff Officer Grade 1. He was the senior member of the GOC's staff and the officer responsible for the planning of operations. In the twenty-first century the GSO1 would be designated 'Chief of Staff'.
9 This was either a prescient remark or the General already knew what the War Office had in mind for the HAC.
10 Statistics are taken from *Two VCs*, by James Colquhoun and published in the *HAC Journal 2007*.
11 Major General CF Townshend CB DSO, during the campaign in Mesopotamia in 1915-1916, was an exception. However, despite his best efforts, he only ever obtained DSOs for his officers.
12 The Assistant Adjutant and Quarter Master General. This is the title of the staff officer responsible for 'A' or personnel and administrative matters (including the award of medals), usually a Lieutenant Colonel. The 'QMG' element of his title indicates his additional responsibility for the logistic support of the Division i.e. 'Q' matters.
13 The *London Gazette*, 8 June 1917.
14 The *London Gazette* is the acme of accuracy but on this occasion it ignored Pollard's post nominal DCM although it made mention of it in the text.

Chapter 12

London and Marriage

'Any part of their uniform that could be polished had been.
Boots and shoes gleamed – and everyone had had a haircut.'

July 1917–June 1918

Haine and Pollard were sent to London and whilst there, had the time of their lives. They were now well known personalities. Darlings of the popular press, wherever they went they were feted. Invitations poured in and they could have eaten three lunches and three dinners every day of the week. If they went to the theatre, at the interval there was a queue of people anxious to buy their drinks. It was heady wine for two young men in their early twenties. AOP recorded that, 'It was much better fun being two than one. One by himself might have felt shy or overwhelmed. With two it was possible to exchange notes and share jests unknown to the others. There was also a psychological effect in having some support. If your heads were to be turned they would have been turned then.' They much favoured the Piccadilly Hotel and lunched there frequently. When they arrived, 'The Head Waiter would unctuously escort us past the inevitable queue to a table in the centre of the room. Everyone paid us homage. There would undoubtedly have been an excuse had we assumed we were some sort of superior beings. Fortunately we were both sufficiently level-headed to appraise the plaudits of the mob at their true worth.'

The Pollard family had obviously responded to the engagement and invited the Lady to stay. This allowed the young couple to spend every spare moment together. Pollard was enormously proud of his 'catch' and enjoyed showing her off. It was now time for a ring to seal the engagement and on one shopping expedition, 'She chose a black pearl set in diamonds on a platinum ring.'

The usual period for leave was a fortnight but the two heroes were warned that they were to be invested with their Crosses on 21 July 1917 at Buckingham Palace. The effect of the warning was to extend their leave for a total of a month.

This was bonus and they decided to spend some time at a seaside resort and settled on Sandown, on the Isle of Wight. There was no question of AOP and his Lady going by themselves. This was 1917 and the conventions of the day did not permit well brought up young men and women to stay in the same hotel, unaccompanied. This had to be a team event and accordingly the party was made up with the Lady, AOP's youngest sister, Amy, who was now twenty-six, Bill Haine and Pollard.

The group stayed at the Sandown Hotel and spent their days boating and bathing. The evenings were filled with concerts and walks after a good dinner. The war was another world and the peace of tranquil summer evenings a balm to the souls of Haine and Pollard. All, however, was not sweetness and light and what followed is best described in Pollard's painfully honest fashion:

> All the same an incident occurred which should have warned both My Lady and I how totally unsuited we were in temperament. One evening, after dinner, we had walked rather further than usual. My Lady was a trifle tired, and to save her as much as possible I suggested attempting a short cut across some fields to where we could see the hotel in the distance. She hesitated for a moment, asking me if I were sure we could get through. Without in the least knowing the country I was positive we could. We nearly did but within a quarter of a mile of our objective, we encountered a 30-foot drainage dyke.
>
> Here was the devil to pay. To go back meant a detour of nearly 3 miles. To go forward without wading was impossible. She was furious. Over-tired, she accused me of not taking proper care of her. I ought not to have taken that way unless I was sure we could pass. I was thoughtless, inconsiderate and neglectful. For my part I could not see what there was to make a fuss about. To me, a short-cut across country was an adventure. Even had she not been tired I should probably have suggested trying it as a matter of course. It was unfortunate that we had met such an obstacle but it was not insurmountable. I would willingly wade through with her in my arms.
>
> I was bewildered by her point of view: she utterly failed to understand mine. Both of us were right according to our temperaments. It was against her nature to take a step in the dark. I almost invariably acted on impulse. In the end we went back the way we had come and round by the road. We walked in silence. The following day I apologized and was forgiven and we resumed our companionship.
>
> Had I been gifted with the power to see into the future I should have broken off the engagement then and there. No happiness can result when two strong natures are hopelessly incompatible. But I was madly, desperately in love. That was why I gave in and apologized instead of

insisting that in following my instinct I was equally in the right with her. She had the advantage in that she was not in love with me, therefore she did not experience that supreme desire to save the one she loved from even a momentary unhappiness.

I gave in then and I gave in many times afterwards but it was from strength rather than weakness. I hated her to be distressed.

It would all come right when we were married. That was the slogan with which I consoled myself. In the meantime I was on leave. When I went back to France I might never return. Live for today: let tomorrow take care of itself. We all enjoyed that holiday. The weather was perfect.

Poor Pollard; it had taken time but slowly the blinkers were falling from his eyes. He was a decisive man, capable of taking life threatening decisions quickly and accurately. In this domestic setting he was the reverse and utterly 'wet'. To his credit, and with the wisdom provided by hindsight, he realized that. In due course he would pay a high price. It should be borne in mind that Pollard was writing years after the event but was still able to recall the detail and put it into the context of the day. He had no need to share the distress of his relationship with the Lady to a wide public – perhaps at the time of writing it was cathartic.

The investiture was arranged solely for the presentation of the Victoria Cross, twenty-four of them. Only eighteen of the recipients were present because six of the Crosses were awarded posthumously and would be given to a mother, wife or brother. For the eighteen it was a daunting experience. Uniforms had been pressed and pressed again. Any part of their uniform that could be polished had been. Boots and shoes gleamed – and everyone had had a haircut. On the day and in the courtyard of the palace, an official busied himself fastening a small hook on the left breast of each man's tunic. In the meantime, the band of the Grenadier Guards played a medley of appropriate music. HM King George V arrived surrounded by the usual coterie of aides and officials. Pollard described the scene and his emotions on the day with these words:

> At last a sharp word of command brought the Guard of Honour to rigid attention. We followed suit. 'Present arms.' The ensigns[1] (sic) dipped. The band played the most stirring tune in the world – the British National Anthem. His Majesty emerged from the Palace.
>
> I stood with my arms straight down by my sides and my chest swelling my tunic. 'God save our gracious King.' Wasn't that what we were fighting for? To save the King and all he stood for – our great Nation? From the highest in the land whose representatives surrounded

their monarch to the middle class and the lowest who formed the crowd pressed against the railings of the forecourt, all were epitomized in that gathering. We represented the Navy, the Army and the Air Force. We even represented those who were fallen in the little group of relatives of those to be posthumously honoured at the end of our line. 'Send Him victorious, happy and glorious.' Well, he would be victorious if human endeavour could make him so. Every one of us had done his damnedest and we were there to receive our rewards. Not that we needed them. People do not go into action with the idea of winning the Victoria Cross. They go with the bare intention of doing their duty. The decoration merely happens. 'Stand at ease!'

The tension relaxed, the proceedings commenced. We were called out in order of seniority. I was the sixth. Ten paces forward and I halted in front of my King. Colonel Clive Wigram read out the particulars of my deeds as published in the *Gazette*. I stood stiffly at attention. When the recitation was concluded His Majesty hooked my medals on to their hooks.

'I've followed the doings of your battalion with the greatest interest,' he said. 'I'm very proud indeed to be your Captain-General and Colonel.'

He shook my hand with a grip of iron. I had scratched the back of my hand rather badly against a rock at the seaside. The scar had only just formed. His Majesty's hand clasp was so powerful that the wound had burst open afresh. I still have the scar. Every time I look at it I am reminded of the occasion when I was so highly honoured.

I stepped back, saluted, and returned to my place to watch Bill going through the same ordeal. At last it was over and we were in a taxi speeding down the Mall. We were to be given a lunch at Armoury House, Regimental Headquarters. That was all right. What we had not anticipated was the reception we received.

As we entered the gates we found the band drawn up waiting for us. We were made to march behind them between two lines of yelling troops to where a platform had been improvised on a couple of carts in the middle of the grounds. I never felt such a fool in my life.

Colonel Lord Denbigh and Colonel Treffry made us get up on the platform whilst they both made speeches. Then we were supposed to speak but we got out of that. At last we succeeded in escaping to the bar.

Even here we were not safe. Someone came along and complained that we were keeping the luncheon party waiting. We were dragged downstairs. The lunch was all right but there were more speeches to

> follow. Colonel Lord Denbigh made a long one recounting the activities of the battalions and batteries who were at the front. Then there was a pause and someone whispered in my ear that I was expected to reply. Well, up to then I had scarcely made a speech in my life so I stood up and said:
>
> 'Thank you very much everybody.'
>
> Then I sat down again. They did not seem to think a lot of my effort so they had a cut at Bill. Bill stood up and said:
>
> 'I think Alf's said all there is to say.'
>
> Then he sat down. I suppose we had knocked the proceedings rather flat for we had peace and quiet for a while. Not for very long though. Colonel Treffry had to have his turn.
>
> Then our fathers enjoyed a little reflected glory by saying a few words each. I suppose one must allow them a certain amount of rope on an occasion like that. Fortunately they kept within bounds. Neither Bill nor I would have stood listening to a moving word picture of the hero, aged six.
>
> The affair was over at last and we were free. We promptly dashed off to the West End to meet my sister and My Lady. One final dinner party at the Piccadilly, a box at 'Cheep'; a night of gaiety. The following day we returned to France.

Pollard's strongly felt pride in his nation, personified by the King, and his willingness to articulate those feelings make him unusual. British people are not by nature flag-wavers, although many of us are stirred, to a greater or lesser degree, to similar feelings. For the most part, patriotism is a private matter rarely discussed and never paraded. That said, in time of war these emotions are rather more public, and during the First World War in particular, that was certainly the case.

Whilst the two officers had been in the UK they had not missed very much in France other than some splendid summer weather. Elsewhere on the Western Front men were still dying in multiples of 10,000, although none wore the badge of 1 HAC. The Battalion dug trenches, moved stores until, on 29 June and accompanied by the bands of 7th Bn the Royal Fusiliers and 4th Bn the Bedfordshire Regiment, it marched to Maroeuil.

General Sir Henry Horne KCB, Commander of 1st Army, addressed the Regiment at some length and during that process remarked inaccurately that 'The Honourable Artillery Company at the commencement of the war were (sic) 740 strong and since that period they have received over 10,000 replacements. They have suffered very heavily - and have found about 3,250 officers for other branches of the Service.' It was interesting that he then went on to extol the virtue of members of the Battalion accepting a commission in another arm or regiment.[2]

Alfred Pollard rejoined to find it in very changed circumstances and he would have enjoyed staying in Maroeuil, where Major Osmond was in command, but 'B' Company was at Hesdin and so that became home. Bill Haine's company was stationed at GHQ and so the two VCs saw little of each other for some months. Pollard had always 'pooh-poohed' suggestions that fellows with a girl at home were more cautious. Now, to his astonishment, he found that actually that was rather how he felt. He said, 'It occurred to me that if I were killed My Lady might be grieved. And because I wished her nothing but happiness, I was glad that for a while she would have no cause to worry.' Pollard did not know it then, but he had thrown his last bomb and killed his last German. This was because pennies were finally dropping in the War Office and at GHQ. Goold Walker put it like this:

> It transpired that the withdrawal of the HAC from the fighting front was primarily due to the serious uneasiness of the General Staff on account of the dearth of suitable material to replace the enormous casualties among the commissioned ranks. Colonel Cooper was asked if he could find 200 suitable candidates for commissions after a short period of special training, and promptly guaranteed to produce 500, if required. The Higher Command was still considering the future of the Battalion.
>
> There were suggestions emanating from certain quarters that its functions should not be confined to the supply of officers for other units, but should include the provision, in the meantime, of specially drilled platoons to exemplify the new methods of training by demonstration.
>
> After due consideration approval was given for a trial of this scheme. Consequently Colonel Cooper and his officers concentrated on the working out of schemes of platoon training to demonstrate the latest ideas in fire control, attack and defence formations, etc. Intensified training on these lines continued without a hitch throughout August.

Major George Mayhew MC, the Quartermaster of 1 HAC, had all the experience and wisdom that went with the territory. His role was administrative but his importance to the domestic and operational efficiency of the Battalion absolutely critical. He was in the thick of all the action and George Mayhew was clearly a military paragon. Colonel Treffry had singled him out during the Battalion's early engagements as being an exceptional officer. He figured high in Pollard's batting order of officers to emulate, along with Treffry, Boyle and Osmond.

AOP had this to say about Mayhew:

> To us he was not the ordinary quartermaster responsible only for his particular job. He was our father and mother, guide, philosopher and friend. Privileged people addressed him as 'Uncle George'. He was the terror of all who merited his displeasure and the pillar of all who needed his assistance. In his own province he was supreme. However short the notice of an intended move, Uncle George was never caught napping. Because of his popularity wherever he went, he could conjure up motor lorries like a magician producing rabbits from a hat. He always got there complete with stores.[3]

Pollard explained to Mayhew the frustration he felt at sitting idle whilst there was fighting to be done elsewhere. He was bored rigid as his company did little else except provide guards and fatigue parties.

Mayhew was amused at Pollard's regular enquiries as to when the Battalion would be moving back into the line. Mayhew told him to enjoy time out of the line because, 'You've already done your bit.' What a wise man – AOP really had done his bit.

The summer of 1917 moved into autumn and then on into winter. Christmas came and went. Letters from the Lady arrived and were eagerly seized upon. Life well behind the line was comfortable but utterly monotonous. 'Ossy' came to the rescue and suggested that AOP should get away on a course - any sort of course that would break the tedium. The first available course was at the Lewis Gun[4] School at Le Touquet, and AOP bid for a place.

The course was great fun. AOP had a wealth of practical experience of deploying and using this light machine-gun, which was the standard issue to British Empire Forces throughout the war.

The students were split into squads of eight; each squad included American officers and the group was led by a sergeant instructor. In Pollard's squad there were two Americans. Pollard was impressed by his nineteen transatlantic cousins on the course. He commented that 'They were all picked officers who had been sent on ahead to learn as much as possible about British methods. They were a quiet, studious crowd more like a party of Bank Inspectors than soldiers.'

The Americans bombarded the British officers with questions and found themselves to be wonderful targets for the British sense of humour and the leg-pull. They were fed some outrageous tales but very soon they would be in a position to see for themselves just how awful modern warfare really was.

The course spanned the New Year and Pollard gleefully recounted a 'rag' he organized against the guests. This was after a 'merry party', which was much enjoyed by the British officers who took a glass while the Americans all chose to study and who then retired to their beds at 2200hrs. Pollard recounted how, at about 0100hrs, he and three others stole into the Americans' rooms and tipped them all out of bed. All rather fourth form stuff but significant enough for AOP to record it.

On a more serious note: Pollard applied himself to the course and he passed out 3rd overall, a very creditable performance. On the last day of the course and for a bit of fun there was a pistol competition. There were to be two practices, six rounds rapid with the right, and then a further six with the left hand. The Sergeant Instructor told AOP that it was the normal form for the senior officer in each course to organize a sweepstake on the result of the competition. AOP arranged for the competition to be fired at five francs per head.

There was little difference in the scores with the right hand but Pollard, who had trained himself to shoot left-handed when he had been wounded, scored twice as many as his nearest competitor and as a result, won the competition. Pollard did the decent thing and bought drinks with his winnings and his bar bill was ninety francs. The very bad news given to him by the Sergeant Instructor, with a drink in his hand, was that the correct form was for the winner to present his winnings – by now converted to liquid form – to … the Sergeant Instructor.

AOP returned to the Battalion a poorer but a wiser man. The course had been as good as a holiday and he said that he felt 'refreshed and invigorated'. Calling on his experience of training bombers, after his own training back in the summer of 1915, he decided to train as many Lewis gunners as he could and he made a start with 'C' Company. Every day Pollard held classes and he felt that he was achieving something when there was a unit move to Montreuil, which completely disrupted his training program.

On 21 March 1918, the German Army launched its final massive assault designed to drive to the sea and bring the war to an end. At first it was crushingly effective as it made enormous territorial gains and inflicted severe losses on the Allies. The war swung in the balance. 1 HAC was not committed to the battle although the Battalion was put at an hour's notice to move. This engendered a mixed reaction. Men who had not yet seen action were excited, those who had were less enthused – and Pollard?

Predictably, he was overwhelmed with joy.

The British Army reeled under the ferocity of the German offensive and was obliged to withdraw. The butcher's bill was ghastly and the war hung in the balance. The attack was held and then the Germans were pushed back. No one knew it at the time but this had been the German's last throw of the dice.

Hereafter, the Allies held the whip hand. 1 HAC was not to be deployed again.

The US Army was now arriving in France in great numbers and four specially trained platoons of 1 HAC were designated to be employed demonstrating British battle drills. Major Osmond was to command the composite company. AOP pressed his case to be the adjutant of this organization and he was duly selected. He was delighted to be able to work alongside a man he thoroughly admired and launched himself into his 'new duties with great zest'. Anything else would have been out of character.

The four platoons were trained to the last detail and Pollard took no credit for that but he ran the administration and by all accounts, he was efficient. When the training was completed each platoon went its separate way to American training areas. There was a feeling of anti-climax as 'Ossy' and his adjutant were left behind in an empty barracks. The Battalion moved yet again, as mere pawns in the great military chess game, this time to a tented camp. However, as the warmer summer weather had arrived conditions were very agreeable.

The first four demonstration platoons had been well received and now instructions were given to form a further six. Pollard remarked that 'If anything, the training was better than before. The men were magnificent. They entered into the spirit of the thing in a way that made our work a pleasure.'

It was evident to Pollard that when these six platoons were deployed 1 HAC would be no more than a skeleton organization. Ten platoons accounted for over 300 men and 1 HAC was not going to provide much stimulation in the near future. Pollard manoeuvred to be given charge of two of the platoons so that he could accompany them to the US Army.

The German offensive continued unabated and although Alfred Pollard was not involved, other members of the HAC were. One of these was Thomas Pryce, who had enlisted with and served alongside Alfred Pollard and Bill Haine in 1 HAC until September 1915.

He had been commissioned into the Gloucestershire Regiment and a year later, in September 1916, transferred to the Grenadier Guards. He was serving with 4th Battalion, Grenadier Guards, on 13 April 1918, when he was killed in action in extraordinary circumstances. The citation published in the *London Gazette*[5] says it all:

> *Thomas Tannatt Pryce, Lieutenant, (Acting Captain), MC 4th Battalion Grenadier Guards. For most conspicuous bravery, devotion to duty and self-sacrifice, when in command of a flank on the left of the Grenadier Guards. Having been ordered to attack a village, he personally led forward his*

platoons, working from house to house, killing some thirty of the enemy, seven of whom he killed himself. The next day he was occupying a position with some thirty to forty men, the remainder of his company having become casualties.

As early as 8.15 am his left flank was surrounded and the enemy was enfilading him. He was attacked no less than four times during the day, and each time beat off the hostile attack, killing many of the enemy. Meanwhile the enemy brought up three field guns to within 300 yards of his line, and were firing over open sights and knocking his trench in. At 6.15 pm the enemy had worked to within 60 yards of his trench. He then called on his men, telling them to cheer and charge the enemy and fight to the last. Led by Captain Pryce, they left their trench and drove the enemy back with the bayonet some 100 yards. Half an hour later the enemy had again approached in stronger force. By this time Captain Pryce had only seventeen men left and every round of ammunition had been fired.

Determined that there should be no surrender, he once again led his men in a bayonet charge, and was last seen engaged in a fierce hand-to-hand struggle with overwhelming numbers of the enemy. With some forty men he had held back at least one enemy battalion for over ten hours. His company undoubtedly stopped the advance through the British line, and this had great influence on the battle.

Tom Pryce was the third member of the HAC to be decorated with the Victoria Cross and although he was wearing the badges of the Grenadier Guards at the time the HAC claim him because, when he died, he was of course, still a member. On the publication of the *Gazette*, members of the Company serving in every theatre took pride in the exploits of an extraordinary and very brave young man.

About the time that Pryce was gazetted, Pollard said succinctly: 'Before that training programme was completed an event took place that affected the whole current of my life. I applied for special leave, went home and got married.'

Alfred Oliver Pollard did not once give a name to his Lady in the 277 pages of his book *Fire-Eater*. She was always Her, My Lady or The Lady. That tells the reader something of their later relationship because *Fire-Eater* did not appear until 1932.

The facts are that AOP married Mary Ainsley of 88, Foxley Lane, Purley, Surrey, on 4 June 1918 at Christchurch, in Purley. Their fathers, James Alfred Pollard and Mathew William Ainsley, were witnesses to the matter. In fairy stories the happy couple live happily ever after – but this is not a fairy story and they most certainly did not.

Notes

1 He almost certainly means 'Colours', probably those of the Battalion of Grenadier Guards furnishing the band. The Royal Navy has ensigns – a different firm entirely.
2 General Horne was initiating new and so far unpublished policy.
3 Major George Henry Mayhew MC (1864-1937) was an extraordinary character, was a regular soldier who served for twenty years with the Royal Artillery.

In 1898 he was appointed Regimental Sergeant Major of the HAC. He held this appointment for thirteen years, an unusually long tenure. He was then appointed 'Honorary Lieutenant'.

On the outbreak of war he sailed on the *Westmeath,* served continuously with 1 HAC and returned to the UK in 1919. He was held in great affection by all the members of his battalion, to whom he was known as 'Uncle George'.

During his war service he somehow found time to record the comings, goings, decorations and deaths of about 3,700 men who served in 1 HAC and this unique and meticulous record is one of the HAC's greatest treasures. This is now known as 'Uncle George's Book'.
4 The Lewis gun was designed by a Colonel Isaac Newton Lewis in 1911. For political reasons it was not adopted by the US Army. Lewis eventually arranged for the gun to be manufactured under license by the Birmingham Small Arms Co. By war's end 145,000 had been built.

The gun weighed 28lbs, had an effective range out to 800 yards, but was sometimes employed at ranges well beyond that. However, in trench warfare the ranges were usually very much shorter.

It could be mounted with either a 47 or 97 round drum. Its rate of fire was between 500-600 rounds per minute. It cost £165 to manufacture, well in excess of the £100 cost of the Vickers machine-gun.

In 1939 the Lewis gun was replaced in the British Army by the Bren LMG, but it continued in use by other forces up until 1952 (www.firstworldwar.com/atoz/mgun_lewis).
5 The *London Gazette*, 23 May 1918.

Chapter 13

The American Experience

'We were demonstrating British methods as a matter of interest.'

June–July 1918

'Bombo' Pollard returned from his special leave a married man. His manoeuvre, which had been successful, ensured that he would take the two platoons to the aid of the US Army.

However, his machinations had unexpected consequences. He made a common mistake in assuming that because the Americans spoke a similar language, because many were descended from British stock, and because they and Britain had a common aim in beating the enemy, they would welcome the type of support that Pollard and his men could provide.

It was not like that. He found that Americans are emphatically not 'Brits with a funny accent'. Despite him making readily available his four years of hard won experience, Pollard found that, far from welcoming him:

> To my utmost astonishment they did not want to listen. Right from the first their general attitude was that they knew as much about conducting a war as we did. The first day I was with them I made a casual remark to one of their officers to the effect that they were lucky to be able to profit by our mistakes. His reply enlightened me as to what I might expect.
>
> 'Ah, wal, loo-tenant, we don't need to be told anything. This division's been under arms on the Mexican frontier since 1906. Our troops are as seasoned as any you've got here.'
>
> The Mexican frontier! Ye Gods! They had probably heard a couple of revolvers fired during the whole period. I wondered how they would appreciate the comparison with a modern artillery barrage as put down by Master Fritz when preparing to attack.

Pollard and his men had to tread very carefully and exercise the utmost tact in dealing with their overly confident hosts. What had seemed to be a straightforward training assignment now had overtones of a diplomatic mission. But a war was raging and in the summer of 1918, the attrition on both

sides had reached astronomic heights. Many thousands more men would die and Pollard knew what these charming but naive Americans were going to face.

They simply had no idea.

A British brigadier was responsible for the whole co-operation /training/acclimatisation/introduction to trench warfare program. There is no record of his name but fortunately he was a wise man and he warned his teams of 'probable pitfalls' ahead. AOP recorded that as a result:

> We were saved from the fatal mistake that we might have made – had we tried to teach them anything. He advised us to take the line that we were demonstrating British methods as a matter of interest without the slightest suggestion that our audience might profit from what they saw.

This advice set the tone for the association between two armies that had a shared aim. AOP commented rather bitterly on the lack of co-operation and he laid the blame squarely at the door of the American officer cadre, which he judged was 'too proud and pig-headed to let us help them'. There was tragedy to accompany their self-sufficiency. The two divisions to which Pollard was temporarily attached he said, 'were decimated in their first action.' AOP's negative comments applied only to the officers and in contrast, he had unreserved admiration for the quality and attitude of the rank and file. These were men he thought were:

> A magnificent set of fellows, big and husky – to use their own word. Properly led they would have been capable of anything. I should have enjoyed taking a company of them over the top. Their officers let them down. They were too full of their own importance, too jealous that we might confuse their lack of knowledge with inefficiency.

Bombo Pollard was asked to give a lecture to the officers of one of American divisions on the subject of 'Bombing and trench clearing'. Pc was an undisputed master of these arcane arts. He had a wealth of expe and he was happy to share it.

Came the day and to his surprise, he found himself addressing an a of lieutenants and below. He surmised that American officers senio would consider it an affront to their dignity to be lectured by a Pollard was not offended and found the affair mildly amusing. Whe with the Brigadier the following evening he recounted the story. Tl was not even slightly amused and immediately after dinner he se and went straight to the American headquarters where, Pollar made the sparks fly.'

In the British Army in 1917 the platoon was consid

foundation stone of an infantry battalion. It was the first level at which an officer commanded and it was a unit capable of independent manoeuvre. It was made up of four sections; these were, a Lewis gun section armed with two weapons, a section of rifle grenadiers who doubled up as 'bombers', and two sections of riflemen. Well led, the platoon was a formidable force and Pollard described it as 'an army in miniature. The Lewis guns supplying covering machine-gun fire: the rifle grenadiers acting as artillery and the riflemen making the infantry assault.'

The HAC demonstration platoons were very well prepared, well rehearsed and inevitably, their party piece was 'Platoon in the Attack'. On one occasion Lieutenant Edward Holder was detailed to stage this particular demonstration. The American soldiers sat on the grass whilst Holder explained what they were about to see. Control of the demonstration was by means of whistle blasts. The 'attack' was halted from time to time so that Holder could enlarge on the tactical lessons. Pollard who was present said that:

> Afterwards a spectacular display was carried out with ball cartridges. The rifle grenadiers were firing live bombs and putting up a smoke screen. The men were drilled to the minute and the result was a masterpiece of co-ordination between different arms.

It was at this juncture whilst Pollard was adding to Holder's commentary to a group of officers, that the Brigadier rode onto the scene. Pollard's remarks were not being well received and in his words he was getting 'a sneering reception'. His audience indicated that it would readily assault any objective without the unnecessary adjuncts of covering fire, smoke or artillery support. One officer went so far as to say of the demonstration, 'In any case it doesn't require much training or practice to do a show like that.'

This remark lit the Brigadier's blue touch paper. 'Very well,' he snapped, 'I should like one of your platoons to give us a demonstration immediately. Pollard watched the debacle that followed and said that:

> The result was a complete fiasco. The men were willing enough but they simply did not understand what they were trying to do. I strolled round to where the Lewis gunners were stationed on one flank. They were trying to fit the magazine on to the gun upside down! The riflemen were shooting indiscriminately in every direction whilst I decided to keep as far away from the bombers as possible. I should not have been in the least surprised had there been one or two casualties. When they had finished the General let them have it hot and strong, pointing out what would have happened had they been facing a real enemy. After that we had a somewhat better reception.

Pollard and his fellow HAC officers enjoyed the company of the Americans off parade and found them sociable and friendly but found their regulations in respect of alcohol baffling. Officially the US Army was 'dry' but in practice, liquor in its many forms was usually available. They found the need for grown men to drink whisky covertly very strange and in stark contrast to the very liberal attitude of the British Army.

One day an officers' club sprang up and how it was supplied remains a mystery. Pollard and Holder visited the 'Club', which was housed in a marquee. The furnishing was minimal, there were no chairs. The only facility was a long bar that ran the length of the marquee. 'Whisky straights' was what everyone drank and the pace was ferocious. It was only the two British officers who asked for water in their whisky as the 'members' consumed as much alcohol as possible in the shortest period of time. AOP remarked that they 'were looked down on because we would not keep up and would insist on a certain amount of dilution.'

The Club did not last very long. The authorities got wind of it and closed it down. Whilst it lasted the promoter, whoever he was, must have coined money. It was no great loss because Pollard did not find it easy to socialize with his American counterparts. Despite ample good will there were insufficient points of mutual interest or shared experiences. 'Bombo' viewed American culture with ill-concealed distaste and like most of his contemporaries, had no doubt as to the inherent superiority of an Englishman over lesser mortals. Nevertheless, AOP admired the American soldiers and he said:

> The Americans are undoubtedly a great nation. They were raw and untrained when I saw them, but I had not the slightest doubt that they would shake down into really first class troops under the refining influence of going under fire. I should have liked to have seen them in action with some of our experienced officers to advise them, provided they would allow themselves to be advised. I think that they would have done well.

AOP spent only a month closely associating with his American allies. Nevertheless, his opinions, honestly expressed, are perfectly valid and go some way to explaining the disproportionate losses suffered by the US Army in its early confrontations with the well drilled and vastly more experienced Germans. The first shot fired in anger by an American soldier was on 27 October 1917 and a few days later, the first three American soldiers were killed in action on 3 November. Thereafter, a further 50,582 were to follow.

Chapter 14

Reinforcement Camp – the Rhine and Peace

'He was lying unconscious in a ditch and he was lucky to be found and even luckier not to have frozen to death.'

July 1918–February 1919

The losses borne by the British Army were such that, in the spring of 1918, after the great German assault, it was necessary to comb through every military establishment and compulsorily transfer men to the infantry. The fitness criteria had been relaxed and the prime source of new infanteers was the logistic chain. It took fifteen men to supply, feed, tend and transport one man in the front line. Pollard estimated that in the RAF it took 400 men to keep one pilot in the air. On 2 August 1918, the Allies halted the great German advance that had commenced in late March and counter-attacked the German salient that had, by now, been driven deep into their lines. The attack rolled back an exhausted German Army with increasing success and a more fluid battlefield was the result. It was the 'open warfare' the generals craved. Nevertheless, the demand for manpower was insatiable.

A reinforcement training camp was established at Quiberville about 10 miles west of Dieppe and Pollard was appointed as adjutant, initially, to a Lieutenant Colonel Bridcutt.

It would seem that he was selected for this job on the recommendation of a Major Baker, a staff officer at GHQ, who had made a number of visits to 1 HAC when the demonstration platoons were being trained. He had observed Pollard at work, liked what he saw and in due course, when the job came up Pollard was on a shortlist of one.

Colonel Bridcutt was a 'ranker' and pre-war had been a company sergeant-major in the Coldstream Guards. He greeted Pollard in his shirtsleeves 'in a sea of canvas'. The day before Pollard's arrival this extraordinary officer took delivery of 2,000 men and umpteen lorries loaded with canvas. It was his task to establish No. 2 Reinforcement Training Camp. He was a human dynamo and vastly impressed young Pollard as he strove to impose order out of chaos and establish a system. AOP says that 'Five minutes after I arrived, I too, was in my shirtsleeves.'

Pollard took on all the adjutantal duties and as soon as Colonel Bridcutt realized that he had a competent aide he was able to concentrate on training the reluctant clerks, drivers, and store men in the arcane mysteries of infantry fighting. AOP worked flat out, he did not leave the camp site for three weeks, and stopped only to sleep. Pollard described his CO as 'A great man … tremendous energy, but his experience and advice were always at my disposal. After a month Colonel Bridcutt was ordered to hand over the reinforcement camp and to take command of 2nd Bn Royal Irish Rifles. He was killed very soon after on 1 October 1918[1] – just five weeks before the Armistice was signed.

Pollard missed Bridcutt but he was replaced by another extraordinary officer. This was 53-year-old Lieutenant Colonel J Payne. Before the war he was the Regimental Sergeant-Major of the Devonshire Regiment. He had won a DCM in the South African war and in France had added an MC and bar. Pollard had by now established a track record in picking his commanding officers, starting with Treffry by way of Boyle, Hanson, Osmond and Bridcutt. Payne was another right out of the top drawer. Of this period Pollard said:

> Under his command I had an absolutely free hand to do as I liked. He simply did not want to be bothered with correspondence and routine matters. That was my department and he relied on me to get on with it. All he asked was efficiency. Almost his whole time was spent in training.

Payne's job was to turn the men into infantry and there was only six weeks to accomplish this. It was a difficult task with willing volunteers but much, much more difficult with recalcitrant, pressed men. That was the material that Payne was dealing with.

The men were not of the highest calibre and Pollard commented that among others they had eleven murderers through the camp. These men, all serving life sentences in the UK, were the subject of regular reporting and Pollard was agreeably surprised to note that they all saw their retraining as an opportunity to restart their lives. They gave no trouble and passed through the system without incident although there was an occasion when, one day and whilst off-duty, a man knocked on Pollard's door and said:

'May I speak to you a minute, sir?'

'What do you want?' Pollard asked sharply. 'Don't you know the proper way to approach me?'

He should have gone first to the sergeant in charge of his platoon, who would have passed his request to AOP through the camp sergeant-major. Discipline was, perforce, very strict in the camp and there was no room for informality.

'Yes, Sir, but this is a very special private matter.' The man was more than a little agitated and Alfred Pollard invited him to speak.

'It's like this, Sir,' he explained. 'I'm a detective in civilian life. Before the war I had occasion to arrest a man for murder. He's just been drafted into my tent and I'm afraid that if he recognizes me he may do me an injury. What I want to know is, may I move to another part of the camp?'

It was not unreasonable and AOP had no difficulty in granting the request.

He effected several changes in the administrative structure of the camp and one of the most important was to remove the camp sergeant-major and ask for a guardsman as a replacement. AOP commented that:

> Sergeant-Major Proctor of the Irish Guards was a tall, well-built man with one of the fiercest ginger moustaches I have ever seen. It was a great asset because in reality he was extremely good-natured. A delinquent had only to catch sight of that moustache, however, and he was immediately intimidated. I never wish to have a better man to support me.

AOP quickly identified a problem in the orderly room, which was grossly understaffed with clerks. Sergeant Parker, who was responsible for running the place, simply could not cope with the constant waves of paper that washed over him. The solution was simple enough and AOP diverted some trained clerks to the orderly room, in batches, for two weeks. The men selected were delighted, Parker was happy and was now able to deal with the routine administration. It was 'win win'. AOP was released from all the boring bits and left 'free to attend to the more important correspondence'. Pollard explained that there was another way in which he:

> Took matters into my own hands was by promoting my servant to be a sergeant. Of course he did not receive any extra pay. I merely bought some stripes and had them sewn on to his sleeve. In this way I killed two birds with one stone. The mess required someone extra efficient to run it. Cannon[2] was eminently suitable. I also wanted to make him as comfortable as possible. As a sergeant he was free (to make use) of the sergeants' mess.
>
> 'Sergeant' Cannon was an amazingly efficient fellow. He came to me one day when I was needing a servant and offered his services. From then onwards he took me in charge. It would be impossible for me to have been better looked after.

Almost his first action was to condemn my tunics as unworthy of me. I meekly promised to order a new one when I was next on leave. He told me there was no need for me to wait until then. He could arrange it immediately. He was a partner in a firm of West End tailors – Messrs. Chappell & Cannon of Sackville Street.

Cannon measured me and sent the particulars to his partner in England. In due course the clothes arrived to be tried on. After the usual business of pins and chalk they went back to be finished. Later I received the completed suit. It was perfect. I had never had such a faultless fit in my life. Chappell is in the first flight as a cutter.

It was not all work and AOP took some time out to savour the sights of Quiberville, a nearby seaside resort that was within easy walking distance. It was high summer and the place was 'packed with matrons and their families'.[3]

Young Alfred took no time to ingratiate himself into the local milieu and the tall, good-looking, young British officer quickly became a favourite with the ladies. He said in *Fire-Eater* that 'Before I knew where I was I found myself being introduced right and left. *L'entente cordiale* was very much in evidence, fostered on our side by lack of female society, on theirs by the fact that all their eligible men were fighting for their country.'

There must have been endless opportunities for dalliances had Alfred been a ladies' man. However, he was not, and Alfred, true to form, did not indulge himself in that direction.

Then a message from 1 HAC told Alfred that the Battalion was to move back into the line and within the hour, his 'resignation' was in Payne's hands. This 'resignation' from a posting is a process not available to the soldiers of today who go where they are sent and stay there until formally moved to another job. Nevertheless, Payne tried to dissuade AOP but he understood, and realising that Pollard's mind was set on rejoining the HAC, did all that he could to help. Pollard was released and published the 'confidential report' written upon him by Colonel Payne in his book. It was, by today's standards, no more than a '*Very Good*' and the text was rather thin.

Pollard left his comfortable job with Colonel Payne. He was accompanied by an incredulous Cannon, who simply could not understand why his officer should actively seek to return to the line in order to put both their lives into mortal danger. The bespoke tailoring business was a deal less hazardous and Cannon would be grateful to get back to Sackville Street.

Did Pollard not realize that the war was almost over?

Pollard reviewed his decision and his motivation when he drafted *Fire-Eater*. He accepted that it was not just a matter of patriotism and concluded that it was a combination of self-respect and the ties of comradeship. He added, 'Apart from that I yearned to feel once more the thrill of "going over the top". I was destined to be disappointed.'

They took train to Peronne and although it was still only October, the weather was inclement and it was bitterly cold. The train was unheated and Pollard could not get warm even when he wrapped himself in blankets. He described the awful journey and said that throughout it 'I shivered violently. My head throbbed with a splitting headache. When I slept, which was in fits and starts, strange nightmares tormented my brain.'

It got worse. When Pollard and Cannon reached Peronne it was 0200hrs on a bitterly cold morning of the second day. There was no one there to meet them despite Pollard having sent a telegram ahead. Peronne was the end of the line. From here any passage was to be by horseback or on foot. The last time Pollard was in the line this small, undistinguished town had been miles behind the German line. Now it was an Allied rail-head. He felt that it was progress to be back in a forward area. Pollard takes up the narrative:

> I wandered on and on. Now I was clear of the town and in a country road. My footsteps faltered but still I went forward. Strange fancies filled my brain. I knew from the stars I was travelling east. If I kept on going enough I must eventually reach the front line trench. Even if I did not find my battalion I should find someone to tell me where they were.
>
> Forward, on and on. My strength was failing now and I was not quite steady on my feet. Once or twice I stumbled: then I fell. I picked myself laboriously up again. Even though my body was weak my mind was steadfast. I must keep on and reach the Battalion. I stumbled again: tried to recover myself: stepped into an abyss: was conscious of falling down, down, down. Oblivion!

Pollard was found by a party of troops. He was lying unconscious in a ditch and he was lucky to be found and even luckier not to have frozen to death. It would have been an ignominious exit for a hero. He was whisked back to base and into hospital.

He had influenza and this was serious.

At the time the entire world was reeling under the effects of the global influenza epidemic. It has been described as the greatest human catastrophe ever. Estimates vary, but 50-100 million people died in the epidemic that lasted from March 1918 until June 1920. Those figures make the estimated sixteen million who died as a result of World War I almost pale into insignificance.

By happy chance Alfred Pollard was one of the umpteen million who survived. He had cheated death twice in as many weeks. But elsewhere, another winner of the VC – Lieutenant RD Sandford VC RN was very ill. He had won his Cross at Zeebrugge on 23 April 1918, a few days before Pollard won his. However, unlike Pollard, he did not live to enjoy his fame and died on 23 November 1918. Courage alone was no defence.

Pollard recovered from his bout of 'flu and discovered that in his absence, on 20 September 1918, 1 HAC had joined 4th Guards Brigade, who were attached to 1st Cavalry Division. However, the formation was never able to be deployed as the ubiquitous barbed wire, the proliferation of trenches and shell holes all served to preclude any mass movement of horses. It is surprising that these very fundamental points seemed to have been overlooked by the planners at GHQ, particularly as these conditions had not changed since 1915. They were, of course, hoping for the great breakthrough and a reversion to 'open warfare'. It was the pipedream of senior officers living in the past and who had been for four long years.

The Battalion spent weeks moving about northern France and in the process suffered their last two fatalities on 8 October, when they were bombed from the air[4] – then still a relatively new and not particularly effective way of inflicting mass pain and misery upon one's opponents. The artillery shell was still the favoured weapon for that.

Although aerial bombing was not employed to any conclusive extent by either side during World War I, by 1936 the balance had changed for ever. Alfred Pollard was one of the first to recognize the potential for aerial warfare once the business in France had been concluded. He predicted with great accuracy that, in a future war, London would be a prime and very vulnerable target.

AOP was discharged from hospital and rejoined 1 HAC just in time to be among friends when the armistice took effect at 1100hrs on 11 November 1918. The war had been fought right to the bitter end and that is evidenced by the British loss of 823 men on the very morning of Armistice Day. The last British soldier to die was forty-year-old, married Private George Ellison of 5th (Royal Irish) Lancers and he was killed at 0930hrs that morning.[5]

A curiosity is that all French soldiers killed on 11 November are shown on their grave markers to have died on 10 November.[6] The reasons for this are not entirely clear. Public relations? Political? At ninety years range who can be sure?

Bill Haine was asked about the atmosphere at war's end and he said, 'It wasn't like London where they all got drunk of course. No it wasn't like that, it was very quiet. You were so dazed you just didn't realize that you could stand up straight and not be shot.'

Bombo Pollard was shown a map that depicted the disposition of German Divisions on the Western Front. He commented that opposite the Belgian

Army, German formations were few and widely spread; in the south and opposing the US Army the density of German troops was a little greater. The French, those obdurate defenders of Verdun, had German divisions two deep to their front. Against the British Army – the opposition was four deep. Pollard commented, 'I felt very proud of being a Britisher as I looked at it (on the map). There was no doubt about which of their enemies Fritz feared most.'

There was chaos in Germany and when volunteers were called for to join the staff of the Provost Marshal[7] of 2nd Army, Pollard was one of eleven selected. He travelled by train, albeit very slowly indeed, through the rear area of the German Army on track freshly laid across the battlefields and over trenches and shell holes. At Spa, where General Plume had established his headquarters, AOP presented himself to the Deputy Provost Marshal, Lieutenant Colonel PC Laurie.

Pollard was given a job across the German border and he confessed to a feeling of superiority over the conquered foe, and especially as it was his function to issue passes to any German who wished to travel. Pollard was not the best man to have in this post and he went out of his way to be bloody-minded. He cheerfully admitted to:

> Hating the Huns as I did, I examined each application that came before me with the most precise and meticulous care. Being unable to understand a word of German I was obliged to rely on an interpreter. The result was that pleadings and entreaties went for nothing. They lose most of their rhetorical force when briefly translated. The worst is that I held up all communications in Germany for ten days … I only issued eleven passes altogether.

Someone noticed … Pollard was relieved of his job, which he had obviously seen as his opportunity to punish all Germans. A few days later he visited his former office and found that the task that he had been given to do by himself now occupied 'Some ten or twelve interpreters and over 100 clerks.' He added, 'I often roar with laughter when I think of it.' Pollard's next job was to organize armed police patrols of the river Rhine before the Royal Navy could take the task on. He was given *carte blanche* to select his vessels and to this end went to see the Burgomaster of Cologne.

This was a shrewd man who realized that if he was to exercise any control and prevent wholesale looting the solution was to provide every material assistance to his conquerors on request. It was masterly – a simple requisition was all that was needed and somehow the Burgomaster kept a measure of control and an accounting system to go with it. Pollard was mightily impressed.

AOP requisitioned eight motor boats and a German official helped him select the best available. A company of infantry was positioned at each end of Pollard's beat on the Rhine and their job was to examine the passes of all craft entering or leaving the British zone. There are times when the Army can be fun and Pollard was enjoying one of those interludes, storming up and down in the biggest and fastest boat on the river. Unfortunately, came the New Year 1919, and along with it came the Royal Navy. A much more professional touch was now to be applied to patrolling the Rhine.

There was still some fun to be had and Pollard got yet another job, this time with the Assistant Provost Marshal of Cologne. This was a Major Ralph Maude, a younger brother of the famous Cyril.[8] He was clearly a wonderful character and Pollard says of him:

> Major Maude had achieved a tremendous popularity at Amiens, which he had policed for the greater part of the war. His star acquired an even brighter lustre at Cologne, where his great gift of firmness tempered with tact had so much more scope. He was absolutely the right man in the right job and as head of the British police he had a large share in the example of how-to-behave-when-on-top, which the British troops showed the rest of the world. In this he was helped considerably by the exemplary conduct of the Guards Division garrisoning the city.
>
> He struck up a firm friendship with me right from the first and after a time I went nearly everywhere with him. He begged me from Colonel Laurie, and as my position as head of the motor-boat controls was really a sinecure, the job ran itself – I was duly transferred. My duties with Major Maude were very light. He used to refer to me as his big bodyguard. He was little more than 5 feet. When he went abroad I travelled with him in the car. We were never once molested, so I had no occasion to go into action. In short I had a very easy time. There was one job, however, which I was never allowed to neglect. Punctually at eleven o'clock each morning I had to burst into the Major's room regardless of whom he might be interviewing. With a punctilious salute I would make a daily announcement.
>
> 'I have that special report you asked for, Sir.'
>
> If the Major had someone of importance with him he would glance at his watch, appear to hesitate, then apparently reach a decision. He had the family instinct for acting. 'Very well, Pollard. Take it to my private sitting room. I'll join you in a few minutes.' It was wonderful camouflage. The private and special report consisted merely of a bottle and two glasses. But we never missed.

Life was very agreeable for Pollard and Maude, who messed at what had been the private house of a wealthy German nobleman. 'The rooms were oak-panelled and hung with rare tapestries.' Colonel Bailey, who was the military chief of 'Navy and Army Canteen', shared their accommodation and his presence ensured that they ate very well.

Pollard took the chance to see as much of Germany as he could. Bonn and Coblenz[9] opened his eyes and he commented that 'I was struck by the healthy vigour of the many children. There were no signs of decadence about them. I could not help thinking forward to the time when they were grown up and able to raise their voices in deciding the destiny of their nation. Would they call for peace or revenge?'

Hitherto, AOP had given no indication that he had any feel for politics and in 1918, at age twenty-five, his political opinions were probably not very sophisticated but by the time he came to write his memoir he was nearer forty, and he made some prescient remarks when speaking of German youth. In 1932 he observed sagely, and as it happens, accurately:

> They are grown up now and banded together in a mighty organization. So far the Treaty imposed on them has prevented them from arming themselves. So far the reorganization of their own affairs at home has debarred them from seriously turning their attention to their relationships with their neighbours and late antagonists. But the time is not very far distant when they will demand a hearing. They will have to receive attention. The call of robust youth cannot be ignored. They will want to be unshackled, to be acquitted of the sins of their fathers. It is up to the statesmen of the leading nations of the world to investigate their claims before a crisis is precipitated with inevitable bloodshed.

Christmas 1918 arrived and everywhere officers like Pollard had to think about what life would have to offer post-war. The Army of 3,500,000 men was being rapidly dismantled and soldiers were flocking back to 'A Land Fit for Heroes'. Demobilization was a constant topic for the non-regular element of the Army. Colonel Laurie made best use of his police experience and took his decision when on leave – he applied for and was appointed as head of the mounted branch of the Metropolitan Police. Pollard reported bleakly:

> I began seriously to think of my own future. My inclination tended towards a commission in the Regular Army, but my wife was opposed to the idea and I reluctantly abandoned it.

Pollard would have found it difficult to fit into the new, very much smaller Army. His VC and other decorations would have been a benefit and curiously also a hindrance. This is because the Army finds it difficult to place a serving

VC. The individual is accorded a quality of respect that is vastly disproportionate to his rank and his appointments do not necessarily relate to the level of his distinction.

AOP was a lieutenant who had experienced command in battle and a peacetime Army would not have been able to provide him with the constant action and danger he craved. Similarly, he was not assured of swift promotion – in fact, the post-war Army was noted for the slow pace of advancement it offered. Pollard would have been frustrated and bored and it may be that Mary Pollard helped him to make the right decision but for the wrong reasons. It is possible to detect in his sparse words that the decision to leave the Army was only reached after some marital discord.

Pollard took leave in February 1919 and made a three-day journey to Ginchy to try to find the grave of his brother Frank. He saw evidence of the fierce fighting and the area was pock marked with shell holes laid bare in the winter weather. His search was fruitless and he accepted that Frank was 'one of the many whose bodies were never traced'.

Whilst on leave AOP explored the job market – along with millions of others. The Alliance Assurance Company had been very good to him. It had kept his job open and paid him his salary whilst he was away. Not unnaturally, Pollard felt an obligation to the Company and went to see a Mr. Owen Morgan Owen.

This gentleman dealt with the young man very graciously indeed saying, 'Consider we have been paying you a premium to insure ourselves against the results of an enemy invasion,' adding, 'you need not return to us if you do not wish, although we should be very pleased to have you.' Pollard was touched and the more so when, having declined the offer, he was given a year's salary as a gift.[10]

AOP had spent four years living the tough life of a soldier exposed to the elements and sharing whatever life had to offer with his comrades. Clerking for the Alliance, although very safe, was simply not for him and although he opted not to go back to the Alliance, nevertheless he realized that he had to leave the Army and find a job, any job, somewhere.

He returned to Cologne and 'put in my papers.' This is an interesting phrase. AOP was not a conscript. He had joined the Army as a volunteer and although he had been commissioned, he was not a regular officer and had no security of tenure. Usually, only regular officers can resign their commissions, and in the usual phrase, they 'put in their papers'. Perhaps volunteers were treated in a similar fashion and semantics apart, the reality is that a week after this 'putting in of papers', on 23 February 1919, Pollard was discharged. He said movingly:

> I ceased to be a unit in the biggest, greatest, and most efficient Army the British Empire has ever put in the field. But I knew in my heart, and I know it now, if ever my King and Country have a further need for my services, I will gladly offer them.

These are the unequivocal words of an unashamed patriot and soldier; a man who had met and overcome every challenge that had confronted him, with distinction. However, two decades later when Great Britain faced the greatest threat in its history, inexplicably and most uncharacteristically, Alfred Pollard did not offer his services.

The CWGC has calculated that the Commonwealth war dead from 4 August 1914 until 31 August 1921 was 1,114,914. This is made up as follows: UK and former colonies 886,342; Undivided India 74,187; Canada 64,944; Australia 61,928; New Zealand 18,050; South Africa 9,463.

Longevity on the Western Front for a junior officer was about three days and Pollard's chances of surviving the war were statistically insignificant. This very slim chance was further reduced by his propensity to put himself consistently in harm's way. However, against all the odds, he survived and the rest of his life stretched ahead of him. What was he to do with it?

Notes

1 Lieutenant Colonel John Henry Bridcutt RIR is buried at Dadizeele New British Cemetery in Belgium. Grave No. 111 E.17.

2 Frederick Charles Cannon joined the HAC on 16 February 1917. Later he was part of the Mission Anglais to Paris.

3 AO Pollard, *Fire-Eater*, p258.

4 Giulio Douhet, an Italian officer, had said back in 1909: 'The sky is about to become another battlefield … In order to conquer the air, it is necessary to deprive the enemy of all means of flying by striking at him in the air, at his bases of operation and his production centres. We had better get accustomed to this idea and prepare ourselves. Ezra Bowen, 'Knights of the Air', *Time Life*, 1980.

5 CWGC.

6 *The Last Day of World War I*, BBC TV programme with Michael Palin, November 2010.

7 The Provost Marshal is the senior military police officer, although, in 1918, not necessarily a policeman himself.

8 Cyril Maude (1862-1951). One of the leading actors of his generation.

9 Pre-1926 German spelling.

10 AO Pollard, *Fire-Eater*, p272.

Chapter 15

A Divorce – RAF – Re-marriage

'Pollard lied - and for a palpably honest man, this was a burden.'

1919–1931

Alfred Pollard, like millions of others, was irrevocably changed by his experiences of war. He had seen sights that turned the stomach and heard sounds that would have chilled the blood of most. It was little wonder that a job as a clerk did not appeal to him.

His post-war life is not well documented and he admitted that he drifted from one form of employment to another. At least he was employed and the probability is that his collection of decorations would have helped him to get to the interview stage. He worked as a salesman, or 'commercial traveller', in the unattractive appellation of the time. However, we have no record of what he 'travelled' in and sought to sell. It is said that a salesman must 'first sell himself and then the sale of the product follows naturally'. Alfred Pollard was an assertive character and he had a track record as a leader. These personality traits must have been assets in the cut and thrust of the sales world.

Three years passed and Alfred had achieved nothing of note. However, on 11 November 1922, the nation marked the internment of 'The Unknown Warrior' in Westminster Abbey and as *The Times* said, 'The Unknown Warrior will be carried to his last resting place between two lines of men who won the Victoria Cross or otherwise distinguished themselves by special valour during World War I.'

Alfred Pollard was selected to be one of that Guard of Honour and on the day he stood alongside the very bravest of the brave. It was a measure of his national standing that he was invited – RL Haine, on the other hand, was not.

If business did not actually flourish at least he got by and he lived with Mary at a house 'The Glimpses', in Woodhall, near Pinner, in Middlesex.

Domestically, however, all was far from well. It was not an equal partnership and the 'adoration' of one by the other is not a desirable basis for marriage. AOP never commented upon his marriage, but he and Mary were not compatible – something that had occurred to him even before they married.

After five unhappy years Mary decided that she had had enough; this marriage was not what she wanted. They separated and she went home to her mother. This did nothing to help an ailing relationship, which got steadily worse. AOP gave up the house in Pinner and moved to 83 Ashburnham Road, Bedford. The significance of Bedford is not known as hitherto AOP had always lived in London. Perhaps it was closer to his place of work at the time.

AOP was a very unhappy man: he had only recently rejoined the HAC and through the Company he would have been able to connect with the '*Westmeath* Association'. This was composed of the survivors of 1 HAC who had sailed to France in the *Westmeath* in September 1914. They were a small group and for Alfred Pollard, the very essence of 'comradeship'. There is not a shred of evidence that Alfred Pollard ever had anything to do with the *Westmeath* Association – this is entirely anomalous and uncharacteristic.

On 22 September 1923 he was prosecuted for 'dangerous driving'. For a normally law-abiding person Pollard had clearly displayed a degree of irresponsibility. Perhaps his domestic circumstances had blunted his awareness of danger for himself and others?

In late 1923 Mary took positive steps and she consulted Young, Jackson Beard & King. This was an expensive firm of solicitors who conducted their business at 46, Parliament Street, London, SW1. Mary now actively sought a divorce from Alfred and instructed her legal representatives to take action to obtain that divorce.

In 1923 a divorce was immeasurably more difficult to obtain than it is nearly 100 years later and appropriate 'grounds' for divorce had to be established and proved to the satisfaction of a judge. The most popular, and certainly the 'grounds' most certain to achieve the desired result, was adultery by one of the partners.

The 'decent thing' was for the husband in an unhappy union to provide the evidence of adultery, usually by booking into a hotel with a woman hired for the purpose and then to be seen in a 'compromising situation'.

Alfred, meantime, obliged to respond to Mary's legal initiative, had also taken legal advice and he chose Bird & Bird of 5, Grey's Inn Square, London WC1 – another expensive firm. This whole process was going to cost a lot of money and the Pollards were not wealthy people, although both families were comfortably off and they may have contributed toward the lawyers' fees. The process of divorce undoubtedly caused both families great distress as in some ways, a divorce is more upsetting than a death. AOP did not contest the divorce and neither did he refute the allegations made by his wife. On 3 December 1923 Mary's solicitors filed the petition and in it she alleged that:

> The said Alfred Oliver Pollard has frequently committed adultery with diverse women whose names are unknown to your petitioner. That on 17th, 18th and 19th days of November 1923, at The Imperial Hotel, Russell Square, London, the said Alfred Oliver Pollard committed adultery with a woman whose name is unknown to your petitioner.

This all seems to be highly unlikely.

Alfred Pollard was something of a prude, did not approve of casual relationships and as far as can be ascertained, Mary was his only sexual partner, but she was also at the very epicentre of his life. Alfred Pollard was always extraordinarily open about his emotions. It is inconceivable that in the five years since the Armistice, he had not only become a predatory sexual athlete but furthermore, had concealed the fact in his memoir. He was not an unduly modest man and had he been enjoying marked success with the ladies, his well developed ego would have encouraged him, at least, to hint at his conquests.

Pollard's affections were unchanged but he recognized that, much as he loved his wife, his affection was not returned now, and probably never had been. He was an honest person and now he took the pragmatic route. Indeed, the only route that was open to him. The fact that he was branded as an 'adulterer' would have distressed him because it was a dishonourable status and it conflicted with his need for 'respect'. Not challenging the charge of adultery demeaned him in the eyes of some, but probably not his friends, who appreciated how dire the relationship had become.

AOP had had to lie in order to release Mary; indeed, he had had to sign a document stating that there was 'no collusion' between the parties. There is every reason to suppose that there was collusion.

Pollard lied – and for a palpably honest man, this was a burden.

The overwhelming probability is that the evidence was an entirely put-up job. The Honourable Sir Maurice Hill, one of the Justices of the Courts of Justice, heard the case in The Strand. The witnesses paraded before him and 'proved' Mary's case. The Judge awarded a decree nisi that same day, 6 May 1924.

AOP went to pieces. He was a single man without apparent purpose 'off course' and he looked around for something worthwhile to do with his life. The Royal Air Force was the coming thing in 1920s' Britain. It was modern, cutting edge and it was a branch of the military. He decided to make a major lifestyle change and on 15 July 1924, in the midst of the divorce proceedings, he applied for a Short Service Commission in the Royal Air Force.

The Royal Air Force snapped him up.

What the RAF could offer AOP is difficult to discern other than the thrill of flying. He was far too old to become a career RAF officer and fortunately, he realized that. He was granted a probationary commission as a pilot officer and he undertook flying training in Lincolnshire, which was a much less arduous regime than it is today. He duly qualified to fly Bristol fighters.

As soon as he qualified his probationary commission as a pilot officer was promptly confirmed. He was then posted to RAF Andover and to No. 13 (Army Co-operation) Squadron RAF. He was a pilot officer with seniority, in that lowest of ranks, of 17 August 1925.

It is interesting to note that his impact upon the RAF was such that the seniority list for 13 Squadron showed ten pilot officers among the complement of twenty-seven. Pollard was named first of these ten POs in the RAF list of 1926, and even more unusually, he was listed as 'VC Alfred O Pollard MC DCM'. This was a curious departure from the norms of 'staff duties'. He was by no means the senior and in the normal course of events, his name would have been listed sixth.

Pollard adapted to life in 'light blue' but failed to come to terms with the break-up of his marriage. On 17 November 1924, the Right Honourable Sir Henry Duke, the President (no less) of the Courts of Justice, had granted Mary a final decree. The marriage was at an end and they went their separate ways. Now there were just the lawyers to pay. Pollard summed up his parlous situation in these words:

> My marriage was a failure. After five years, my wife divorced me. The circumstances which led up to such a climax are naturally not for the public eye. The result was that deprived of my lodestar I went completely off my course. For two or three years I did every conceivable damned silly thing imaginable. Then some latent spark of common sense within me whispered, 'Why be such a fool?' I put on the brake to regain my self-control. My luck still held.

These are not the words of a man anxious to end his marriage, not a man with a string of notches on his bed post – far from it. There is a note of desperation and despair that begs sympathy. His 'fixation' – perhaps not too strong a word in the circumstances – with Mary had lasted from his late teens until he was thirty-one. She had provided him with a focus, a motivation and with heartbreak.

Later he was serving at RAF Sealand, just outside Chester. It was good to be back in uniform but he was finding it hard to settle. He lived in the mess among officers of a similar rank but who were younger and in many cases had no wartime experience. His multiple decorations and campaign medals marked him out as 'different', as he most clearly and deservedly was. One of his brother officers was called Frank Togood, who was very taken with a girl living near Chester. The young lady invited Togood to bring two of his chums the next time he came to tea. Charitably, Togood asked Alfred to join him and interested to meet the object of Togood's aspirations, Alfred went to tea.

Violet Irene Swarbrick took one look at the tall, rugged, confident Alfred Pollard and Togood's aspirations were dashed for ever. Equally, AOP was smitten by the lovely blond with the attractive personality.

Irene Violet Swarbrick, whose family lived in Ealing, West London, appeared to be all the things that the now unlamented Mary was not. Their friendship developed into love and they were married on 5 September 1925, just before his promotion to Flight Lieutenant on 16 February 1926.

Violet buckled down, briefly, to Service life and together they saw out Pollard's remaining time in uniform – probably in an RAF married officer's quarter in the Andover station. He left the RAF on 15 December 1926 in the rank of flying officer. Below is a simple family tree to show how AOP related to the Swarbrick/Chown families:

Descendants of Robert Alfred Swarbrick

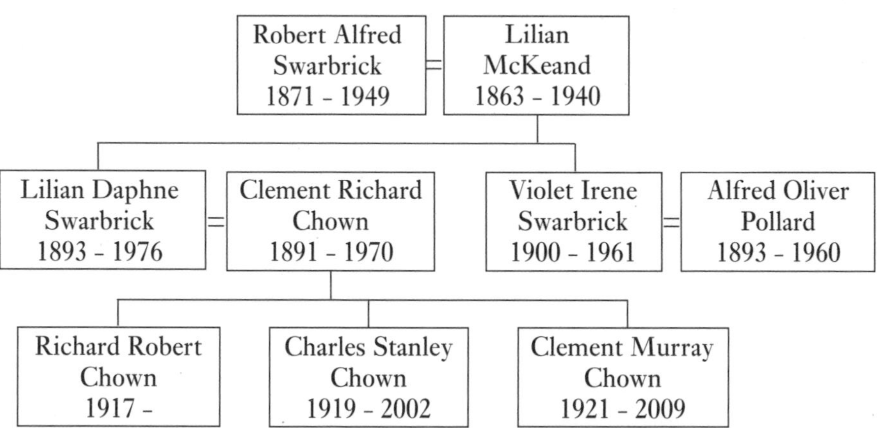

AOP still had a reserve commitment to the Army, and the RAF list of 1926 showed, in brackets under his name, the legend (Capt TA Res). This reflects his joining the TA reserve of officers in late 1921 and does confirm that AOP had been raised to substantive captain since his demobilization back in 1919.

Those two and a half years[1] in light blue had inculcated in him a love of aviation and all that surrounds it. It had altered his perspective of life and aviation was to be a constant in what lay just ahead.

Mary faded into the background and today she is no more than a footnote in the life of Alfred Pollard. Where she went, what she did and when she died have no place in this narrative over which she has already cast a lengthy cloud of unhappiness. Pollard commented in 1931:

> I met and married my present wife. She is the perfect mate. We have now been married for six years and are greater lovers than on the day that we were first joined together. More important still, we are friends. To her never failing sympathy, courage and help, I owe the fact that I am a better man today than I have ever been in my life before.

What a charming, unequivocal testimonial that is. As it happens, they remained very happily married for the rest of their lives. The family explained their apparently sparse social life by saying that[2] 'They were complete in themselves, they really did not need anyone else.'

Notes

1 This was a highly cost-ineffective commission. By the time he had learned to fly and started to be a productive member of the RAF, he was back in 'Civvy Street'.
2 Conversation Author/Dick Chown, 11 October 2010.

Chapter 16

Authorship and *Fire-Eater*

'I enjoyed the war, both in and out of the line.'

1931–1960

Pollard had to earn a living and initially he worked for an American company as a trainer of salesmen. Although he had a background in 'sales' and this job fitted his profile, post-RAF, he really wanted to be associated with aviation. He moved on to the Low Engineering Company, which had produced a small two-stroke aero engine. Pollard became a director of the company and although he had no engineering background, he was an aviator and he did have a VC to adorn the Company literature. Low Engineering was a successful enterprise and whilst working there AOP decided to try his hand at authorship.

He chose a very overpopulated craft and he then compounded the issue by opting to write thrillers and adventure stories. Fiction writing is a special talent and for every book of that genre that is published there are a host that never see light of day, and earn their author not a penny.

AOP wrote his first book in 1929 and he submitted it to the leading publishers, Hutchinson, with the title *Pirdale Island.* It had an aviation theme and Walter Hutchinson, the head of the publishing firm, could see that he could exploit this new author. Unfortunately, the dust jacket of the book bore the title in lurid typeface followed with '*by Captain AO Pollard VC MC* DCM*'. There cannot be any doubt that Pollard's name and decorations had a commercial attraction for Hutchinson but it was a device that lacked dignity and AOP would have been advised to have demurred.

A raft of war memoirs and novels appeared after the war. Some were carefully crafted and balanced, others were not and many of the latter category gloried in the bestiality of war and the degradation of all who were involved. One book in particular had provoked strong reactions, and this was *Over the Top – A. P. B. I. in the HAC* (PBI stands for 'poor bloody infantryman'), by Arthur Lambert, who had served in the 2nd Battalion of the HAC. Excerpts of the book had been published in the *HAC Journal* in 1928 and had either passed unnoticed or been ignored as the washing of this dirty linen was 'in house'.

Later, in 1930, Lambert's experiences were published as a book and although it drew some muted support, that support was drowned out by virulent criticism. It was reviewed in the *HAC Journal*.[1] The reviewer, who had been a member of 2 HAC, was scathing and he described the book as:

> This wholly deplorable book … crude and sensational ... good taste is outraged … persistent misinterpretations of his battalion as composed of men who went about their work with semi-mutinous and malicious thoughts in their mind.

The Times Literary Supplement observed in May 1930 that: 'Bitterness is the prevailing tone of the book unrelieved by the humour which made it possible for others to endure the years of "mutual and physical misery" to which the author constantly refers.'

Alfred Pollard wrote to the *Morning Post* on 6 February 1930 in support of Major Ian Hay, the author of *The First Hundred Thousand*, who had spoken publicly about his own war experiences and in doing so had regretted that so many of these memoirs, not the least those of Lambert, presented a very unattractive view of the soldier. Pollard was never a man for sitting on the fence and in his letter, he said among other things:

> War runs the gamut of physical and mental horror … and those who descended to the level of beasts wallowing in their beastliness were rare ... If we must have war novels, let us have stories emphasizing the spirit of comradeship, which was greater between 1914 and 1918 than it has ever been before or since.

Lambert's book ran counter to Pollard's somewhat idealistic position and it hardened his view; he saw a need to correct the balance. His pronounced feeling for and admiration of 'comradeship' were to be features of the rest of Pollard's life. Although, curiously, his regard for comradeship did not extend to practising it.

It is something of a paradox that AOP, who felt 'neither pity nor fear' and who only expressed regret at the death of one of his many comrades, should demonstrate such trenchant views on the topic, if only as a theorist.

Pirdale Island was published later that year and was reviewed in the September 1930 edition of *Bookfinder*. The author was very fortunate that a first book should attract any attention at all and the review was broadly positive. It liked his descriptions of flying, which, it said, he wrote with an authentic touch. *Bookfinder's* view of the plot was less enthusiastic and it added:

> It has those elements of thrills which in addition to the air interest of the

story will make it enjoyable for many. It is an old plot, well worn, but not worn out.' The review concluded tepidly, 'We can recommend reservedly to those who have a taste for this sort of thing.

Hmmm! – the message was 'try harder'.

The book sold well enough and during 1931 Pollard wrote and had published two further books. Hutchinson obviously saw their new author as an asset because they only ever publish books that will turn a profit. These two latest books were *Rum Alley* and *Murder Hide-and-Seek*. They were both 'favourably received' and were aimed at men and women in their late teens. The story lines were not dissimilar in style to Capt WE Johns' Biggles series or the Sexton Blake stories; a later generation would read Simon Templer – 'The Saint'. *The Oxford Dictionary of National Biography*, many years later, summarized his style as being in 'A lively *Schoolboys' Own* style'.

Pollard's heroes had many of the author's characteristics. They are determined, forthright, courageous, moral and unashamedly patriotic.[2] The girls are good sports, attractive, athletic and plucky.[3] It has to be said that Pollard did not write great literature. Instead he produced workmanlike, commercially viable yarns that satisfied a niche market and Hutchinsons were just the people to capitalize on Pollard's energy – and his name.

Murder Hide-and-Seek attracted a favourable press and the *Morning Post* of 3 November 1931 commented, 'There is no need to recommend the work of this writer to those who are on the look-out for real excitement.'

The reader might be unaware of the difficulties that authors have always had, Shakespeare and Plato apart. The easy bit is writing the book. From then on it gets more difficult. A compliant publisher has to be found and the published book has to be marketed to a degree that ensures its commercial success. AOP had moved, apparently effortlessly, into this brutally competitive world.

Those first three books established AOP as an author and importantly gave him the confidence to write his war memoirs. Since 1919 the market had been swamped with the reminiscences of hundreds of officers and soldiers of all ranks and all nationalities. Some of these books have justifiably been acclaimed as classics of their type. Eric Maria Remarque's superb novel *All Quiet on the Western Front* (1929), Siegfried Sassoon's *Memoirs of an Infantry Officer* (1930), Ernst Jünger's *The Storm of* Steel (1920) and his *Copse 125* (1925) are all typical of post-war literature.

AOP started to write his memoir in 1931 and he was motivated, in part, with a desire to offset those negative impressions left by Arthur Lambert, among several others. In his introduction to the book, which he chose to entitle

Fire-Eater,[4] he echoed his earlier letter to the *Morning Post* and delivered a homily to his reader, in which he said this:

> I have chosen a title which aptly expresses my attitude throughout the campaign. *I enjoyed the war, both in and out of the line. Despite the discomfort and hardships of life in the trenches, I found pleasure in wandering about "no man's land" at night. "Going over the top" struck some chord in my nature which vibrated strongly to the thrill of the attack. Men called me mad. Perhaps I was.* [Author's italics.] In this narrative I have endeavoured to set down a true account of my thoughts and sensations when going into action.
>
> Many books have been written about the war, both fact and fiction. Those that I have read … nearly all stress the sordidness and suffering which were inevitable in such a gigantic struggle. But there is another aspect of the picture which has not received the notice it deserves – the spirit of comradeship which pervaded all front-line troops and the unselfishness with which men shared any extra comforts sent out from home with less fortunate comrades, or helped a weaker brother to 'carry on'.
>
> Many men gave their lives, generously and unhesitatingly, either to rescue or protect other men. True, they were often acting under discipline, but a high-minded spirit was there, or their efforts would have been half-hearted and the result a failure. The war is said to have brought out the beastliest instincts in man. It certainly brought out the noblest self-sacrifice, unselfishness, comradeship. Today, in peace time, we have men striving against one another for money and power. 'Every man for himself and the devil take the hindmost' is the general slogan. It is not considered 'business' to give a chance to an applicant for a job unless it is a certainty that he can 'deliver the goods'. He may have the responsibility of a wife and family and no money to supply them with necessities. That's his affair. If he has fallen in the race for success no one has time to stop and help him rise. He must be trampled underfoot. There is no parallel in commerce with a soldier risking his life to succour a wounded comrade.
>
> If we had more of the spirit exhibited by Tommy when up against it, in dealing with post-war problems, the task would be easier, the achievement infinitely greater. Difficulties would be swept away by a tide of humanity actuated by the will to win through. The motif of this book is to show what that spirit was that bound together the British Army and made it possible for them to ignore defeat and gradually wear

down the resistance of the toughest troops they have ever been up against in the history of the nation. The story has naturally to centre round myself, although I would have preferred to have been able to write it in the third person. The thoughts and impressions are mine and are intended to point out a lesson that war taught us - that, as a nation, we can accomplish anything so long as we work together. Nobody wants another war. All the glamour and romance cannot make up for the misery occasioned by the terrible loss of life. The fact still remains that those who gave their glorious lives in the defence of the British Empire, gave them in vain unless the nation profits by their sacrifice.

There are two interpretations of this uncompromising opening statement. It is either the view of a very angry and disillusioned man or the considered thoughts of an author with a higher, national purpose. The answer probably lies somewhere in the middle. Certainly life had not treated Pollard well and there were millions of his comrades who were now enduring a world-wide depression, unemployment, poverty, malnourishment, and facing early death.

Britain in 1931 was most emphatically not 'a home fit for heroes'. Pollard's sense of 'comradeship' is a topic to which he repeatedly refers and which he believed to be a fundamental element in citizenship. This biography quotes from *Fire-Eater*, and in the pages of that book, there are any number of references to this component of trench life. He was not alone and the value placed on comradeship is to be found in many other war memoirs.

The foreword to the book was written by Major General, The Rt. Hon. JEB Seely MP.[5] Pollard went 'first class' when he asked Seely to write the foreword because Seely was one of the most distinguished men of his day. He had not been associated either with Pollard or 1 HAC during the war and quite how Pollard enlisted his support is not recorded, but then a VC does open doors that are closed to others.

Seely was himself a capable, distinguished and brave soldier, as a DSO and five 'mentions' demonstrate. The General did not find favour with Dominic Harman[6], who highlighted Seeley's description of himself as 'A brass hat whose boldest claim is to have been *quite* near the enemy'. [Harman's italics.] Seely was possibly being ironic. However, his record stands close scrutiny and he wrote a foreword that Harman recognized as being entirely germane. Seely said:

That attacks on those who serve their country in close contact with the enemy are always written by those who have never been near the real Front.... War is as ennobling to the actual combatants as it is degrading to the idle onlooker. Some people think that these deeds of unselfish courage are done by desperate men with nothing to lose. In my experience it is those who have the most to lose who are the bravest in war. The writer of this book had everything to lose.

The *Daily Telegraph* reviewed *Fire-Eater* on 5 February 1932, and it said that Pollard's book 'Possesses a strong strain of romantic sentiment and a disarming naïveté. (It) conveys the thrills of his Army career with a vigorous touch.'

The Times followed, and on 12 February 1932 it said of Pollard that his book 'Records his experiences, and occasionally his sentiments, in a straightforward way. The experiences are very exciting: in fact very few of its kind more thrilling can be recalled.' *The Times* went on in similar vein, as if Pollard were writing an adventure story, but it concluded, 'The whole book is marked by a very pleasant spirit, independence of thought with regard to the tactics of trench warfare, but no grumbling and no unreasonable criticism, and always the best of comradeship.'

A further review in *The Times* of 18 February 1932 said, 'It is impossible to read these simply but forcibly written pages without an uplifting of the heart and it must be added that, if he is candid, he has none of the perverted and unmannerly candour which sets itself to shock. His pleasure and pride in his own exploits are expressed as naturally as though he were thinking aloud. Those people named are mostly described as "good fellows" and those not of this standard are not named, but even of them, few hard things are said.'

Fire-Eater is without doubt the best of AOP's sixty-two works. It is drafted with a light touch and is eminently readable – even eight decades later. However, Pollard could and should have written an even better book. This is because, in many places, his lack of research is very obvious. He gets names wrong and in many cases forgets them. His chronology is confused. He had at his disposal the considerable resources of the HAC, which unquestionably he should have put to better use. One can only suppose that he did not seek help – and it shows.

Pollard's book is not of the same literary quality as those of Graves, Sassoon, Jünger, Chapman, Clapham, Carrington, Blunden et al. However, it is very much better than Lambert's. AOP made no claim to literary greatness and did not set out to do anything other than set out his experiences between 1914 and 1919.

He succeeded in his aim although, along the way, his obsession with Mary Ainsley and the manner in which he documented this obsession, is bordering on bizarre. Nevertheless, it is revealing and it provides a window into the heart and mind of a man who might otherwise be judged as being without normal emotion. The paragraph [author's italics, page 206] sets AOP apart from the overwhelming majority of other men because he really did function on a different plane.

Pollard's words, although unusual, are, by no means, unique. Guy Chapman,[7] for example, wrote the following lyrical passage about the attraction of war:

> Once you have lain in her arms you can admit no other mistress. You may loathe, you may execrate, but you cannot deny her. No lover can offer you defter caresses, more exquisite tortures, such breaking delights. No wine gives fiercer intoxication, no drug more vivid exaltation. Every writer of imagination who has set down in honesty his experience has confessed it. Even those who hate her most are prisoners of her spell, they rise from her embraces, pillaged, soiled, it may be ashamed: but they are still hers.

AOP would never have expressed himself in such poetic terms. However, it is sentiments like those that have attracted the attention of historians such as Catherine Boylan, who in 2004 wrote a masterly paper[8] for the *Journal of the Society for Army Historical Research*, in which she sought parallels to Pollard's attitude. To do this she drew attention to Brigadier-General FP Crozier's[9] books *A Brass Hat in No Man's Land* (1930) and *The Men I Killed* (1937). Boylan describes Pollard's book as 'a lively, literary pleasure', but Crozier's 'anger and remorse' make the second of his books 'an uncomfortable read'.

Crozier wrote of fear – an emotion that Pollard never admitted to feeling. In his first book the Brigadier wrote:

> An important part of your intellectual discipline is your conquest of fear. All soldiers – except the dense and unintelligent – are frightened in action, at times. There comes that pain in the tummy. That you have to master. Funk in itself is nothing; when unchained it becomes a military menace and for that men die at the hands of their comrades.

By his own account Crozier shot many of his own men in order to achieve compliance with his orders. He suffered agonies of remorse afterwards. On the other side of the line Ernst Jünger did something similar on a smaller scale. Pollard, it would seem, was able to achieve much the same aim by dint of his personality and his innate leadership skills. At war's end AOP felt no remorse.

Boylan refers to Robert Graves and his book *Goodbye to All That*, in which he comments that 'I used to speculate on which of my contemporaries would distinguish themselves after they left school. The war upset these calculations. Many dull boys had brief, brilliant military careers.'

Boylan's view that Pollard was 'neither dense nor dull' is not fully supported. Certainly, there is no parallel either with Crozier, certainly not with Graves, and Sassoon. That trio had sleepless nights after 1918 – Pollard slept like a lamb. Crozier's shame and remorse converted him to pacifism. Pollard remained a militarist, convinced that national survival was entirely dependent upon the ability and willingness of its people to defend themselves. However, and despite his eloquence on political issues, the value of comradeship and the use of air power etc., Alfred Pollard was neither a warm, extroverted character nor was he an entertaining, gregarious person with a wide circle of friends.

The sad and incontrovertible fact is that although Alfred Pollard was not 'dense' he was nevertheless a rather 'dull' dog.

Catherine Boylan was not alone in finding AOP an interesting subject and, in 2008, Professor Brian Bond also examined Alfred Pollard. He drew on Boylan's research and endorsed her view. He concluded that:[10]

> It is tempting to compare Pollard with Ernst Jünger, author of *Storm of Steel*, *Copse 125* and a great variety of publications on philosophy, politics and literature, but the comparison should not be pushed too far.
>
> Both were staunch patriots, and much-decorated front-line heroes who, surprisingly, did not achieve field officer rank. But Pollard was conspicuously lacking in Jünger's wide-ranging scientific interests and his mystical Teutonic approach to philosophy and politics. They were also superficially alike in praising the spirit of comradeship and sense of national unity which the war had produced and which Pollard, in particular, felt to be depressingly lacking in peacetime Britain in the 1920s. But Jünger's ecstatic philosophising in *The War as Inner Experience* (1922) lay entirely beyond Pollard's relatively unsophisticated mental horizons.
>
> War, for Jünger, was not a cause of man's unhappiness, but an expression of his eternally unchanging nature and at the same time a revelation of things to come. War was a creative force. Perhaps one could sum up by saying that Jünger was an internationally famous writer and militarist whereas Pollard was a simple patriotic fire-eater with only moderate literary ability.

Little did Pollard realize, in 1931, as he drafted his memoir that eighty years later his motivation and his form of words would attract so much attention. He did not set out to write a work of great literary merit – nor did he have the talent to do so. His aim was merely to record events as he saw them and to use his book as a platform for his simple, unadorned patriotism.

He continued his work for Low Engineering but now dedicated more of his time to journalism and authorship. He contributed articles to any number of newspapers and journals but there was a constant and rather negative flavour to his work.

In October 1932, only eight months after the publication of, and the excellent reception accorded to, *Fire-Eater,* AOP wrote an article in the *London Star* with the provocative title, *My Useless VC.* In this piece he alleged that 'There is no walk of life where my decorations have given me an advantage over other men.'

This posture does him no credit because it is patently untrue. Would he have been a director, no less, of an engineering company? Would he have had his first book published had he not been Pollard VC? Would his war memoir have been worthy of publication if he had just been Tommy Atkins? Would his books sell without the slogan on the cover advertising his decorations?

Possibly, but probably not.
or
Perhaps, but possibly not.

The reader must decide where the line should fall. What cannot be disputed is that the decorations Pollard won were solely intended to mark his gallantry: they were not intended to be an annuity for life providing him with unremitting fame, respect and success in any field of his choosing. However, in part, that is what those decorations did provide. Once Pollard wore that maroon ribbon his life changed for the better, he benefited immeasurably as a result, but seems never to have acknowledged the fact.

Just a few weeks after his article in the *London Star* he entered the debate that had ensued when it became clear that in some places Public Assistance Committees were abating financial support to holders of the VC because they were in receipt of a £10 annuity. Understandably, AOP wrote in forceful terms to the *Daily Herald* on 15 December 1932.

The books continued to roll off his typewriter and in 1932 *The Cipher Five* and *The Death Flight* followed hard on the heels of *Fire-Eater*. The success of his authorship allowed the Pollards to move to Hillingdon, Middlesex, and a desirable address in 1932.

In the 1930s, while Pollard cranked out his books, his prognosis of the future of Germany started to fall into place. *Death Flight* was published in 1932, followed in 1933 by two further books and in 1934 by yet two more. These books were of a remarkably standard, 288 pages, and at 12cms x 18cms, just a little smaller than A5. Publishers' costs are, of course, dictated in part by the length of the book. It is the length that determines not only how much editing energy will be needed in the publication process, but also the quantities of paper required and the cost of packing and transporting the finished book across the country. The reader expects value for money and 288 pages would be sufficient for a yarn amounting to around 73,000 words. (As a measurement, the text of this book is 103,000 words.) Pollard's later books started to carry the banner '500,000 copies sold' and from this we can deduce that he was by any standard a successful author, selling several thousand copies of each of his books.

It is difficult to compute his income and relate it accurately to 2011 prices but as a guide, generally an author can aspire to 10% of the 'sticker price'. Pollard had a 'literary agent' in Robert Crewe and it was his job to negotiate the best arrangement for his client with Hutchinsons.

Mrs. Doreen Montgomery, now the joint Managing Director of Robert Crewe, remembers Pollard visiting the office toward the end of his life and recalls that he was known as 'Jumbo'; this was a family nickname. AOP was still 'Bombo' to hundreds of people and as this author well knows, nicknames do stick. It may be that 'Bombo' had evolved into the less martial 'Jumbo'.

Robert Crew exploited Pollard's sales success and worked diligently to obtain the desirable 10%. A simplistic calculation is that if Pollard's books, most in hard-back covers, sold for an average of £10 at 2011 prices, then his income over thirty years would have been something over £500,000 or £16,666 per annum. If, however, the books retailed at £7 at 2011 prices, which is more likely, his annual income would have been an average of £11,666. That is insufficient and he found it necessary to supplement his income by writing for newspapers and magazines.

The erstwhile fire-eater settled into domesticity with his wife Violet. The *Middlesex Advertiser* of 16 October 1932, presumably because AOP was a local celebrity, ran a small piece about him and in it reported that he occupied his time with dogs, handicrafts and gardening. This was a far cry from bombing German trenches and then shooting dead any of the surviving occupants. It was a very suburban existence.

The newspaper report also recorded that AOP was building a model of a three-masted tea clipper. The model was a substantial beast 4 feet 6 inches in length and 3 feet in height. It seems that it eventually took seven years to complete and Catherine Boylan discovered that the same newspaper carried a photograph of the model in its edition of 15 November 1935. This inconsequential information merely adds to the profile of this paradox of man.

In 1934 Pollard completed *The Royal Air Force: A Concise History*. It was published by Hutchinsons and retailed at 18/9d.[11] The book was Pollard's second non-fiction book and it would establish him as rather more than just a writer of 'rollicking yarns'. Pollard had set himself a stern test and in just 288 pages it was always going to be difficult to get the balance of the content right and the degree of detail correct. AOP indulged himself by wandering into the political use of air power and used a 'slightly hectoring tone'[12] in expressing his heartfelt views. If nothing else, he was consistent.

The book was reviewed on 19 April 1934 by *Flight*, the aviation journal of the day. The review was not unlike the curate's egg of legend. Criticism of Pollard's penmanship was muted, but criticism there was. The good news was that the reviewer started by applauding Pollard's initiative. He said:

> An official history is being prepared, of which the fourth volume has just been published and other volumes will doubtless follow in due course. This great work is too large and detailed for the ordinary reader and so a concise history of the Royal Air Force is to be welcomed …
>
> The author knows his subject and his style is easy. He has covered his ground well and missed little. On the whole this book is welcome and deserves high praise. It should be widely read. The early chapters are particularly good for he sets forth very well the different objects which the RFC and RNAS set before themselves at the outset….That of the RNAS was much more complex and Capt Pollard describes the various activities of that Service very well …
>
> He is less good in describing by which each policy was carried out. He does deal with the tactical method by which General Trenchard set about carrying out the policy laid down for the RFC, namely protecting British reconnaissance and artillery machines by sending offensive patrols of fighters far across the lines to engage the Germans at a distance from the infantry battle.

The reviewer then went into a degree of detail that need not trouble this reader but which clinically itemized AOP's deficiencies and will have troubled him no end as it cut to the very heart of his book by opining:

> It is on the technical factor that Capt Pollard is least satisfactory … that a history of the Royal Air Force which does not lay great stress on such points (assorted technical issues) seems to propound a mystery without solving it.
>
> In the chapter "Afterwards" a very succinct account is given of some post-war expeditions of the Royal Air Force. The next three chapters deal with flying in general and are hardly necessary in the history of a fighting Service. The last chapter gives accounts of the nineteen Victoria Crosses won by members of the flying Services in the war, and is a distinctly valuable addition to this book.

Another professional journal, *Aircraft Engineering*, considered the book and expressed doubts as to its value by saying:

> This is a book that is a little difficult to place. It will hardly satisfy those with any deep knowledge, while one fears that it is too concise to appeal to the general public.

The Times, which had been warm in its opinion of *Fire-Eater*, was less entranced by the history when it was reviewed on 17 April 1934. *The Times* recognized the vast canvas that Pollard's book sought to cover and observed that the reader 'would feel hurried about the world and supplied with much detail which is ill-proportioned to the scope of this work …' It concluded more positively, 'And he will find that Captain Pollard supplies him with the material for a fairly complete framework of ideas.'

In November 1934 Alfred Pollard took great offence when the local branch of the British Legion issued an edict that on Remembrance Day, officers should wear top hats and frock coats and other ranks should turn out in bowler hats and lounge suits. An article in *Reynold's Illustrated News* published after the event and entitled *Top Hat Snobbery*, gave AOP's trenchant views national exposure. He said, quite correctly, that at times like this 'there should be no distinction between officers and men.' He had worn a bowler hat to the parade!

War clouds were gathering during 1939 as Jumbo laboured over his latest book, which was to re-launch him onto the serious literary stage. Pollard's *Epic Deeds of the Royal Air Force* might have helped to establish him as a military historian and opened up an entirely new field. It appeared in 1940, followed swiftly by a shorter book, *Leaders of the Royal Air Force*, published the same year. However, neither book captured the readers' attention, sales were modest, and Alfred's ambitions as a historian were thwarted once more. He wrote well and with conviction but these books did not satisfy the informed public.

It might have been expected that an acclaimed warrior with Jumbo Pollard's credentials would have rushed to re-enlist in 1939/40 and would have been willing to serve in any capacity. He had said that 'If ever my King and Country have a further need for my services, I will gladly offer them.'[13] He may have offered and perhaps he was rejected. Perhaps he was medically unfit? There is no record of either an application to rejoin the Service or of a rejection by the Service.

Dick Chown is most emphatic that his uncle did not serve in a uniformed Service during the Second World War.[14] Had Pollard joined the Home Guard he would, at the very least, have qualified for the War Medal. As it is, Second World War medals are noticeably absent from his medal group.

The fact is, he wrote fifteen books during the war – and that is a full-time occupation. It must be bourne in mind that in 1939 AOP was forty-six and well over the age for active service. He was fifty-two at war's end and he had done a lot more than 'his bit' in the previous unpleasantness. Nevertheless, his lack of a contribution in World War II is surprising, curious and unexplained. His protestations in *Fire-Eater* of his future willingness to spring to the defence of the Realm sound hollow.

Robert Swarbrick, Violet's father, was widowed in 1940 and he opted to move from Ealing, in London, and join Alfred and Violet, who had moved to Stockbridge, in Hampshire, as far from the ongoing blitz as possible. They stayed in Stockbridge until 1946, when they eventually settled in Bournemouth. They spent the rest of their lives there.

AOP was able to sit back and admire the feats of the RAF during the early days of the war at a distance. Nevertheless, *Epic Deeds of the RAF* and *Leaders of the Royal Air Force*, both of which were published in 1940, were premature and swiftly overtaken by events. Pollard was not to know that they would be obsolescent when he was drafting them in 1939. It might have been expected that he would update those books after the Second World War and reissue them – but surprisingly, he never did.

AOP supplemented his income from books by writing articles for newspapers and magazines. Catherine Boylan described these as 'ponderous'. He was much given to taking the moral high ground and his articles were given weighty titles such as *The Purpose of Life*, *The Art of Living*, *When Courage is Determination*, *Are You Afraid of Fear?* Ponderous sounds about right.

In addition to his writing Alfred also served as a BBC pundit and had a series called *Talks in the Train*. The *Daily Telegraph* summed up by saying that Pollard 'had very decided opinions of war and disarmament.' That, one must presume, was why he was invited to make the series.

AOP's novels are a window into the world in which they were written and consequently today, they are dated, displaying as they do the styles, manners and attitudes of a world that is now long gone. Pollard incorporated flying elements in many of his books (not necessarily evident from the book title) and he readily admitted that 'If my fiction helps to make our nation slightly more air-minded I am performing a national duty. If by making them (the Soviet Bloc) the villains in my books I can put even the tiniest obstacle in their way I am glad.'[15] This statement, which was made eight years before the Second World War and seventeen years before the building of the Berlin Wall, does add credibility to Pollard's views on the world scene. He foresaw the growth of a fascist Germany if steps were not taken to forestall it, and similarly, he anticipated the appalling relations between the Communist states and the Democratic West that lay ahead.

Red Hazard appeared in 1950 and on the dust cover was the oft repeated slogan 'Over half a million copies of AO Pollard's books have been sold'. It added the gratuitous intelligence that 54,000 copies of *Black Out* (1938) had been sold – obviously one of his best sellers. *Red Hazard* went to a second edition in 1951 (every author's dream), and it was reviewed among others by *Books of Today*, which opined that 'This is a brisk story that moves at a fast clip.' The *Liverpool Evening Express* said gushingly, 'A hectic start, but only the beginning of a succession of hair raising adventures which flow freely from the pen of one who writes with plenty of kick.' The *Manchester Evening Chronicle* was a little more restrained saying that the book was 'a nicely baited thriller'. The *Glasgow Evening Citizen* thought that it was 'a fast moving story of murder and sabotage which kept me gripped in the teeth of tension till the last word.'

The book is about communist activities in Britain and the hero, countering that threat, is Flight Lieutenant Robert Peel-Townsend RAF. The threat to Britain from the communist world was a theme that AOP returned to regularly and at the time the book was written, the Cold War was at its peak and the Berlin Wall was two years old. AOP was responding to contemporary issues and doing so with considerable success and his capacity for predicting political trends was remarkable. *The Death Parade* (price 9/6d), which followed hard on the heels of *Red Hazard*, also has a political setting and centres on a communist plot to assassinate Marshal Tito of what was then 'Jugoslavia'. The hero is again an ex-RAF officer.

Hutchinson and Co. (Publishers) Ltd., who published almost all of AOP's books, are now part of Random House. They had destroyed all of their correspondence with AOP; however, they were able to provide from their archive some copies of correspondence with AOP's literary agent, Rupert Crew.[16]

The earliest record is a contract between AOP and the Publisher dated 28 October 1948 concerning *The Poisoned Pilot*. This was a book for which AOP agreed to produce a typescript of not less than 60,000 words by 31 March 1949 as a 'Juvenile edition'.

In 1949 the Pollards had moved to Bournemouth. There they remained until the end of their lives as Alfred sought to maintain them with his pen. It was an uphill struggle.

The value of money is much changed and 1948 prices are difficult to relate to sixty-odd years later. The book was to retail for 6/- (30p), Pollard's royalty was to be 7½% of the 'sticker price', that is to say, 5½d per copy (2.25p). That arrangement applied to the first 10,000 copies, but sales over that number attracted 10%. The contract is a complicated document and the reader will not be troubled by the caveats or the 'ifs' and 'buts'.

On 1 February 1954, AOP agreed to accept a royalty of 2d (less that 1p) in respect of a reprint of the book in a 'cheap edition'; the print run was to be 25,000 and publication date in the short term. However, in September that year, Crew wrote to Hutchinson to say that Captain Pollard was 'disappointed that the cheap edition of the book has not yet seen the light of day. I think he was counting upon some royalties from this edition on your next statement of accounts due in October *as he is very hard up these days.*' [Author's italics.] Rupert Crew continues by adding, 'I am wondering if you might be able to push this title forward and perhaps grant the author something on account … *He is very badly in need of some cash* [author's italics] and if you have any suggestion to make I shall be most grateful … .'

This letter had the desired effect and a cheque for £100 followed immediately as an advance on the 'cheap edition' of *The Poisoned Pilot* to be retailed at 2/6 (12p) and on sale in March 1955.

Pollard sometimes got a better deal and on 2 January 1950, he signed a contract giving him 10% for *The Golden Buddha*. Unfortunately, 10% of not much is very little and although Pollard was a prolific author, he was writing for the cheap end of the market and was finding it difficult to make ends meet.

AOP's income must have been not much above subsistence level and in August 1951, Crew wrote to Hutchison to accept a royalty of 1d (less that ½p) per copy of a cheap edition of *The Death Game*. The Literary Agent had 'played a blinder' in the negotiations because the Publisher's initial offer was ¾d per copy. This is a sum too small to convert to modern currency and by any yardstick is derisory, bordering insulting. It amounts to a royalty of 4.16%.

Publishing houses are not altruistic organizations and they drive hard bargains. Pollard does not appear to have been treated by Hutchinson in anything other than a crisp and businesslike manner. There is no indication from the source material that his association with the firm over thirty years generated any personal relationships.

On 26 March 1952, Hutchinson wrote to Crew and said that they were unable to agree to the reprint of *Black Out*, *Hidden Cipher*, *Phantom Plane*, *ARP Spy*, *Blood Hunt*, *Death Squadron* and *The Royal Air Force: A Concise History*. On that basis, they said, 'We have no option but to allow the reprint rights to revert to the author on 18 September 1952.'

This was not what Crew and Pollard wanted to hear. If these books were going to continue to produce royalties they had to be available on the bookshelves. Pollard did not have either the will or the resources to reprint the books – nor did he have the machinery to market any book he reprinted personally.

The sixty-two books written by AOP can be found today on the internet. They are invariably in hard cover, but they are all long out of print and only available second-hand. The novels are very inexpensive (£2 at 2011 prices is the average). His other books cost rather more and an original edition of *Fire-Eater* is very expensive. A survey of Pollard's titles at Appendix 1 reveals that those that included the words air/wing/plane/flight account for thirteen of his books, a clear indication of his interests, and there are other books with an aviation theme that is not apparent from the title. 'Dead' and 'death' are his next favoured and eleven books include these words in the title. Close behind come 'secret', with eight, 'murder', with five and 'Spy', also with five.

AOP pressed on with his authorship and his output of about two books a year in the pre-computer age is laudable. He had to type, correct and re-type all of his books, and then had to correct and agree the publisher's draft. It was a lengthy process.

Productivity slowed as he reached his sixties; in 1954 he published only one book (*Homicidal Spy*); in 1955 another (*The Missing Diamond*), and followed that in 1956 with *Sinister Secret.* In 1957, for the first time since 1930 he had a fallow year, the first not to see a new Pollard on the bookshop shelves.

Things looked up in 1958, with two titles published, namely *The Secret Pact* and *Smugglers' Buoy*. The following year, 1959, was another blank year but 1960 saw the publication of *Wrong Verdict*.

These blank years are significant because they heralded a further diminution in AOP's income and contraction in Alfred and Violet's lifestyle. Violet took a job selling stationery and office equipment for a firm called Kalamazoo in order to eke out their income. She had a natural flair for salesmanship and fortunately was sufficiently successful to keep the family's head above the financial waves.

Jumbo Pollard's final book, *Forged Evidence*, was written in 1960 and published about eighteen months after his death; it appeared in 1962 and the copyright of this and all his other books passed first to Violet and through her to the three Chown boys, her nephews. Dick Chown is the survivor of these boys and thus he is the copyright holder.

Violet was diagnosed with cancer in 1960, and her health was a concern to them both. They were utterly devoted to each other and level of Jumbo's care for Violet demonstrated that relationship.

Notes

1 *HAC Journal*, 7/79, April 1930.

2 Pollard's central character in *Murder Hide-and-Seek,* Flight Lieutenant Richard Peel-Baring, 'Possessed the indefinable air of command of the best type of British officer.' Pollard had absolutely no doubts as to the desirable qualities in a man.

3 Pollard knew what qualities a girl should have and Alma, in *Murder Hide-and-Seek* was described as 'A forthright young lady' who is prepared to give people 'a piece of her mind'.
4 A definition of a fire-eater is 'an aggressive, angry, or argumentative person'.
5 Major General, the Rt. Hon. JEB Seely PC CB CMG DSO, MP (1868-1947). A former Secretary of State for War.
6 Dominic Harman, *The Truth about Men in the Front Line.*
7 Guy Chapman, *A Passionate Prodigality.*
8 Catherine Boylan, *Fearless Fighter, Tender Romantic: The Paradox of Alfred Oliver Pollard.*
9 Brigadier FP Crozier CB CMG DSO (1879-1937) Commander, 119 Brigade of BEF.
10 Professor Brian Bond, *Survivors of a Kind.*
11 18/9d in 1935 was worth very much more than the 2011 94p. £3 or less was a weekly wage for many.
12 Catherine Boylan, *'Fearless Fighter, Tender Romantic: The Paradox of Alfred Oliver Pollard'.*
13 AO Pollard, *Fire-Eater.*
14 Discussion Chown/Nash, 11 October 2010.
15 *Bookfinder*, 1931.
16 Correspondence and telephone calls with Mrs. Jean Rose, Random House Archivist and Librarian, July-August 2010.

Chapter 17

Epilogue

At 0900hrs, 4 December 1960 … AOP came back into the house; his thin hair was plastered to his head soaking wet as he had spent some time outside in the storm wrestling with the downed panel. He had succeeded in getting it vertical despite the attempts of the wind to wrest it from his grasp.

Who needs this sort of exertion on a Sunday morning?

He sat down on a chair in the kitchen and reached for the Sunday paper. The headlines were, as always, wall-to-wall doom and gloom. The Cold War was at its coldest and the threat from the USSR – always a fount of copy for the newspapers – was once more being painfully rehearsed. AOP appraised the front page and then gave a short gasp. Suddenly and inexplicably, he dropped the paper and his heavy 6 foot 2 inch frame fell sideways to the floor. Violet rushed to his side, then fled to the telephone and called an ambulance.

It was to no avail.

Bombo/Jumbo Pollard warrior, author and a man honest to a fault, died on that kitchen floor, aged sixty-seven, to the deep distress of Violet, who had been an unwilling and very distressed witness.

* * *

A post mortem was ordered by Mr. TC Thompson, the Coroner for the County Borough of Bournemouth. Two days later, on 6 December, the death of Alfred Pollard was duly registered and the cause was specified as being a coronary thrombosis. The internet carries a spurious suggestion that a splinter that he had carried in his body for forty-three years moved, pierced a vein and Alfred Oliver Pollard died of the resulting gangrene. It is not the case and the suggestion that the Germans got him in the end, although it might make for a good story, is fiction.

Alfred died intestate and Violet, who was bereft and terminally ill with cancer, died only three months later. In her will she left Alfred's medals and his sword to the Honourable Artillery Company. Her nephew, Dick Chown, carried out her wishes and those medals are now on display at Armoury House.

The *HAC Journal*, published in the spring of 1961,[1] carried an obituary. It was not signed but was clearly written by a member of 1 HAC and it said:

> Alfred Pollard was a man of great character and was able to adapt himself to any situation. If when away from the trenches he was light-hearted and gay. Almost irresponsible at times, and always ready for a party, in the line he was cool came from a sudden impulse but was the result of careful study of all matters affecting a given situation followed by a wise and quick decision to act regardless of personal danger. He would never commit men under his command to a task without first having satisfied himself that everything possible had been done to ensure success. He would carry out a personal reconnaissance and not only rely on reports from other sources. He was a great believer in the use of the hand grenade and was himself a fine bomber … When in the line he would never touch alcohol. He was never overawed by higher command and was quite regardless of his own personal position when the welfare of his company or platoon was concerned.
>
> As a man he was a most loveable character. His loyalty to his friends, in which category one can include everybody who served with him, was outstanding. He never sneered at those less efficient or less brave than himself but went out of his way to help them … there is no doubt that in battle or even in ordinary trench duty he inspired all those near him with a feeling of confidence. He had a great sense of humour which never deserted him and which he passed on to others at times when it was most needed.

Alfred Pollard's life was shaped and irrevocably altered by those nineteen months between September 1915 and April 1917. Like many other war heroes he peaked at an early age and then spent the rest of his life living up to his reputation. The sad fact is that after he threw his last bomb, the remainder his life was without reportable incident.

In combination, journalism, public speaking, broadcasting and the writing of novels and Service-related books provided AOP's livelihood. He was never going to be a rich man, but apparently he did not aspire to be so. It was as well, because he and Violet were entirely content with their lot. He held strong, right of centre opinions and seems to have had a particularly well-tuned antenna for political affairs. Given the strength of his convictions it is surprising that he did not enter the political arena.

Alfred Pollard is something of a mystery. He had his failings, of course he had, but they were modest when set against his positive qualities, not the least of which was his extraordinarily open and self-deprecating style.

He was fluent, erudite and principled. In addition he was blessed with ample self-confidence and determination. Despite his talents Alfred Pollard did not exploit them to the full. Instead he settled for being a writer, but he did not have the specific skills to excel in that field. The consequence of that was that he did not prosper in material terms. Perhaps his lifestyle would have been enhanced had he chosen to do something else.

The question is what?

He was very happily married but was childless and his warrior gene died with him. He had particular affection for his nephew, Richard Chown (always known as 'Dick'), and their relationship was close; indeed, Dick filled the space of a son in his life. Fifty years after AOP's death, Dick Chown speaks of his Uncle 'Jumbo' with unabashed pride and affection and he summed up Alfred as being 'A cheerful person and a thoughtful man with a sense of humour'. But, he added, 'He was not the life and soul of the party.'

AOP's interests were prosaic and parochial. He particularly enjoyed gardening, a glass of beer and handicrafts. He was an aficionado of the cinema and kept up to date with all the latest films. Dick Chown speculated[2] that he drew ideas from the cinema for the plots of his novels. He and Violet were dog lovers; an Old English Sheepdog captured their hearts, to be followed by a brace of Sealyhams called 'Soldier' and 'Sailor'. Dog walking provided the Pollards with exercise and AOP was never tempted to take up golf – an expensive game that he could not afford.

James Colquhoun, an admirer of AOP, worked to bring his life to a wider audience and to this end he spoke to his old friend and fellow member of the HAC, Leo Cooper, the publisher. The object of the exercise was to reprint *Fire-Eater.* Leo Cooper, very reasonably, sought and took the advice of the military historian, AJ Smithers.

Smithers wrote to Cooper in 1997[3] and in effect, reviewed the book. He wrote in caustic and unforgiving terms.

Smithers first acknowledged Alfred's bravery, but then dismissed it by saying:

> The man was, of course, a psychiatrist's case. A photograph of him (in Hammerton's *The Great War*, taken in about 1930) shows a great, brutal, stupid looking face.[4] I doubt whether the book justifies resurrection …. I have to feel that if half-forgotten books are to be disinterred for the occasion there are better books than this. And funnier ones.

Smithers was quite entitled to his views but the vehemence and contempt with which he expressed them throws his judgement completely out of balance and damages his credibility. Quite what Alfred's looks had to do with it all baffles this biographer, as does the curious reference to 'funnier books'. Smithers seems to have had a private agenda that went beyond making a professional appraisal.

Notwithstanding all of that, the consequence was that, inevitably, Leo Cooper shied away from the project and James Colquhoun had to look elsewhere. He interested *The Naval and Military Press*, which in due course produced a cheap paperback version of the original, but without maps or illustrations. The ownership of the copyright of *Fire-Eater* was always and is firmly and incontrovertibly lodged with the Chown Family.

Leo Cooper Ltd. changed its form and became Pen & Sword Ltd., and it is they who have published this biography of Alfred Pollard. 'What goes around comes around', as they say.

AOP's life from 1914 to 1919 is very well documented; however, the last forty-one years of his life are not. He left no written testament other than his books, only three members of his family have any memory of him and all of his contemporaries are dead.

AOP and his 828 comrades who sailed on the *Westmeath* in September 1914 and who survived the war formed an association. They met for dinner once a year and in September 1933, for example, 374 survivors were encouraged to attend. Only eighty-eight did dine and AOP was not one of them.

The *Westmeath* dinner was held until well after Alfred Pollard's death and numbers peaked at 128 in 1938. There is no record that AOP ever attended a *Westmeath* dinner – a curious record for one of the Battalion's most celebrated members and especially so as he was eloquent on the subject of 'comradeship'.

To be fair, he was not alone in eschewing this event and there were others who preferred not to rake over old coals. In 1960, just before AOP's death, seventy-one members dined together. Later, in 1964, Bill Haine took the chair – it was the fiftieth anniversary of the sailing of the *Westmeath*.

Dick Chown avers that AOP was very close to Bill Haine and one would have expected that these two men would have been chums for life. They did meet occasionally at meetings and events of the 'VC and GC holders Association'. However, the comprehensive archives of the HAC do not have any record of their ever meeting at a regimental event. These two men together would have provided a wonderful photo opportunity.

It did not happen.

The indications are that the two men were very different and the Victoria Cross was about all they had in common. Those who knew Bill Haine say that he was a gregarious, amusing person and he participated in the life of the HAC until his death in June 1982. Alfred Pollard was made of different stuff and in the course of researching this biography, no one has emerged as being his particular friend or regular companion – other than Brigadier Jackie Smyth[5] VC, a contemporary whom AOP admired and whose company he enjoyed at infrequent intervals.

Alfred was an enigma.

The conclusion is that he was something of a loner. He did not seek the company of men and was absolutely not a ladies' man. The fact is that, in later life, Alfred Oliver Pollard was actually a colourless and somewhat introverted personality. It is difficult to reconcile the ferocious warrior of 1915-17 with the sedate, reclusive, prolific, impecunious author of 1930-60.

He conducted himself with consummate bravery during the nineteen months between September 1915 and April 1917. This period was the highlight of his life and he was only twenty-four years of age when he won national and lasting fame. He had described himself, accurately, as a 'fire-eater' and during his war service he was just that. After the hostilities ceased in 1918, AOP lived a quiet, unremarkable life in which his courage, fortitude, determination and leadership skills were never tested again. His sterling martial characteristics could have, should have translated readily into a civilian context and a successful business career would have followed. It was not to be. Instead, a forceful, courageous, effective soldier and leader evaporated; an author and journalist took his place.

Perusal of this text will emphasize one other element that shaped Alfred Pollard and set him on the road to fame. He was either:

Blessed by his God
Very, very lucky
or
extremely fortunate.

He stood on the threshold of death's door at frequent intervals. He survived shell bursts, grenade explosions, shrapnel strikes on his helmet and incompetent German shooting. He could have, indeed should have, been killed half a dozen times. To counter that he made the best use of his good luck and a German who shot at him and missed did not get a second chance. It seems that his personal weapons were the bomb and the revolver, with which he was an above average shot.

AOP was an honest, principled man whose oft stated devotion to his sovereign and country never wavered. His life's work was his authorship but sadly, his literary legacy is of little consequence today. However, he will always be remembered as one of 'the bravest of the brave', a patriot to his boot straps and in the carefully understated words of Dick Chown, 'A thoroughly good chap'. There are none who would dispute that, and most men would settle for such an unequivocal epitaph.

This book set out to 'provide a record of Alfred Pollard's exploits putting his courage into the wider context of his life and the times in which he lived.' It is hoped that a brave man and a patriot has been fairly and objectively assessed.

Notes

1 *HAC Journal*, 28/327.
2 Telephone conversation, Nash/Chown, 8 August 2010.
3 I was given sight of this document by James Colquhoun on 7 July 2010.
4 AO Pollard was a very well built, striking young man and the ladies would say that he was good looking.
5 Brigadier Sir John Smyth VC MC MP Bart. (1893-1983) First President of the VC & GC Holders Association on its formation in 1956.

Appendix 1

The Pubished Works of AO Pollard

Title	Pages		Publisher
Pirdale Island	286	1930	Hutchinson & Co.
Rum Alley	288	1931	
Murder Hide-and-Seek	288	1931	
Fire-Eater	278	1932	
The Cipher Five	288	1932	
The Death Flight	288	1932	
The Havenhurst Affair	287	1933	
The Riddle of Loch Lemman	287	1933	
The Royal Air Force: A Concise History	288	1934	
The Phantom Plane	287	1934	
The Boy's Romance of Aviation	326	1935	
Murder in the Air	287	1935	
The Secret of Castle Voxzel	288	1935	
Unofficial Spy	288	1936	
The Death Game	288	1936	
Romantic Stories of Air Heroes	299	1937	
Hidden Cipher	288	1937	
The Murder Germ	288	1937	
Flanders Spy	286	1938	
Air Reprisal	272	1938	
Black Out	256	1938	
The Secret Formula	256	1939	
The Boy's Romance of Aviation	319	1939	
Murder of a Diplomat	256	1939	
Epic Deeds of the RAF	287	1940	
Leaders of the Royal Air Force	130	1940	
The Secret Pact	256	1940	
ARP Spy	254	1940	

The Army Today	48	1940	Ralph Tuck & Co.
Bombers over the Reich	208	1941	
The Secret Weapon	224	1941	
Wanted by the Gestapo	195	1942	
The Death Squadron	178	1943	
Invitation to Death	192	1944	
Gestapo Fugitive	184	1944	
The Fifth Freedom	175	1945	
Blood Hunt	191	1946	
Double-Cross	192	1946	
A Deal in Death	224	1947	
The Iron Curtain	224	1947	
The Death Game	176	1947	
The Murder Germ**	160	1947	
David Wilshaw (Air Detective) Investigates	252	1948	
The Death Curse	208	1948	
The Secret Vendetta	271	1949	
Dead Man's Secret	231	1949	
The Poisoned Pilot	272	1950	
Red Hazard	251	1950	
The Death Parade	224	1951	
The Golden Buddha	244	1951	
Death Intervened	256	1951	
The Dead Forger	240	1952	
Counterfeit Spy	232	1952	
The Buckled Wing	264	1953	
Criminal Airman	239	1953	
Homicidal Spy	232	1954	
The Missing Diamond	240	1955	
Sinister Secret	208	1956	
The Secret Pact	159	1958	Brown, Watson
Smuggler's Buoy	207	1958	Hutchinson & Co.
Wrong Verdict	187	1960	John Long
Forged Evidence	287	1962	John Long

** A reissue of the original, published in 1937

Appendix 2

The Inventor of the Baton Round

It is only as you get older that you can look back and take a dispassionate view of those who have influenced your life, be it for better or worse. In my case such a person was a man called Ernest Stanley Simmons.

When I left school I decided to make a career in the food business in general and the baking industry in particular. At that time J Lyons & Co. Ltd., always referred to as 'Joe Lyons', not only ran a national chain of retail shops, hotels and tea shops but also several large bakeries to support these outlets.

The largest of these bakeries was where Hammersmith starts to get serious pretensions about being Kensington. The site was called Cadby Hall and it employed perhaps 2,000 people. It had an almost military hierarchy, with various grades of supervisors wearing different distinguishing marks on their uniform protective clothing.

The Lyons organization was, in many ways, just like the Army. It took the view that you shouldn't ask someone to do something you can't do yourself. Thus it was that despite the mechanization in the industry, all aspiring managers had first to develop the skills that would allow them to lead tradesmen and craftsmen with confidence.

I found myself as one of about eighteen students in the J Lyons Bakery School in Cadby Hall. It came as a considerable shock when I plunged from my feather-bedded public school into a very robust factory environment. For example, I'd never scrubbed and mopped a floor in my life but I learned very quickly and it's a skill I still have, though rarely use.

A tyrant ran the school. He was the Ernest Simmons of the opening paragraph. Simmons was known only as 'Sir' to his face and 'The Old Man' behind his back. He only ever called me 'Nash' and when I arrived he made it clear to me that only the very best would do and if I couldn't produce the best then I'd do it again and again and again … until I could.

He was a Master Baker himself and an unashamed seeker of excellence in his field. Blessed with incredible personal skill and vast experience, he was impossibly demanding of those less gifted. Top of the 'less gifted list' was me. His oft-stated aim in life was to turn us all into competent bakers before we were let loose on an unsuspecting workforce and he was happy to break our hearts if that was what it took.

It sounds very prosaic, and it was. However, making by hand, forty-eight absolutely identical hand-raised jam tarts was a test. If one single tart in the batch did not meet his strict criteria then it was time to start again. I made hundreds and hundreds, perhaps thousands of jam tarts.

I did not like Ernie Simmons. He seemed to me to be unreasonable, unsympathetic and often unfair. He was a hard man in more ways than one. Bad workmanship could well give rise to his launching a rolling pin across the school at the miscreant. I suppose he could be celebrated as the inventor of the baton round. The effect was the same. A rolling pin in the groin really does make your eyes water and it serves to focus your thoughts on the matter in hand. The Old Man's ire was awful to behold: I held him in considerable awe and had unqualified respect for his ability.

After several months of wall-to-wall harassment and unrestrained criticism, I asked 'Sir' if I could leave a few minutes early on the morrow. 'Why, Nash?' he interrogated, in his gravelly voice, gazing at me over his half-moon glasses.

I explained that the next evening I was going to Armoury House in London and expected to 'Enlist. In a thing called the HAC … it's a sort of TA unit,' I explained nervously. He looked at me bleakly, twiddled his pencil between his fingers and said, 'Yes … I do know what the HAC is.'

Permission was given. I went. I enlisted.

I noticed a subtle change in The Old Man's attitude toward me. Perhaps I was actually getting better. It seemed unlikely, but he didn't shout quite as loudly or as often and the incoming baton rounds were less frequent. He put no obstacles in my path and so I was always first away on Thursday, which was 'drill night'.

The first summer approached and it was with trepidation that I went to see him to explain that I was required to attend summer camp with No. 3 Company, of the HAC Infantry Battalion. I was flummoxed when he readily agreed, and what was more, made an immediate note in his diary.

A couple of days later we were working together and he casually raised the matter of the HAC. He said, 'I was in the HAC in the Great War, you know.' He paused and continued, 'I was a sergeant, very proud to be so too.' He turned and gave me the benefit of one of his rare smiles. 'Heard of Pollard, have you?'

'Yes,' I replied promptly, 'he's one of the Company's VCs. Wasn't he the chap who was chucking bombs at the Germans? He cleared a trench, didn't he?'

The Old Man reached for a handful of dusting flour and with a practiced flick of his wrist spread it across our workbench in a very fine and even film.

'Pollard was my officer,' he volunteered. 'I was with him in those trenches, near Arras it was, in April 1917. I was priming the bombs for him, and he did the throwing ....'[1]

I have always regretted not questioning him more closely about this famous action, in which he not only played a key part but which is now a part of regimental folklore.

There didn't seem to be much to say at the time as Ernie Simmons reflected for a moment on events of forty years before. Then he cleared his throat and added, 'When you next go into the Long Room at Armoury House, look up and study the magnificent plaster work. An absolute master of his craft created that. I want you to sketch the design and then come back here and recreate it, in sugar, as a test piece.'

I never was up to the task and could not match that 18th century plasterer no matter how hard I tried. Nevertheless, I finished my time with Ernie Simmons and was sent out to manage a small independent bakery in one corner of the Cadby Hall complex. It was a first intoxicating taste of 'command'.

From time to time I'd pop in to see The Old Man and would receive a terse, gravelly and almost warm greeting. He was obviously keeping tabs on me because his questions on the running of my department were inevitably shrewd and well directed. He took an interest in my HAC activity, and the Company was something that gave us a link of sorts.

It took time for the penny to drop but slowly I came to realize that The Old Man had taught me rather more than the craft skills of a baker. I found that I was able to manage my staff with the easy confidence that comes from sound training. Above all else he had taught me to be 'organized'. In fact, I realize now but didn't then that he'd played an important role in my transition to manhood.

National Service beckoned and I went to register. The clerk was most enthused and he judged, 'If you work for Joe Lyons you're ideal for the Army Catering Corps.' I protested and said, rather pompously, that I was a corporal in the HAC, and I insisted on joining the infantry.

The Royal Fusiliers drew the short straw.

I told Ernie Simmons about the registration process and he remarked, 'I was a captain in the ACC during the Second War but much prouder to have been a sergeant in the HAC in the First.' He wished me well and concluded with a twinkle, in his eye, 'You're already a soldier, Nash. If you try and work hard you could just make an officer. Mark you,' the gravelly voice judged, 'it takes a very good man indeed to be a sergeant.'

The Long Room, Armoury House, showing the ornate plasterwork that the author failed to recreate. (*HAC Journal*)

I did try, and was commissioned, very pragmatically, for the remainder of my two years in the Army Catering Corps. It was in May 1961 that I went on 'commissioning leave'. On my first day of that leave I set off to visit The Old Man; I knew he'd be pleased at my success.

I climbed the fire escape stairs, pushed open the double doors and walked into the Bakery School. I arrived at his office and sitting at his desk was a former student, about fifteen years senior to me. 'I've come to see The Old Man,' I said cheerfully.

'Sorry, he died three weeks ago and I'm trying to hold the fort. It was a heart attack ... S'pose he was about sixty-three.'

I was absolutely stunned and it must have shown. 'Funny thing, he was talking about you in the Managers' Mess about ten days before he had his heart attack. Quite complimentary, he was. Thought the world of you, apparently. Y'know, the Army and all that sort of thing.'

I made my way back down the fire escape into the maelstrom of the Cadby Hall yard. Trucks, trolleys, carts, barrows and people were going in all directions. Several former colleagues hailed me and I waved back.

The Old Man, that skilled, tough, indestructible, bloody-minded, gravel-voiced, demanding, unreasonable, shrewd, pin-throwing, bomb-priming member of the Company and of my new corps was dead and I'd never said 'thank you'.

I wept.

I deeply regret my oversight and feel remorse even to this day.

There is a sad postscript to all of this. When researching this article I discovered that the heart attack in April 1961 had not killed Ernie Simmons. He lived for two more years and eventually died in 1963. Had I but known …

ES Simmons was admitted to the Honourable Artillery Company on 6 November 1916. He embarked for France on 15 April 1917. He joined 'B' Company and immediately afterwards, Lieut. Pollard assumed command. Simmons was a private during the action on 28 April 1917, but by June 1918, was a lance-sergeant. He was Acting Sergeant when, in January 1919, he transferred to the staff of the Deputy Assistant Provost Marshal (DAPM). He last appeared in the membership list of the Honourable Artillery Company in 1922.

Today, Ernest Simmons is no more than a footnote in the long history of the HAC. The names of the small group who supported Pollard when he won his VC are recorded but there were many others in 'B' Company at the time who are long since forgotten. Ernest Simmons is the one who is not. This brief vignette, which was first published in the HAC Journal in the autumn of 2000, is the very least I can do in his memory.

Notes

1 The facts are that ES Simmons was not directly present when Pollard won his VC – the three men who were, were identified and decorated for bravery. He may have been close enough behind the action to witness it. This piece was written forty-three years after the original conversation and ten years before I embarked on writing the biography of Alfred Pollard.

The most likely explanation is that, given the proximity Ernest Simmons had to Pollard in 'B' Company, he supported his officer in some other foray. Along the way, perhaps time dulled his memory and the precise chronology of events. I may have misquoted him. I chose to think that this is the case because 'The Old Man' would not have deliberately misled me – although it does rather spoil a good story.

Appendix 3

On Decorations

For a serviceman there are five essential ingredients that need to be present if he/she is to win a decoration for gallantry.

The first of these is opportunity – in that there has to be situation in which the safety of the group or a comrade is at risk or a tactically important state of affairs exists.

Secondly: the individual has to have the will and the ability to influence events and the courage to do so.

Thirdly: having decided to influence events the individual needs a disproportionate amount of luck. He/she has to avoid being hit in the process and disabled before the event has been influenced.

Fourthly: someone has to witness the act of bravery and report it up the regimental command chain to the Commanding Officer.

Fifthly: at commanding officer level a well written and finely judged citation has to be submitted even further up the chain of command. That citation then has to be endorsed at every level without equivocation.

It is only when all of those conditions have been satisfied that a gallantry award is made. The decoration finally awarded may not be what the Commanding Officer sought and the downgrading from, say, a VC to a DCM (as in the case of Alfred Pollard) was a matter of routine to prevent 'decoration inflation'. The high probability is that many of those eventually awarded a DCM were initially recommended for a VC.

An extreme case is that of 2nd Lieutenant SF Jeffcote (see page 162); he was recommended for a VC but was awarded merely a posthumous 'Mention in Despatches'. To illustrate at least one of the points made above, Mr. W Finch (late Corporal 1 HAC) wrote the following:[1]

> For some months in 1915 I was very matey with a cockney corporal of the 3rd Worcesters named Vaughen, and in July of that year his battalion and mine were holding the front line across the Menin Road. We had been subjected to some twelve hours of severe shelling.
>
> I got slightly hit in the morning, and lay in the trench all day waiting for darkness to hobble down to the dressing station. In the afternoon

Vaughen appeared round the traverse. He said 'Hello kid, how are yer?' I said, 'Lucky.'

'Well,' he said 'my luck's clean gone. I had a go for the DCM today – bin aht mendin' bleedin' wires for hours in this blinkin' shellin' and now the bloke wot sent me as gorn and got hiself killed.'

Such is the vagary of winning or not winning a decoration. To win one medal marks a soldier as different. To win two makes him special and to win three is exceptional. Very rarely does anyone win four decorations, or more, for gallantry and Alfred Pollard is one of that very select band.

The members of the HAC were widely employed across the face of the Army during the Great War and earned a proportionate number of decorations, 760 in total.[2] Lieutenant Humphrey Gilkes won an MC and three bars serving with three units: 1 HAC, 2 HAC and 21st London Regiment. He is the only member of the HAC to win four awards apart from Alfred Pollard. Had the latter won the two VCs for which he was recommended then he would have been in an entirely different bracket.

A host of other HAC soldiers won three awards in various combinations and the probability is the awards to the HAC were in much the same proportion as to other British regiments.

The most decorated British soldier in World War I was Lance Corporal William Coltman of the North Staffordshire Regiment with five gallantry decorations, which are Victoria Cross, Distinguished Conduct Medal & Bar, and Military Medal & Bar (VC DCM* MM*). This man was no fire-eater, quite the reverse, but his courage was of the very highest order - he was a stretcher bearer and never fired a shot.

There are two Australians, of whom the first is Captain Henry Murray, Australia's most decorated serviceman and the most decorated soldier in the British infantry in World War I, with five awards. As well as the VC, Murray was awarded the DCM, DSO* and the French Croix de Guerre. In 1919 he was made a Companion of the Order of St. Michael and St. George. However, the CMG was not for gallantry.

Murray's decorations are not quite matched by those of the courageous Captain Joe Maxwell VC MC* DCM of 1st Bn AIF.

Four decorations was unusual but not unique and mention must be made of Major Dudley Johnson VC DSO* MC of the South Wales Borderers, and Colour Sergeant John Williams of the same regiment, who was awarded the VC DCM MM*.

All of the above are foot soldiers and won their medals in the mud of the trenches. However, there is one man who won his decorations in the air and he is indisputably the most decorated member of the Forces of the British Empire in World War I.

Without a peer is Lieutenant William Baker RCAF, who incredibly won VC DSO* MC** Croix de Guerre, Silver Medal of Military Valour (Italy) and Bar. A total of nine awards for gallantry.

Notes

1 *HAC Journal*, 7/81, June 1930.
2 AH Eades produced a summary and found that the Regiment won three VCs, one officer won four MCs, two officers won three MCs, nineteen won two MCs and 396 others won a single MC. There were also 122 MMs, twenty-five DCMs and forty DSOs. A miscellany of other decorations made up the total.

Bibliography

Arthur, Max, *Lest We Forget,* Ebury Press, 2007.

Blunden, Edmund, *Undertones of War*, Cobden-Sanderson, 1928.

Bond, Prof Brian, *Survivors of a Kind,* Continuum UK, 2008.

Boylan, Catherine, *Fearless Fighter, Tender Romantic: The Paradox of Alfred Oliver Pollard VC MC DCM, Journal of the Society for Army Historical Research*, 83, 2004.

Cage, Nigel, *Sanctuary Wood and Hooge*, Leo Cooper, 1993.

Carrington, Charles, *A Subaltern's War,* Peter Davies, 1929.

Chapman, Guy, *A Passionate Prodigality,* Nicholson and Watson, 1933.

Clapham, HS, *Mud and Khaki: The Memoirs of an Incomplete Soldier*, Hutchison, 1930.

Coles, Alan, *Three Before Breakfast*, Kenneth Mason, 1979.

Crozier, Brigadier FP, *A Brass Hat in No Man's Land*, Jonathan Cape, 1930.

Crozier, Brigadier FP, *The Men I Killed*, Jonathan Cape, 1937.

Corrigan, Gordon, *Mud Blood and Poppycock*, Cassell, 2003.

Fryer, Evelyn, RM, MC, *Reminiscences of a Grenadier*, Digby Long, 1921.

Gazette, The London.

Graves, Robert, *Goodbye to All That*, Jonathan Cape, 1929.

Goold Walker, Major G, DSO MC, *The Honourable Artillery Company in the Great War 1914-1919*, Seeley Service & Co., 1930.

Goold Walker, Major G, DSO MC, *The Honourable Artillery Company 1537-1947*, Gale and Polden, 1954.

Harman, Dominic, *The Truth About Men in the Front Line. Imagining the Experience of War. Memoirs of the Western Front*, University of Sussex, *Journal of Contemporary History*, 2001.

HMSO, *The Official History of World War I.*

Hynes, Samuel, *The Soldier's Tale.*

Idriess, Ion, *The Australian Guerrilla, Book 2, Sniping*, Sydney, 1942.

Jünger, Ernst, *Storm of Steel*, London, 1920.

Lucy, JF, *There's a Devil in the Drum*, Naval and Military Press, 1992.

Honourable Artillery Company Journal Volumes 1-7.

Honourable Artillery Company, War Diary, 1st Battalion, 1914-1918.

Honourable Artillery Company, The Great Vellum Roll (list of members).

Keegan, John, *The First World War*, Hutchinson, 1998.

Lambert, Arthur, *Over the Top – A PBI in the HAC.*

Laffin, John, *The British Butchers & Bunglers of World War One*, Sutton Publishing, 1988.

Mayhew, Major George, MC, 'Uncle George's Book', HAC Archive, unpublished, 1914-1919.

Mitchell, Major TJ Smith, Miss GM, *Official History of the War, Casualties and Medical Statistics*, Imperial War Museum (reprinted) London, 1997.

Mottram, RH, *Journey to the Western Front – Twenty Years After*, G Bell and Sons Ltd., 1936.

Pollard, Alfred Oliver, *Fire-Eater, The Memoirs of a VC*, Hutchinson, 1932, reprinted by the Naval & Military Press.

Richards, Frank, *Old Soldiers Never Die*, Faber and Faber, 1933.

Pegler, Martin, *Out of Nowhere – A History of Military Sniping*, Osprey Publishing, 2004.

Sassoon, Siegfried, *Memoirs of an Infantry Officer*, Faber and Faber, 1930.

Scannell, Vernon, *Argument of Kings*, London, 1987.

Terraine, John, *To Win a War,* Sidgwick and Jackson Ltd., 1978.

Times, The

Telegraph, Daily

Townshend, CVF, Major General, KCB DSO, *My Campaign in Mesopotamia,* Thornton Butterworth Ltd., 1920.

Tsouras, Peter G, *The Greenhill Dictionary of Military Quotations*, Greenhill Books, 2000.

Oxford Dictionary of National Biography.

Random House Publishing Group Archives.

De Vauban, Sebastien, Marshal of France, *A Manual of Siegecraft*, 1740.

Index